DK EYEWITNESS

TOP10
ROME

Top 10 Rome Highlights

The Top 10 of Everything

CONTENTS

Rome Area by Area

Streetsmart

Within each Top 10 list in this book, no hierarchy of quality or popularity is implied. All 10 are, in the editor's opinion, of roughly equal merit.

Title page, front cover and spine *The Trevi Fountain at dusk*
Back cover, clockwise from top left *Street in Trastevere; interior of the Colosseum; Trevi Fountain; Colosseum and Roman Forum; Vatican Museum roof*

The rapid rate at which the world is changing is constantly keeping the DK Eyewitness team on our toes. While we've worked hard to ensure that this edition of Rome is accurate and up-to-date, we know that opening hours alter, standards shift, prices fluctuate, places close and new ones pop up in their stead. So, if you notice we've got something wrong or left something out, we want to hear about it. Please get in touch at **travelguides@dk.com**

Welcome to
Rome

Vespas parked by Baroque portals. Ancient ruins near statues of Roman kings and holy paintings of madonnas. Strong espresso and delectable gelato. The eternal city is a feast for the eyes, soul and stomach. Tourists, artists and pilgrims have been flocking here since antiquity, and with DK Eyewitness Top 10 Rome, it's yours to explore.

Once the most powerful city in the world, Rome has been 2,800 years in the making. Ancient Roman columns are embedded in Renaissance palazzo walls, Egyptian obelisks are recycled in Baroque fountains and Christian churches have been built over pagan temples. Experience the city purposefully by exploring the **Forum** or the **Vatican**, or sample it casually while pausing under the **Pantheon's** massive portico (providing shade since AD 125) or going for a spin around Bernini's fountains on **Piazza Navona**, once Emperor Domitian's racetrack.

Despite its heritage, Rome feels nothing like a dusty museum, mostly thanks to its flamboyant citizens who live much of their life outdoors in cafés and piazzas, negotiating cobbled alleyways, going for their *passeggiata* and always intent on *fare la bella figura* – that very Italian concept of looking fabulous and making an impression.

Whether you are coming for a weekend or a week, our Top 10 guide brings together the best of everything that Rome has to offer, from grand sights such as the **Sistine Chapel** and **Colosseum** and tiny piazzas and views you will never forget to stupendous works by **Michelangelo** and **Caravaggio** hidden away in churches and the best spots for *pizza al taglio* and hearty Roman cuisine. The guide has useful tips throughout, from seeking out what's free to places off the beaten track, plus 11 easy-to-follow itineraries, designed to tie together a clutch of sights in a short space of time. Add inspiring photography and detailed maps and you've got the essential pocket-sized travel companion. **Enjoy the book and enjoy Rome.**

Clockwise from top: **Musei Capitolini, Fountain of Neptune (Piazza Navona), Spanish Steps, MAXXI, mosaic at Museo Nazionale Romano, Colosseum, Sistine Chapel fresco**

Exploring Rome

Rome is packed with magnificent piazzas, beautiful palazzi, ancient monuments and churches. There is a lot to see and do, and to help you make the most of your visit here are some ideas for a two- and four-day Roman holiday. Bear in mind that you can save time by reserving tickets beforehand, and that advance booking is obligatory at Galleria Borghese.

| 0 metres | 800 |
| 0 yards | 800 |

Key
— Two-day itinerary
— Four-day itinerary

St Peter's Basilica towers magnificently over Rome and is not only a beautiful church, but is also packed with works of art by the great masters.

Two Days in Rome

Day ❶
MORNING
See the **Colosseum** (see pp26–7), then walk past the **Roman Forum** (see pp20–21) and **Imperial Fora** (see pp26–7) to the virtually-recreated villa of a patrician family at **Palazzo Valentini** (see p49). Visit **Musei Capitolini** (see pp28–31), and don't miss the bird's-eye view of the Forum.

AFTERNOON
Stroll through the *centro storico* to **Piazza Navona** (see p62) and the **Pantheon** (see pp18–19) for atmos-phere, ice cream and window shop-ping. Cross the Tiber by Ponte Sisto to lively Trastevere for a drink.

Day ❷
MORNING
Get up early to see **St Peter's** (see pp12–17) without the crowds when it opens at 7am – an unforgettable experience. Then visit the **Vatican Museums** (see p54), preferably having booked tickets in advance.

AFTERNOON
Spend some time at the lovely **Villa Borghese** park (see p117) followed by a visit to the Bernini sculptures at **Galleria Borghese** (see pp24–5) and the Etruscan finds at **Villa Giulia** (see pp40–41). Walk back through the park to **Piazza del Popolo** (see p116) to visit **Santa Maria del Popolo** (see pp38–9), before ending the day at **Piazza di Spagna** (see p115).

Four Days in Rome

Day ❶
MORNING
Begin with the **Pantheon** (see pp18–19), then wander over to **Piazza Navona** (see p62), stopping to admire Caravaggio's works in **San Luigi dei Francesi** (see p89) and **Sant'Agostino** (see p90). Marvel at the Bernini foun-tains and street performers, then browse the shops around the piazza.

AFTERNOON
Head to the fantastic **Museo Nazionale Romano's Palazzo Massimo alle Terme** (see pp34–7),

The Colosseum, built in the 1st century AD, has served as the prototype for all stadiums since.

The Pantheon, constructed in the 1st century BC, is the world's best preserved Roman temple.

which has an entire frescoed room from the Villa of Livia. Wind down with an evening in appealing Monti.

Day ❷
MORNING
Explore Ostia Antica *(see pp42–3)* and return in time for lunch in Testaccio.
AFTERNOON
Visit Santa Maria del Popolo *(see pp38–9)*, then explore the Piazza di Spagna area *(see p115)*. Climb the Spanish Steps *(see p115)* for a great city view. Walk back to the centre via the Trevi Fountain *(see p115)*.

Day ❸
MORNING
Explore the Colosseum *(see pp26–7)*, then visit Palazzo Valentini *(see p49)*

and the Musei Capitolini *(see pp28–31)*, stopping for lunch in the museum's roof terrace café.
AFTERNOON
See the evocative ruins of the Roman Forum and Palatine Hill *(see pp20–23)*, then wander through the Jewish Quarter and vibrant Campo de' Fiori.

Day ❹
MORNING
Start early to see St Peter's and the Vatican *(see pp12–17)* – the children's audio guide is highly recommended for adults too – then take the tram to the stop outside Galleria Nazionale d'Arte Moderna *(see p55)* for lunch.
AFTERNOON
Visit Villa Giulia *(see pp40–41)* before taking a stroll through the park to Galleria Borghese *(see pp24–5)* – make sure to book in advance.

Top 10 Rome Highlights

Theatrical mosaic masks of Comedy
and Tragedy, Musei Capitolini

🔟 Rome Highlights

The unique appeal of Rome is that it is a 2,800-year-old indoor-outdoor museum, with ancient monuments, art treasures and timeless architecture. With religion at its heart and history in its soul, it dazzles and inspires visitors time and time again.

1 Vatican City
This is home to the Pope, the world's largest church, and the most incredible work of art ever created – the Sistine ceiling (see pp12–17).

2 The Pantheon
The most perfectly preserved of all ancient temples, this marvel of engineering has a giant oculus forever open to the sky (see pp18–19).

3 Roman Forum
Formerly at the heart of ancient power, the forum is now evocatively empty, broken by grand arches, solitary columns and carved rubble (see pp20–21).

4 Galleria Borghese
This stunning palace is filled with Graeco-Roman, Renaissance and Baroque works (see pp24–5).

5 Colosseum and Imperial Fora
Imperial Rome built many impressive monuments, including this splendid amphitheatre (see pp26–7).

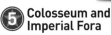

6 Musei Capitolini

At the ancient centre of religious Rome are some of the world's greatest masterpieces, from 4th-century BC Greek sculptures to Caravaggio's revolutionary, even scandalous, paintings *(see pp28–31)*.

7 Museo Nazionale Romano

These collections, housed at five sites, feature some of the world's finest ancient art, including stunning frescoes and mosaics and Classical sculpture *(see pp34–5)*.

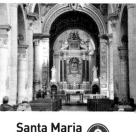

Santa Maria del Popolo 8

Built over emperors' tombs, this church offers a rich display of Renaissance and Baroque art, including masterpieces by Bernini, Raphael and Caravaggio *(see pp38–9)*.

Villa Giulia 9

This elegant 16th-century villa is home to the national collection of Etruscan antiquities *(see pp40–41)*.

10 Ostia Antica

Extending over several square kilometres, the remarkable ruins of ancient Rome's main port city hold many surprises and convey a powerful sense of everyday Imperial life *(see pp42–3)*.

TOP 10 ⭐ Vatican City

The Vatican is the world's smallest nation, covering just 50 ha (120 acres), and is a theocracy of just over 550 citizens, headed by the Pope, but its sightseeing complex is beyond compare. Within its wall are the ornate St Peter's Basilica, the astonishing Sistine Chapel, apartments frescoed by Fra Angelico, Raphael and Pinturicchio, and some 10 museums. The latter include collections of Egyptian, Greek, Etruscan and Roman antiquities; Paleochristian, Renaissance and modern art; and a world-class ethnographic collection.

③ Sistine Chapel

Michelangelo's ceiling **(right)** is one of the most spectacular works of art in the world *(see pp14–15)*.

④ Etruscan Museum
Finds from the Regolini-Galassi tomb of a noble woman (7th century BC) are the highlights here, including gold and amber jewellery **(left)** and a bronze bed.

① Raphael Rooms
Raphael decorated Julius II's rooms with frescoes that included the School of Athens, a convention of ancient philosophers bearing portraits of Renaissance artists such as Leonardo da Vinci as bearded Plato in the centre.

⑤ Chapel of Nicholas V
The Vatican's hidden gem is this closet-sized chapel colourfully frescoed in 1447–50 with early martyrs by Fra Angelico.

⑥ Raphael's Transfiguration
Raphael was labouring on this gargantuan masterpiece (1517–20) when he died at 37, leaving students to finish the base. It shows Christ appearing to the Apostles in divine glory.

② Pio Clementino Museum
This museum has several famous Classical sculptures, including the contorted, Hellenistic Laocoön **(right)**, found in an Esquiline vineyard – Michelangelo saw the unearthing. There are also the Apollo Belvedere and Belvedere Torso, both huge influences on Renaissance artists.

Vatican City

9 Egyptian Museum

The collection consists mostly of sculpture brought from Egypt for temples and private villas and gardens. There are also decorated mummy cases **(below)**, mummies and finds from a tomb that include a nit-comb.

8 Caravaggio's Deposition

Caravaggio's *chiaroscuro* technique accentuates a diagonal composition (1604) filled with peasant figures and grisly realism.

10 Borgia Apartments

Borgia pope Alexander VI had these beautiful rooms frescoed by Pinturicchio (Raphael was once his junior collaborator) between 1492 and 1495. The walls are now hung with lesser pieces from the Modern Art collection.

7 Leonardo da Vinci's St Jerome

Sketchy and unfinished – Leonardo was often a distracted genius – this 1482 painting is nevertheless an anatomical masterpiece.

NEED TO KNOW
MAP B2 ■ www.vatican.va
Museums and Sistine Chapel: Viale Vaticano 100; 06 6988 3145; open 9am–6pm Mon–Sat (last admission 4pm), 9am–2pm last Sun of the month (free); closed 1 & 6 Jan, 11 Feb, Easter, Easter Mon, 1 May, 29 Jun, 15 & 16 Aug, 1 Nov, 25, 26 & 31 Dec; adm: €17 (€8 ISIC under 26s, under 18s)

St Peter's Basilica: Piazza San Pietro; 06 6988 3731; dome open 7am–7pm

daily (to 6pm in winter), treasury open 7:30am–5pm daily; adm: free (basilica); €5 (treasury), €8 (dome via steps), €10 (dome via lift)

■ The Vatican museums offer a multi-sensory tour for the visually impaired, as well as tours in sign language, and allow the use of electric scooters for wheelchair users.

■ When in town, the Pope gives a mass audience on Wednesday mornings. Book free tickets in advance *(Prefecture of the Papal Household, fax 06 6988 5863)*.

Museum Guide
The Vatican Museums (a 15-minute walk from St Peter's) consist of 10 collections, the Sistine Chapel and the Papal Apartments. To see highlights only, first visit the Pinacoteca, to the right of the entrance turnstile. The Sistine and other collections are to the left.

Sistine Chapel Works of Art

Detail from Michelangelo's fresco *The Creation of Adam*

1 Adam and Eve
God imparts the spark of life to Adam in one of western art's best known scenes, *The Creation of Adam*, then pulls Eve from Adam's rib.

2 Creation
God separates darkness from light, water from land and creates the Sun and Moon. Michelangelo veers towards blasphemy by depicting God's dirty feet.

3 The Sacrifice, Flood and Drunkenness of Noah
After disassembling his scaffolding and gazing up from floor level, Michelangelo noticed that these three tumultuous scenes were too minutely drawn.

4 Life of Moses Scenes
Left wall highlights include Botticelli's *The Trials of Moses* and Signorelli and della Gatta's *Moses Giving his Rod to Joshua*.

5 Sibyls and Prophets
Hebrew prophets, including Jonah, mingle with the Sibyls who foretold Christ's coming.

6 Old Testament Salvation Scenes and Ancestors of Christ
Portraits from Jesus's family tree are above the windows, and bloody Salvation scenes, including David and Goliath, are on corner spandrels.

7 Life of Christ Scenes
The chapel's right wall stars Botticelli's *Cleansing of the Leper*, Ghirlandaio's *Calling of Peter and Andrew*, and Perugino's *Christ Giving the Keys to St Peter*.

8 Christ Giving the Keys to St Peter
Classical buildings form the backdrop to this pivotal scene of transferring power from Christ to the popes. Each scene is divided into three parts.

9 Botticelli's Punishment of the Rebels
Schismatics question Aaron's priestly prerogative to burn incense. A vengeful Moses opens the earth to swallow them.

10 Last Judgement
This vast work depicts figures nude, equalized and stripped of their earthly rank. This was considered indecorous and the figures were covered by fig leaves. Saints are identified by their medieval icons.

Sistine Chapel Works of Art

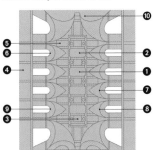

UNDERSTANDING THE SISTINE CHAPEL ART

The Sistine Chapel's frescoes are not merely decorations by some of the greatest artists of the Renaissance – the images tell a story and make a complex theological argument. Pope Sixtus IV commissioned wall frescoes for the Pope's Chapel in 1481–83. They were intended to underscore papal authority, in question at the time, by drawing a line of power from God to the pope. In the Life of Moses cycle, Moses' and Aaron's undisputed roles as God's chosen representatives are affirmed by the fate of those who oppose Aaron – significantly and anachronistically wearing a papal hat – in the *Punishment of the Rebels*. Directly across from this work, Perugino's *Christ Giving the Keys to St Peter* bridges the Old Testament with the New as Christ hands control of the church to St Peter – and therefore to his successors, the popes (who are pictured between the Sistine windows). Michelangelo's breathtaking frescoes on the ceiling (1508–12) later added Genesis, Redemption and Salvation to the story.

TOP 10 PAINTERS OF THE SISTINE CHAPEL

1 **Fra Diamante** (1430–98)

2 **Rosselli** (1439–1507)

3 **Sandro Botticelli** (1445–1510)

4 **Bartolomeo della Gatta** (1448–1502)

5 **Domenico Ghirlandaio** (c 1449–94)

6 **Luca Signorelli** (c 1450–1523)

7 **Perugino** (1450–1523)

8 **Pinturicchio** (1454–1513)

9 **Piero di Cosimo** (1462–1521)

10 **Michelangelo** (1475–1564)

The Fall and Expulsion from the Garden of Eden, from Michelangelo's Genesis cycle, shows Adam and Eve being expelled from Eden for eating fruit from the forbidden Tree of Knowledge.

The Trials of Moses by Botticelli depicts scenes from the life of the prophet.

Features of St Peter's Basilica

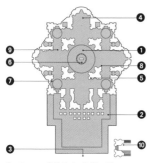

Features of St Peter's Basilica

mournful, stately and ethereal. It has been protected by glass since 1972, when a man screaming "I am Jesus Christ!" attacked it with a hammer, damaging the Virgin's nose and arm.

The magnificent Piazza San Pietro

1 Dome

When Michelangelo designed a dome to span St Peter's massive transept, he made it 42 m (138 ft) in diameter, in deference to the Pantheon's 43.3 m (142 ft) dome. You can ride an elevator much of the way, but must still navigate by foot the final 330 stairs between the dome's inner and outer shell to the 132 m high (435 ft) lantern and sweeping vistas across the city.

2 Pietà

Michelangelo carved this statue (see p56) in 1499 at the age of only 25. It is at once graceful and

Michelangelo's *Pietà*

3 Piazza San Pietro

Bernini's remarkable semi-elliptical colonnades transformed the basilica's approach into a pair of welcoming arms embracing the faithful. Sadly, the full effect of entering the piazza (see p63) from a warren of narrow medieval streets was spoiled when Mussolini razed the neighbourhood to lay down pompous Via della Conciliazione. The obelisk came from Alexandria.

4 Apse

Bernini's exuberantly Baroque stained-glass window (1666) centres on a dove representing the Holy Ghost, surrounded by rays of the sun and a riot of sculptural details. Beneath the window sits the Chair of St Peter (1665), another Bernini concoction; inside is a wood and ivory chair said to be the actual throne of St Peter. Bernini also crafted the multicoloured marble *Monument to Urban VIII* (1644) to the right, based on Michelangelo's Medici tombs in Florence. It is of far better artistic quality than Guglielmo della Porta's similar one for Pope Paul III (1549) to the left.

5 Statue of St Peter

A holdover from the medieval St Peter's, this 13th-century bronze statue by the sculptor Arnolfo di Cambio has achieved holy status. The faithful can be seen lining up to rub (or kiss) Peter's well-worn foot for good luck.

6 Baldacchino

Whether you view it as ostentatious or glorious, Bernini's Baroque sculpted canopy above the high altar is at least impressive. Its spiralling bronze columns are said to have been made from the revetments (portico ceiling decorations) of the Pantheon *(see pp18–19)*, taken by Pope Urban VIII. For his desecration of the ancient Roman temple the Barberini pope *(see pp60–61)* and his family were castigated with the

waggish quip: "What even the barbarians wouldn't do, Barberini did."

7 Treasury

Among the ecclesiastical treasures here is a 6th-century, jewel-encrusted bronze cross – the Crux Vaticana – various fragments of the medieval basilica including a ciborium by Donatello (1432), and Antonio Pollaiuolo's masterful bronze slab tomb (1493) for Sixtus IV, the pope's effigy surrounded by representations of theological virtues and liberal arts.

Crux Vaticana or the Cross of Justin II

8 Grottoes

Many of the medieval basilica's monuments are housed beneath the basilica's floor. During excavations in the 1940s, workers discovered in the Necropolis the legendary Red Wall behind which St Peter was supposedly buried. The wall was covered with early medieval graffiti invoking the saint, and a box of bones was found behind it. The late Pope John Paul II was buried in the crypt after his death in 2005.

9 Alexander VII's Monument

One of Bernini's last works (1678) shows figures of Justice, Truth, Chastity and Prudence gazing up at the pontiff seated in the deep shadows of the niche. A skeleton crawls from under the flowing marble drapery to hold aloft an hourglass as a reminder of mortality.

10 Vision of Constantine

The most dramatic statue in the basilica, this rearing equestrian figure shows Emperor Constantine at the moment in which he had a vision of the Cross at the Battle of the Milvian Bridge in 312 AD. Victorious, Constantine converted to Christianity and made it the official religion of the Empire.

Bernini's ornate *baldacchino*

🔟⭐ The Pantheon

When Emperor Phocas donated this pagan temple to Pope Boniface IV in 608, he unwittingly ensured that one of the marvels of ancient Rome would be preserved unaltered in its new guise as the Christian church of Santa Maria ad Martyres. Designed by Emperor Hadrian in AD 118–25, it has been lightly sacked over the ages, yet the airy interior and perfect proportions remain, a wonder of the world even in its own time.

1 Dome
The widest masonry dome in Europe is precisely as high as it is wide: 43.3 m (142 ft). Its airy, coffered space, cleverly shot through with a shaft of sunlight from the oculus, is what lends the Pantheon an ethereal air.

4 Oculus
The bold 8.3 m (27 ft) wide hole at the centre of the massive dome **(right)** provides light and structural support: the tension around its ring helps hold the weight of the dome.

6 Doors
The massive bronze doors are technically original, but were so extensively renovated under Pope Pius IV (1653) that they have been practically recast.

2 Walls
The 6.2 m (20 ft) thick walls incorporate built-in brick arches to help distribute the weight downwards, relieving the stress of the heavy roof.

5 Portico
The triangular pediment **(above)** rests upon 16 pink and grey granite columns, all original save the three on the left (17th-century copies).

7 Marble Decorations
Red porphyry, giallo antico, as well as other ancient marbles grace the interior **(below)** of the Pantheon. More than half the polychrome panels cladding the walls are original, the rest are careful reproductions, as is the floor.

3 Royal Tombs
Two of Italy's kings are honoured by simple tombs. Vittorio Emanuele II (1861–78) unified Italy and became its first king. His son, Umberto I, was assassinated in 1900, shot four times by an Italian American anarchist, Gaetano Bresci.

🔟 Fountain

Giacomo della Porta designed this stoop; Leonardo Sormani carved it in 1575. The marble basin was replaced by a stone one and the Egyptian obelisk **(left)** of Rameses II was added in 1711.

Raphael's 8 Tomb

Raphael, darling of the Renaissance art world but dead at 37, rests in a plain, ancient stone sarcophagus **(right)**. Poet Bembo's Latin epitaph says: "Here lies Raphael, whom Nature feared would outdo her while alive, but now that he is gone fears she, too, will die." Other artists buried here include Baldassare Peruzzi.

9 Basilica of Neptune Remains

Of the Pantheon's old neighbour, all that remains are an elaborate cornice and fluted columns against the Pantheon's rear wall.

THE FIRST PANTHEON

Emperor Augustus's son-in-law, Marcus Agrippa, built the first Pantheon in 27 BC, replaced in AD 118–125 by Hadrian's rotunda. The pediment's inscription *"M. Agrippa cos tertium fecit"* ("M. Agrippa made this") was Hadrian's modest way of honouring Agrippa. The pediment also provided the illusion of a smaller temple, making the massive space inside even more of a surprise (the Pantheon was originally raised and you couldn't see the dome behind). Bernini's "ass ears", tiny towers he added to the pediment, were removed in 1883.

NEED TO KNOW

MAP M3 ■ Piazza della Rotonda
■ 06 6830 0230

Open 9am–7pm daily (to 1pm during hols); Mass: 10:30am Sun & 5pm Sat; closed 1 Jan, 1 May, 25 Dec

■ If you're hungry, there's a good gelateria, Cremeria Monteforte (see p102), on the Pantheon's right flank, and an excellent coffee shop, La Tazza d'Oro (see p79), just off the square.

■ Rather than bemoan a rainy day in Rome, head to the Pantheon to watch the water fall gracefully though the oculus and spatter on the marble floor and down a drain. Snowfall is even better.

🔟 ⭐ Roman Forum

Gazing on the picturesque ruins today, one would hardly guess that the Forum was the symbol of civic pride for 1,000 years. Its beginning, more than 3,000 years ago, was as a cemetery for the village on Palatine Hill. When the marshy land was drained in the 6th century BC, the Forum took on a more central role. It was at its most elegant starting with the reign of Augustus, who is said to have turned the city from brick to marble.

1 Temple of Vesta and House of the Vestal Virgins

A graceful round temple and its adjacent palace were the centre for one of the city's most revered cults. Noble priestesses tended the sacred flame and enjoyed the greatest privileges.

2 Curia

The 3rd-century-AD Senate retains its original polychrome inlaid floor, its risers, where the 300 senators sat in deliberation, and the speaker's platform. For 2nd-century views of the Forum, examine the large marble reliefs, showing Emperor Trajan's good works.

5 Arch of Septimius Severus

This well-preserved triumphal arch **(below)** commemorates the emperor's Middle Eastern victories. It was erected in AD 203 by his sons, Geta and Caracalla, then co-emperors.

3 Temple of Castor and Pollux

Three Corinthian columns remain of this temple **(left)** to the Dioscuri – twin brothers of Helen of Troy and sons of Jupiter and Leda. It marked the spot where they miraculously appeared in 499 BC to announce a crucial Roman victory.

6 Arch of Titus

The oldest extant arch in Rome was built in AD 81 by Emperor Domitian to honour and deify his brother, Titus, who suppressed the Jewish rebellion in Judea. Reliefs show the sacking of Jerusalem's Holy of Holies and sacred objects, such as a golden menorah, being taken.

4 Basilica of Maxentius and Constantine

Three vast, coffered barrel vaults proclaim the Forum's largest structure, built around AD 315 and used as the legal and financial centre of the Empire.

Roman Forum

IMPERIAL FORA
see page 27

VIA DEI FORI IMPERIALI

8 Temple of Vespasian
Until 18th-century excavations, these graceful columns (AD 79) from a temple to the former emperor stood mostly buried beneath centuries of detritus.

7 Temple of Antoninus and Faustina
Dedicated by Antoninus Pius in AD 41 to his deified wife Faustina, this is one of the best preserved temples **(above)**. With its Baroque-style top-knot, it is also one of the oddest. Note the carvings of griffins along the side frieze.

9 Via Sacra
Paved with broad, flat, black basalt stones, Rome's oldest road wound from the Arch of Titus through the Forum and up to the Capitoline. Triumphal processions were staged here, but it degenerated into a hangout for gossips, pick-pockets and other idlers.

10 Temple of Saturn
Eight grey-and-red Ionic columns **(left)** constitute what's left of this temple (also the state treasury) to the ruler of agriculture and of a mythic "Golden Age." Saturnalia, cele-brated each December, was very similar to modern-day Christmas.

NEED TO KNOW

MAP Q5 ■ Via dei Fori Imperiali ■ 06 3996 7700 ■ www.coopculture.it

Open 9am–1 hour before sunset; closed 1 Jan, 25 Dec

Adm €16 (includes Palatine & Colosseum for 24 hr; €22 for 48 hr); €9.50 for afternoon entry; €2 EU citizens (18–25); free for under 18s; free for all first Sun of the month

■ For drinks and snacks try the mobile refreshment vendors. For something more substantial, there are plenty of cafés and restaurants on Via Cavour.

■ In summer, it's best to visit the Forum either early or late in the day, to avoid the intense heat.

Forum Guide
You can access the Forum from Via Dei Fori Imperiali. However, for a great view of the whole site, enter from one of the high

points at either end. From the north-west end, begin on the Capitoline (to the right and behind the huge, white Victor Emmanuel Monument) and take the stairs down from Largo Romolo e Remo. From the southeast end, start at the Colosseum (see pp26–7) and climb the small hill just to the northwest. Enter by the Arch of Titus, which is near the main gate to the Palatine.

Palatine Hill Features

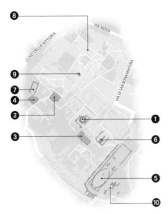

Palatine Hill Features

1 Domus Flavia

Marked today primarily by the remains of two fountains, this imposing edifice was once the official wing of a vast emperors' palace, built by Domitian in AD 81.

2 Livia's House

This 1st-century BC structure, now below ground level, formed part of the residence of Augustus and his second wife. Here you can examine a number of mosaic pavements as well as wall frescoes.

3 Palatine Museum and Antiquarium

This former convent houses a wealth of artifacts unearthed here, including pottery, statuary, ancient graffiti and very fine mosaics. You can also study a model of the Iron Age Palatine.

4 Romulus's Iron-Age Huts

At this location, traces of three 9th-century BC huts were uncovered in the 1940s. Legend says that this tiny village was founded by Romulus (see p46), who gave Rome its name.

5 Stadium

Possibly a racetrack, or just a large sunken rectangle formed part of Domitian's palatial 1st-century abode.

6 Domus Augustana

All that remains of the private wing of Emperor Domitian's imperial extravaganza are the massive sub-structure vaults.

7 Temple of Cybele

The orgiastic cult of the Great Mother was the first of the Eastern religions to come to Rome, in 191 BC. Still here is a decapitated statue of the goddess. Priests worshipping Cybele ritually castrated themselves.

8 Farnese Gardens

Plants and elegant pavilions grace part of what was once an extensive pleasure-garden, designed by the noted architect Vignola and built in the 16th century over the ruins of Tiberius's palace.

Pavilions at the Farnese Gardens

9 Cryptoporticus

This series of underground corridors, their vaults decorated with delicate stucco reliefs, stretches 130 m (425 ft). It connected the Palatine to Nero's fabulous Domus Aurea or Golden House (see p133).

10 Domus Septimius Severus

Huge arches and broken walls are all that remain of this emperor's 2nd-century AD extension to the Domus Augustana.

A DAY IN THE LIFE OF A ROMAN HOUSEHOLD

Most Romans lived in *insulae*, apartment buildings of perhaps six floors, with the poorest residents occupying the cheaper upper floors. An average Roman male citizen arose before dawn, arranged his toga, and breakfasted on a piece of bread. Then out into the alleys, reverberating with noise. First, a stop at a public latrine, where he chatted with neighbours. Next a visit to his honoured patron, who paid him his daily stipend. Lunch might be a piece of bread dipped in wine or olive oil, perhaps with a bit of cold meat. Bathing waited until late afternoon, when he met his friends at the public baths. There he lingered – conversing, exercising, reading, or admiring the artwork – until dinnertime. The main meal of the day was taken lying on couches, with enslaved people in attendance. Then it was bed-time. Roman matrons, apart from their time at the baths (usually earlier than the men), spent the entire day at home, running the household.

Roman toga

TOP 10 ANCIENT ROMAN BELIEF SYSTEMS

1 State Religion of Graeco-Roman Gods (especially the Capitol Triad: Jupiter, Juno, Minerva)

2 Household Gods: Ancestors and Genii

3 Cult of Cybele, the Great Mother

4 Deification of Emperors, Empresses and Favourites

5 Orgiastic Fertility Cults

6 Mithraism

7 Cult of Attis

8 Cult of Isis

9 Cult of Serapis

10 Judeo-Christianity

Feasts held by wealthy Romans were usually extravagant, served by enslaved people and eaten lying on couches, sometimes under garden pergolas.

🔟 ⭐ Galleria Borghese

The Borghese Gallery is one of the world's greatest small museums. Some of Bernini's best sculptures and Caravaggio's paintings sit alongside Classical, Renaissance and Neo-Classical works in a beautiful frescoed 17th-century villa set in the Villa Borghese park, all of which once belonged to the great art-lover of the early Baroque, Cardinal Scipione Borghese. He patronized the young Bernini and Caravaggio, in the process amassing one of Rome's richest private collections.

⑤ Sleeping Hermaphroditus
A Roman marble copy **(left)** of a Greek bronze sculpture depicting Hermaphroditus, son of Hermes and Aphrodite, who is known for bearing both female and male characteristics.

① Bernini's Apollo and Daphne
A climactic moment frozen in marble (1622–5). As Apollo is inches from grabbing Daphne, the pitying gods transform her into a laurel.

③ Bernini's David
Young Bernini's *David* (1623–4) was the Baroque answer to Michelangelo's Renaissance version. The frowning face is a self-portrait.

⑥ Canova's Pauline Bonaparte
Napoleon's sister caused a scandal with this half-naked portrait (1805–8), lounging like a Classical goddess on a cushion carved of marble.

② Titian's Sacred and Profane Love

Titian's allegorical scene (1514), painted for a wedding **(above)**, exhorts the young bride that worldly love is part of the divine, and that sex is an extension of holy matrimony.

④ Bernini's Rape of Persephone
Bernini carved this masterpiece **(right)** at the age of 23 (1621–2). Muscular Hades throws his head back with laughter, his strong fingers pressing into the maiden's soft flesh as she struggles to break free of his grasp.

7 Caravaggio's Self-Portrait as a Sick Bacchus

This early self-portrait (1593) as the wine god was painted with painstaking detail, supposedly when the artist was ill. It shows finer brushwork than later works.

8 Raphael's Deposition

The Borghese's most famous painting (1507), although neither the gallery's nor Raphael's best **(below)**. The Perugian matriarch Atalanta Baglioni commissioned it to honour her assassinated son (perhaps the red-shirted pall-bearer).

Galleria Borghese

Key to Floorplan
- First floor
- Ground floor

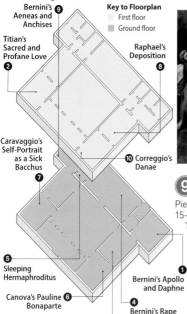

- Bernini's Aeneas and Anchises **9**
- Titian's Sacred and Profane Love **2**
- Raphael's Deposition **8**
- Caravaggio's Self-Portrait as a Sick Bacchus **7**
- Correggio's Danae **10**
- Sleeping Hermaphroditus **5**
- Canova's Pauline Bonaparte **6**
- Bernini's Apollo and Daphne **1**
- Bernini's Rape of Persephone **4**
- Bernini's David **3**

9 Bernini's Aeneas and Anchises

Pietro Bernini was still guiding his 15-year-old son in this 1613 work. The carving is more timid and static than in later works, but the genius is already evident.

10 Correggio's Danae

A sensual masterpiece (1531) based on Ovid's Metamorphoses. Cupid pulls back the sheets as Jupiter, the golden shower above her head, rains his love over Danae.

THE BORGHESE COLLECTORS

Scipione used this 17th-century villa as a showplace for a stupendous antiquities collection given to him by his uncle, Pope Paul V, to which he added sculptures by the young Bernini. When Camillo Borghese married Pauline Bonaparte, he donated the bulk of the Classical sculpture collection to his brother-in-law Napoleon in 1809. They now form the core of the Louvre's antiquities wing in Paris.

NEED TO KNOW

MAP E1 ■ Villa Borghese, off Via Pinciana ■ 06 328 10 ■ www.galleriaborghese. beniculturali.it, www. gebart.it/musei/galleria-borghese (for reservations)

Open 9am–7pm Tue–Sun; closed 1 Jan, 25 Dec

Adm €13; €4 EU citizens (18–25); €2 under 18 and journalists (exhibition prices may differ); free first Sun of the month; maximum viewing time 2 hours (mandatory exit after that)

■ There's a decent café in the museum basement, although the Caffè delle Arti (06 3265 1236) at the nearby Galleria Nazionale d'Arte Moderna is better, with a park view.

■ Entrance to the gallery is strictly by reservation. Make sure you book well ahead of time – entries are strictly timed and tickets often sell out days, even weeks, in advance, especially if an exhibition is on.

[TOP 10] ★ The Colosseum and Imperial Fora

Trajan's Column

This rich archaeological zone, rudely intruded upon by Mussolini's Via dei Fori Imperiali, contains some of the most grandiose and noteworthy of Rome's ancient remains. Dominating the area is the mighty shell of the Colosseum, constructed in AD 72–80 under the Flavian emperors and originally known as the Flavian Amphitheatre. The Comune di Roma is constantly working on excavating the area and new discoveries are made every year.

① Trajan's Forum and Column

Trajan's Forum left all who beheld it awed by its splendid nobility. Now cut off by modern roads, all that stands out is the magnificent column, commemorating in fine graphic detail the emperor's victories in what is now Romania. Access to part of it is through Trajan's Market.

③ Trajan's Markets

The emperor and his visionary architect, Apollodorus of Damascus, built this attractive, very modern looking shopping and office mall **(below)** in the early 2nd century AD. There were 150 spaces in all, the top floor utilized by welfare offices, the lower levels by shops of all kinds.

⑤ Colosseum

Built by enslaved Jewish people, this magnificent structure *(see p48)* was where the imperial passion for bloody spectacle reached its peak of excess. When Emperor Titus inaugurated the amphitheatre **(above)** in AD 80, he declared 100 days of celebratory games, some involving the massacre of 5,000 wild beasts, such as lions. This slaughter-as-sport was finally banned in AD 523.

② Domus Aurea

A result of the mad emperor Nero's self-indulgence, this "golden house" *(see p133)* was the largest Rome ever saw, yet it was for amusement only. It covered several acres and had every luxury. Currently closed for restoration.

④ Mamertine Prison

Legend holds that Sts Peter and Paul were imprisoned here *(see p65)*. Prisoners were dropped down through a hole in the floor and the only exit was death, often from starvation.

6 House of the Knights of Rhodes

This 12th-century priory was owned by the crusading order of the Knights of Rhodes. Inside are the original portico, three shops and the Chapel of St John.

7 Arch of Constantine

This arch marks the victory of the first Christian emperor over his rival emperor Maxentius (see p46). Yet it is mostly a pastiche of pagan elements taken from several earlier monuments – the beautiful hunt-scene roundels come from a temple dedicated to Emperor Hadrian's male lover, Antinous.

The Colosseum and Imperial Fora

8 Forum of Julius Caesar

The first of Rome's great Imperial Fora. Caesar's line, the Julians, traced their ancestry back to Venus herself, so he erected the Temple of Venus Genetrix in 46 BC and placed there statues of himself and his great love Cleopatra, the queen of Egypt.

9 Palazzo Valentini

In 2005 two imperial Roman villas, retaining a spa bath, courtyards and traces of frescoed walls and mosaic floors, were found below Palazzo Valentini (see p49).

10 Forum of Augustus

Julius Caesar's successor (see p38) made the focus of his forum the Temple of Mars the Avenger **(above)**, identified by the broad staircase and four Corinthian columns.

NEED TO KNOW

Colosseum: MAP R6; Piazza del Colosseo; www.coopculture.it; open 9am–1 hour before sunset daily; closed 1 Jan, 1 May & 25 Dec; adm: €16 (includes the Palatine & Forum for 24 hr; €22 for 48 hr); €9.50 for afternoon entry; €2 EU citizens (18–25); free for under 18s; free for all first Sun of the month

Trajan's Markets: MAP P4; Via IV Novembre; www.

mercatiditraiano.it; open 9:30am–7:30pm daily; closed 1 Jan, 1 May & 25 Dec; adm: €16; concessions €14; free for under 6s; free for all first Sun of the month

Mamertine Prison: MAP P5; Clivo Argentario 1; 06 698 961; www.tullianum.org; open 9am–5pm daily

■ A friendly place for a light meal is Caffè Valorani at Largo Corrado Ricci 30.

■ Student guides at the Colosseum work for tips and bring the place to life.

■ Via dei Fori Imperiali is pedestrianised to let visitors walk around the site.

Area Guide

Allow 3 hours to explore the site and expect to stand in the queue for the Colosseum. The Forum of Augustus can be viewed from Via dei Fori Imperiali.

🔟 ⭐ Musei Capitolini

Ancient Rome's religious heart, Capitoline Hill now houses a magnificent museum. Take the Cordonata uphill, a theatrical experience planned by Michelangelo in the 16th century. At the top stands a statue of Marcus Aurelius in a star-shaped piazza, which is bordered by twin palaces containing some of Rome's greatest treasures. The collections in the Palazzo Nuovo (this page) and Palazzo dei Conservatori (overleaf) were established in 1471 with a donation of bronzes by Pope Sixtus IV.

Fresco depicting Hannibal crossing the Alps

 Hall of the Emperors

The hall contains several portraits of the emperors and empresses of the Imperial Age. Among them is a bust of the brutal ruler Emperor Caracalla from the 3rd century AD.

④ Resting Satyr

Used to adorn an ancient grove or fountain, this young mythological creature is a copy of a 4th-century BC original by Greek sculptor Praxiteles. His pointed ears, panther-skin cape and flute are attributes of the nature god Pan. It inspired Nathaniel Hawthorne's novel *The Marble Faun (see p58)*.

 Mosaic of the Masks

This floor mosaic of two Greek theatre masks is probably from the 2nd century AD. The use of perspective, light and shadow is highly skilled, employing small squares of marble to create dramatic effects.

 Capitoline Venus

This fine 1st-century BC copy of a Praxiteles Aphrodite from the 4th century BC shows the goddess of love risen voluptuously from her bath, attempting to cover herself, as if reacting to someone's arrival.

NEED TO KNOW

MAP N5 ■ Piazza del Campidoglio ■ 06 0608 ■ www.museicapitolini.org

Open 9:30am–7:30pm daily; closed 1 Jan, 1 May, 25 Dec

Adm: €17; free for under 6s; exhibition prices included

■ Capitolini Card costs €14.50 (valid for 7 days) and also gives admission to Centrale Montemartini *(see p156)*.

■ The café behind the Palazzo dei Conservatori (Caffè Capitolino) has a terrace with a spectacular panorama of the city.

■ Part of the underground passage between the two museums is the ancient Tabularium, imperial Rome's Hall of Records, which offers an unusual view of the Roman Forum.

Museum Guide
The Palazzo Nuovo, on the left as you enter the piazza, contains mostly restored ancient sculpture. The finest pieces are on the upper floor. Take the stairs down to the underpass leading to the Palazzo dei Conservatori *(see pp30–31)* – the courtyard displays ancient marble fragments. The next floor up displays 16th-and 17th-century decorations and Classical statuary. On the top floor are paintings from the Renaissance and Baroque periods.

Marforio ⑤
This hirsute reclining giant **(right)** was originally a river god, and is believed to have come from the Forum of Augustus *(see p27)*. A Renaissance sculptor added the attributes of the god Ocean and placed him here, as overseer of this courtyard fountain.

⑥ Mosaic of the Doves
Once the centrepiece of a floor decoration in Hadrian's Villa *(see p158)*, this jewel-like composition **(above)** uses tiny marble and glass *tesserae* (chips) to achieve a sense of texture and volume.

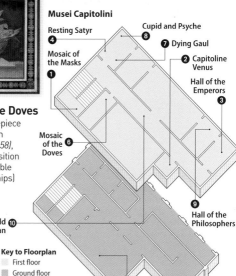

Musei Capitolini

Resting Satyr ④

Cupid and Psyche ⑧

⑦ Dying Gaul

Mosaic of the Masks ①

❷ Capitoline Venus

Hall of the Emperors ❸

Mosaic of the Doves ⑥

⑨

Hall of the Philosophers

Drunken Old Woman ⑩

Key to Floorplan
First floor
Ground floor

⑤ Marforio

⑦ Dying Gaul
The collection's most renowned piece conveys great pathos. It is probably a 1st-century AD Roman copy of a Hellenistic bronze from the 3rd century BC.

⑧ Cupid and Psyche
The Roman god of love embraces the personification of the soul; here, the lovers are eternally united **(left)**. This Roman copy of a Hellenistic original has inspired a great many sentimental variations.

⑨ Hall of the Philosophers
This room is filled with Roman copies of idealized Greek portrait busts of the greatest Hellenic poets and thinkers, including the blind epic poet Homer.

⑩ Drunken Old Woman
This copy of a Hellenistic original dating from the 3rd century BC is from a series of sculptures, which represent the wages of vice.

Palazzo dei Conservatori Exhibits

Head, Colossal Statue of Constantine

1 Colossal Statue of Constantine Fragments

Found in the ruins of the Basilica of Maxentius and Constantine, these surreal outsized body parts (c AD 313–24) formed the unclothed segments of an overwhelming seated effigy of the first Christian emperor, recognizable by his protuberant eyes. The rest of the sculpture was made of carved wood dressed in sheets of bronze.

2 Lo Spinario

One of the precious bronzes that comprised Sixtus IV's donation to the people of Rome, this charming sculpture dates from the 1st century BC. Hellenistic in its everyday subject matter, the head recalls more archaic models. The boy's unusual and graceful pose inspired many works during the Renaissance.

3 Caravaggio's St John the Baptist

Shocking in its sensuality, the boy's erotic pose, his arm around the ram, created an iconographic revolution when it was unveiled around 1600. Masterful *chiaroscuro* brought the holy image even more down to earth.

4 Bronze She-Wolf

The most ancient symbol of Rome, from the 5th century BC, of Etruscan or Greek workmanship. The she-wolf stands guard, at once a protectress and a nurturer, as the twins Romulus and Remus *(see p46)* feed on her milk. This was also part of the 1471 donation of Pope Sixtus IV.

Bronze statue of the Roman She-Wolf

5 Guercino's Burial of St Petronilla

The influence of Caravaggio is clearly evident in this huge altarpiece, executed for St Peter's Basilica between 1621 and 1623. Powerful effects of light and dark combined with pronounced musculature and individuality of the figures bring the work directly into the viewer's physical world.

6 Caravaggio's Fortune Teller

An earlier work by Caravaggio, but just as revolutionary as his St John

Palazzo dei Conservatori Exhibits

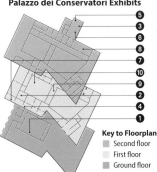

Key to Floorplan
- Second floor
- First floor
- Ground floor

Pietro da Cortona's Baroque artwork *Rape of the Sabines*

the Baptist. This subject is taken from everyday street life in late 16th-century Rome, which the painter knew intimately. Notice that the fortune teller is slipping the ring from the unsuspecting young dandy's finger.

7 Bust of Lucius Junius Brutus

Dating from between the 4th and 3rd centuries BC, this bronze bust is possibly the rarest object in the museum. Its identification as the first Roman consul is uncertain, because it also resembles Greek models of poets and philosophers. Its intense, inlaid glass eyes make it one of the most gripping portraits.

8 Pietro da Cortona's Rape of the Sabines

Baroque painting is said to have begun with this work (c1630), where symmetry is abandoned and all is twisting, dynamic movement. It shows an early episode in Roman history: the new city had been founded but the population lacked women, so they stole those of the neighbouring Sabine tribe (see p46).

9 Bust of Commodus as Hercules

The 2nd-century emperor, who loved to fight wild animals in the Colosseum, had himself represented as the demigod Hercules, to promote his own divinity. The club held in his right hand, the lion's mantle and the apples of the Hesperides in his left hand are all symbols of the labours of Hercules.

10 Equestrian Statue of Marcus Aurelius

A copy of this 2nd-century AD bronze masterpiece stands in the centre of the Capitoline star; the larger-than-life original is displayed in a glassed-in courtyard within the Palazzo dei Conservatori.

Equestrian statue of Marcus Aurelius

Museo Nazionale Romano

The National Museum of Rome (MNR) is split across five sites. Much of the sculpture is at Palazzo Altemps (overleaf), while some of the best individual pieces, mosaics and frescoes are at Palazzo Massimo alle Terme (this page). Aula Ottagona has oversized bathhouse statues and the Baths of Diocletian house the epigraphic and *stele* collection. Crypta Balbi features remnants of ancient Roman city blocks and a 13 BC portico.

1 Statue of Augustus

The statue of Rome's first emperor once stood on Via Labicana. It shows him wearing his toga draped over his head – a sign that, in AD 12, he added the title *Pontifex Maximus* (high priest) to the list of honours he assigned himself.

2 Boats of Nemi

These elaborate bronzes (including lions, wolves and a head of Medusa) once decorated the two luxury boats that Emperor Caligula kept on the Lake of Nemi. The boats, used for parties, even had central heating.

3 House of Livia

These frescoes (20–10 BC) depicting a lush garden came from the villa of Augustus's wife, Livia **(above)**. They were in the *triclinium*, a dining room half-buried to keep it cool in summer.

4 Leucotea Nursing Dionysus

Discovered in 1879, a luxuriously frescoed villa included this bedroom scene of a nymph nursing the wine god **(above)** with additional scenes around.

5 Ivory Mask of Apollo

This exquisite mask was found by illegal excavators in 1995 near Lake Bracciano, and intercepted by the Carabinieri. It was part of a larger chryselephantine statue – whose face, hands and feet were made of ivory, placed on a wooden frame and "dressed" with textiles and gold.

6 Discus Thrower

This 2nd-century AD marble copy **(right)** of the famous 450 BC Greek original by Myron is faithful to the point of imitating the original bronze's imperfect dimensions.

7 Wounded Niobid

Sculpted for a Greek temple around 440 BC and later acquired by Julius Caesar, this hauntingly beautiful figure of Niobid (daughter of Queen Niobe) is reaching for the fatal arrow that killed her siblings.

Previous pages The ruins of the Roman Forum

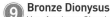

8 Four-Chariotters Mosaic

The imperial Severi family must have been passionate about sports to have decorated a bedroom of their 3rd-century AD villa with these charioteers **(below)**. They are dressed in the traditional colours of the four factions of the Roman circus.

9 Bronze Dionysus

Very few large Classical bronzes survive in modern times, making this 2nd-century AD statue special beyond its obvious grace, skill and preserved decoration. You can still see the figure's yellow eyes, red lips as well as a comb band in the grape-festooned hair.

10 Boxer at Rest

No idealised athlete, this is a muscled, tough, middle-aged man **(below)**, resting between bouts, naked except for the leather strips binding his fists. Red copper highlights make his bruises look fresh.

NEED TO KNOW

Palazzo Massimo alle Terme: MAP F3; Largo di Villa Peretti 1; 06 480201; www.museonazionale romano.beniculturali.it; open 11am–6pm Tue–Sun (booking recommended); closed 1 Jan & 25 Dec

Palazzo Altemps: MAP L2; Piazza Sant'Apollinare 46; 06 684851; www. museonazionaleromano. beniculturali.it; open 11am–6pm Tue–Sun; closed 1 Jan & 25 Dec

Adm €10; extra €3 for exhibitions; €2 EU citizens (18–25); free for under 18s; free first Sun of the month; €12 combined ticket (3-day validity)

■ **From Palazzo Massimo alle Terme, walk down Via Nazionale for bars and restaurants. After exploring Palazzo Altemps, go to Tre Scalini (see p94) on Piazza Navona for refreshments.**

■ **Call ahead for Palazzo Massimo alle Terme tickets, as the frescoes and mosaics on the top floor are timed-entry only. Ask for the virtual reality goggles at the entrance.**

■ **Gallery Guide**
Palazzo Massimo alle Terme exhibits its Republican and Early Imperial Rome (up to Augustus) statuary on the ground floor, along with a few older Greek pieces. The first floor art exhibits reflect the political, cultural and economic spheres of Imperial Rome up to the 4th century. The second floor has ancient mosaics and frescoes. In the basement, the numismatic collection reflects the history of money from its origins. There is also gold jewellery and a mummified eight-year-old girl.

Palazzo Altemps Collection

Dionysus with Satyr

1 Athena Parthenos
The 1st-century BC Greek sculptor Antioco carved this statue to match the most famed sculpture in antiquity, the long-lost Athena in Athens' Parthenon.

2 "Grande Ludovisi" Sarcophagus
This mid-3rd century AD sarcophagus, deeply carved and remarkably well-preserved, shows the Romans victorious over the barbarian Ostrogoth hordes.

3 Orestes and Electra
This 1st-century AD statue was carved by Menelaus, an imitator of the great Greek artist Praxiteles. The scraps of 15th-century fresco nearby depict some wedding gifts from the marriage of Girolamo Riario and Caterina Sforza.

4 Garden of Delights Loggia
The loggia frescoes (c 1595) are a catalogue of the exotic fruits, plants and animals then being imported from the Americas.

Garden of Delights Loggia

5 Dionysus with Satyr
Imperial Rome was in love with Greek sculpture, producing copies such as this grouping of Dionysus, a satyr and a panther.

6 Ludovisi Throne
This set of 5th-century BC reliefs came to Rome from a Calabrian Greek colony and were discovered in the 19th century.

7 Apollo Playing the Lute
There are two 1st-century AD Apollos in the museum, both restored in the 17th century.

8 Suicidal Gaul
This suicidal figure supporting his dead wife's arm was part of a trio, including the Capitoline's Dying Gaul (see p28) commissioned by Julius Caesar to celebrate a Gaulish victory.

9 Egyptian Statuary
The Egyptian collections are divided into three sections related to that culture's influence on Rome: political theological, popular worship and places of worship. The showpiece is the impressive granite *Bull Api*, or *Brancaccio Bull* (2nd century BC).

10 Colossal Head of Ludovisi Hera
Goethe called this his "first love in Rome". It is believed to be a portrait of Claudius's mother, Antonia.

ANCIENT ROMAN ART

Ancient Rome's art was as conservative as its culture. From the middle Republican to the Imperial era, Romans shunned original sculpture for copies of famous Greek works. The Caesars imported Golden Age statuary from Greece, and Roman workshops churned out toga-wearing headless figures in stock poses to which any bust could be affixed. Romans excelled at bust portraiture, especially up to the early Imperial age when naturalism was still in vogue. Roman painting is divided into styles based on Pompeii examples. The First Style imitated marble; the Second Style imitated architecture, often set within the small painted scenes that became a hallmark of the Third Style. The Fourth Style was *trompe l'oeil* decoration. Mosaic, first developed as a floor-strengthening technique, could be simple black-on-white, or intricate work with shading and contour. *Opus sectile* (inlaid marble) was a style that was imported from the East.

The Ludovisi Throne is a sculpted marble block depicting the birth of Aphrodite. The goddess is seen rising from the sea wearing finely carved diaphanous drapery.

A 2nd-century BC Roman mosaic at the Museo Nazionale Romano

🔟 ⭐ Santa Maria del Popolo

Few churches are such perfect primers on Roman art and architecture. Masters from the Early Renaissance (Bramante, Pinturicchio), High Renaissance (Raphael) and Baroque (Caravaggio, Bernini) exercised their genius in all disciplines here: painting, sculpture, architecture and decoration. It's also one of the few churches with major chapels still intact, preserving the artworks that together tell a complete story.

2 Crucifixion of St Peter

Caravaggio has avoided the goriness of his earlier works and filled this *chiaroscuro* work (1601) with drama **(left)**. The naturalistic figures quietly go about their business – the tired workers hauling the cross into place, Peter looking contemplative.

1 Pinturicchio's Adoration

Raphael's contemporary retained more of their teacher Perugino's limpid Umbrian style in this 1490 work in the della Rovere chapel. Also in the chapel is Cardinal Cristoforo's tomb by Francesco da Sangallo (1478), while Domenico's tomb (1477) features a *Madonna with Child* by Mino da Fiesole.

3 Conversion of St Paul

Again, Caravaggio leaves all drama to the effects of light, depicting an awe-struck Paul transfixed by blinding light (1601).

4 Sansovino Tombs

Tuscan Andrea Sansovino gave a Renaissance/Etruscan twist to the traditional lying-in-state look (1505–07). These effigies of Cardinal della Rovere and Cardinal Sforza recline on cushions as if merely asleep.

Santa Maria del Popolo

5 Daniel and Habakkuk

Sculpture as theatre by Bernini, as an angel seizes Habakkuk by the hair **(right)** to fly him to the imprisoned, starving Daniel, shown kneeling with a lion licking his foot.

6 Raphael's Chigi Chapel

Pagan and Christian imagery are fused in this exquisite chapel designed for Agostino Chigi. The skeleton inlaid in the floor **(left)** plays a role in Dan Brown's *Angels and Demons*.

⑧ Marcillat's Stained-Glass Window

The only Roman work by Guillaume de Marcillat (1509), the undisputed French master of stained glass **(left)**, this depicts the Infancy of Christ and Life of the Virgin.

THE PEOPLE'S CHURCH

The ghost of Nero, buried in the Domitia family crypt on the Pincio *(see p66)*, is said to have terrorized this neighbourhood in the form of demon crows that lived in a cursed tree. Pope Paschal II reassured the locals in 1099 by replacing the tree with a chapel paid for by the people *(il popolo)*. It was enlarged in 1227 and rebuilt in Lombard style in 1472–7. Andrea Bregno may have added the Renaissance façade, and Bernini a Baroque touch to the interior.

Santa Maria del Popolo

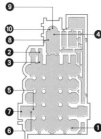

⑦ Sebastiano del Piombo's Nativity of the Virgin

This altarpiece in the Chigi Chapel (1530–34) is in contrast to the dome's Neo-pagan themes, the Eternal Father blessing Chigi's horoscope of planets symbolized by pagan gods.

NEED TO KNOW

MAP D2 ▪ Piazza del Popolo 12 ▪ 06 361 0836; 392 3612243

Open 7am–noon, 4–6pm Mon–Fri, 4–7pm Sat & Sun

▪ Canova and Rosati cafés *(see p122)* are both on Piazza del Popolo.

▪ Some of the church's treasures are behind the high altar in the choir and apse. When mass is not in session, go behind the curtain to the left of the altar and switch on the lights to see them.

⑨ Bramante's Apse

The Renaissance architect's first work in Rome, commissioned by Julius II around 1500, was this beautiful light-filled choir and scallop shell-shaped apse.

⑩ Delphic Sibyl

Pinturicchio, one of the most fashionable artists of the early 16th century, decorated the apse with antique grotesqueries including Sibyls and an intricate tracery of freakish and fantastic beasts.

TOP 10 ⭐ Villa Giulia

Villa Giulia was built in the mid-16th century by Vignola as a pleasure palace for Pope Julius III, who used to float up the Tiber on a flower-decked barge to the building site to keep an eye on progress. It is now a museum devoted to the Etruscans, whose upper classes at least shared Julius's love of luxury. Occupying the area bounded by the Arno and Tiber, they dominated Rome until ousted by an uprising in 509 BC.

5 Euphronios Krater

This exquisite red-figured Greek *krater* **(right)** – used for mixing wine and water – holds 45 litres and depicts a scene from the Trojan War, in which the Olympian deity Hermes directs Hypnos, the god of sleep, and Thanatos, the god of death, to carry away the body of a slain warrior. It was sold to New York's Metropolitan Museum of Art after being looted from a tomb in the 1920s, and was returned to Italy in 2008.

1 Frescoed Tomb from Tarquinia

A reconstruction of a tomb **(above)** at the Etruscan necropolis at Tarquinia, this is frescoed with scenes from a banquet, with dancers, acrobats and athletes providing entertainment.

3 Lion Sarcophagus

This marvellous 6th-century BC terracotta sarcophagus **(below)**, with four roaring lions on its lid, was so huge that it had to be cut in two in order to fit in the kiln for firing.

2 Hydria

This vase **(below)**, used for carrying water, was imported from Greece by the Etruscans and shows a lion and panther attacking a mule.

4 Ficoroni Cista

A cylindrical bronze coffer in which women stored mirrors, cosmetics and beauty accessories, incised with intricately detailed scenes from the myth of Jason and the Argonauts.

6 Ex Votives

As with similar practices in contemporary Catholicism, models of body parts, including feet, uteri and various other internal organs were offered to Etruscan Gods by sick people and their families, in the hope that they would be cured.

7 Sarcophagus of the Spouses
When it was discovered in 1881, this splendid 6th-century BC sarcophagus **(right)** was in 400 pieces. Painstakingly reconstructed, the intimate portrait of a married couple reclining on the lid, smiling as if sharing a joke, is perhaps the most evocative and human work of Etruscan art in existence.

9 Etruscan Temple
In the gardens is a 19th-century reconstruction of the Temple of Alatri.

10 Chigi Vase
Imported from Corinth, Greece, this vase is painted with hunting and battle scenes, including a fascinating frieze showing hoplites (foot soldiers) in formation with decorated shields.

8 Faliscan Krater of the Dawn
The Faliscans, who lived in southern Lazio, were an Indigenous Italic tribe with their own language and culture. This elaborate 4th-century BC vase is decorated with scenes showing a personification of Dawn rising in a chariot.

NEED TO KNOW

MAP D1 ■ Piazzale di Villa Giulia 9 ■ 06 320 1706 ■ www.museoetru.it

Open 9am–8pm Tue–Sun

Adm €10; €2 students (18–25); under 18s free; free for all first Sun of the month

■ Villa Giulia's vast collection continues in the Villa Poniatowski *(see p68)*, which also hosts temporary exhibitions. Check the website for more information.

■ The Villa Giulia Café has tables on a terrace shaded by orange trees, and serves coffees, cold drinks pastries and sandwiches.

■ There are excellent audio guides available in English and Italian.

Museum Guide
This is a lovely museum with a lot to see and pleasant gardens to stroll around when you need to take a break. There are two main floors, plus a small basement section – an atmospheric home for the reconstructed tombs from Etruscan necropolises at Tarquinia and Cerveteri. The ground floor is organised geographically, with sections devoted to the main Etruscan archaeological sites, including Cerveteri, Vulci and Veio. The first floor has a room devoted to important objects that have been returned after being illegally excavated and sold, as well as private collections that have been donated to the museum. There is also an interesting and well-explained epigraphic section.

🔟⭐ Ostia Antica

Some 2,000 years ago, this lively international port city was at the seashore (*ostium* means "river mouth"), but over the millennia the sea retreated and the river changed course. Ostia was founded in the 4th century BC as a simple fort, but as Rome grew, the town became important as an import hub. Its heyday ended in the 4th century AD, and it died completely as an inhabited area about 1,000 years ago.

③ Museum
Beautifully organized, the displays include precious sculptures, sarcophagi and mosaics found among the ruins. A highlight is a statue **(left)** of the god Mithras about to sacrifice the Cosmic Bull.

④ Forum
The rectangular heart of officialdom was originally encircled by columns. In the centre was a shrine to the Imperial Lares (household gods).

① Decumanus Maximus
You enter this vast archaeological park by way of the ancient Via Ostiensis. The white marble goddess on the left marks the start of city's main street, lined with buildings, the Decumanus Maximus.

⑤ Mithraeum of the Serpents
One of 18 Ostian temples to Mithras. The cult was popular with Roman soldiers, and flourished especially well in port towns. The snake frescoes invoked the earth's fertility; the platforms were for lying on during mystic banquets.

⑥ Theatre
The original theatre was twice as tall as it now stands **(above)**. Behind the stage was a temple, of either Ceres (goddess of grain) or Dionysus (god of theatre).

⑦ Piazzale delle Corporazione
This large piazza is surrounded by the ruins of what were once the offices of various maritime businesses, each with a black and white mosaic advertising its trade – chandlers, ropemakers, importers of grain, ivory, wild animals. One has a charming elephant mosaic.

② Casa di Diana and Thermopolium
You can climb up to the top of this *insula* (apartment block) for a great view across the site. Across the street is the Thermopolium, a tavern with a delightful wall painting **(above)** of menu items.

9 Terme di Nettuno

Built in the 2nd century, this bath complex **(left)** was enhanced with fine mosaics of sea gods and sea monsters, which you can view from a small terrace. You can also go down to the left to study close-up the ingenious heating system of the baths.

10 Terme dei Sette Sapienti

This elaborate bath complex contains a painting of Venus; floor mosaics of hunters, animals, nude athletes and marine scenes; and humorous texts in Latin.

8 House of Cupid and Psyche

The wealthy had villas like this refined example of a 3rd-century AD *domus* **(right)**. You can still admire the Doric columns, the fountain *(nymphaeum)* and the inlaid marble decorations.

NEED TO KNOW

MAP G2 ▪ Viale dei Romagnoli 717 ▪ 06 5635 8099 ▪ www.ostiaantica. beniculturali.it

Metro B, trams 3 and 30, or buses 23, 75, 95, 280 to Piramide, then local train from Porta San Paolo Station (next to the metro station) to Ostia Antica

Open Nov–Feb: 8:30am–3:30pm Tue–Sun; Mar–Aug: 8:30am–4:30pm Tue–Sun; Sep–Oct: 8:30am–5:30pm

Tue–Sun (last admission 1hr before closing); closed 1 Jan, 1 May, 25 Dec

Adm: €14; €2 EU citizens (18–25); free for under 18s; free first Sun of the month

The port area (Trajan's Port) can be visited on request, 06 6501 0089

▪ The ruined walls look similar – rent an audio guide at the ticket counter to spot the differences and learn more about each one.

Park Guide

The trip by local train is easy, short and costs the same as one regular bus ticket. From the Ostia Antica train station, walk straight out to the footbridge that goes over the highway. Continue past the restaurant until you get to the ticket booth. The park is extensive and a decent visit will take at least 3 hours. Wear sturdy shoes, and bring sunscreen and water on hot days.

The Top 10 of Everything

Museum staircase at the Vatican

🔟 Moments in History

1 Romulus and Remus

The foundation of Rome is said to have occurred in 753 BC. Twins Romulus and Remus, sons of Mars and a Vestal Virgin, were set adrift by their evil uncle and suckled by a she-wolf. They then founded rival Bronze Age villages on the Palatine, but Romulus killed Remus during an argument, and his "Rome" went on to greatness.

2 Rape of the Sabine Women

To boost the female population in the 750s BC, Romulus's men kidnapped women from the Sabine kingdom. As Rome began to expand, however, the kingdoms were united. Rome was later conquered by the Etruscan Tarquin dynasty. In 510 BC, a patrician-ruled Republic was formed that lasted more than 450 years.

3 Assassination of Caesar

A series of military victories, adding Gaul (France) to Rome, increased General Julius

Joseph Court's *The Death of Caesar*

Caesar's popularity. He marched his army to Rome and declared himself Dictator for Life, but on 15 March 44 BC he was assassinated. Caesar's adopted son Octavian changed his name to Augustus and declared himself emperor in 27 BC.

Julius Caesar

4 Rome Burns

In AD 64 fire destroyed much of Rome (see p49). Emperor Nero rebuilt many public works, but also appropriated vast tracts of land to build his Domus Aurea or Golden House. Hounded from office, he committed suicide in AD 68.

5 Battle at Milvian Bridge

In 312 Emperor Constantine's mother, had a vision of victory under the sign of the Cross and defeated co-emperor Maxentius at Milvian Bridge. He declared Christianity the state religion.

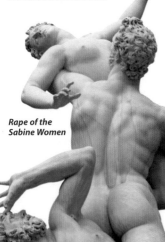

Rape of the Sabine Women

6 Fall of the Empire

By the late 4th century Rome was in decline, as Barbarians from across the Rhine and Danube conquered outlying provinces. In 476, the last emperor was deposed and the Empire fell.

(7) Papacy moves to Avignon

Following the departure of the papacy to France in 1309, the city became a backwater ruled by petty princes who built palaces out of marble from the great temples. In 1377 the papacy returned to Rome, and the city was reborn.

(8) Sack of Rome

Rome was conquered for the first time in more than a millennium in 1527. Emperor Charles V's Germanic troops held the city for seven months until Pope Clement VII surrendered and promised to address the concerns of the new Protestant movement.

(9) Unification of Italy

Piemontese King Vittorio Emanuele II and his general, Garibaldi, spent years conquering the peninsula's kingdoms and principalities to create a new country called Italy. In 1870, Garibaldi breached the Aurelian Walls and took the ancient capital, completing Italian Unification.

Mussolini with the Quadrumvirs

(10) Mussolini Takes Power

Benito "Il Duce" Mussolini, leader of the Fascist Party, marched on Rome in 1922 with the Quadrumvirs (four leaders he appointed), and was declared prime minister. Delusions of imperial grandeur led him to excavate many ruins. He allied Italy with Hitler, but when the tides turned, Mussolini was deposed and Italy joined Allied troops. The current Republic was set up after a referendum in 1946.

TOP 10 INFLUENTIAL POPES

1 St Peter
The Apostle (AD 42–67) called by Jesus to lead the church. After his martyrdom in Rome the city became the epicentre of Christianity

2 St Leo the Great
Rome's bishop (440–61) made himself *pontifex maximus* of the Christian church.

3 St Gregory the Great
Affirmed the papacy as the western secular leader and converted England to Christianity (590–604).

4 Innocent III
This medieval pope (1198–1216) hand-picked emperors and approved monkish orders.

5 Boniface VIII
Imperious, pragmatic and power-hungry, Boniface (1294–1303) instituted the first Jubilee to make money.

6 Alexander VI
Ruthless Borgia pope (1492–1503), who used the pontificate to destroy rivals.

7 Julius II
A warrior pope and patron of the arts (1513–21), he hired Michelangelo for the Sistine Chapel and Raphael to decorate his apartment *(see p12)*.

8 Paul III
Scholarly and secular, but fighting Protestant reforms, Paul III (1534–49) founded the Jesuits and the Inquisition.

9 Sixtus V
Cleansed Papal States of corruption (1585–90) and masterminded a Baroque overhaul of Rome.

10 John Paul II
The first non-Italian Pope for over 400 years, John Paul II (1920-2005), was famed for his extensive travelling.

Pope John Paul II

TOP 10 Ancient Sites

The ruins of the Colosseum, the imposing 1st-century AD amphitheatre

1 The Colosseum

The intense labour to build the greatest of amphitheatres *(see p26)* was carried out by enslaved Jewish people, brought here after the suppression of their revolt in Judaea. It has been the archetype for the world's sports stadiums ever since.

2 Trajan's Markets and Column

Trajan's Markets *(see p26)* were the world's first shopping complex – 150 shops on five levels selling everything from fish (kept fresh in tanks), spices and fruit to wine, oil and fabrics. It opened onto Trajan's Forum, dominated by Trajan's Column. Bas reliefs spiral around the column, describing two Roman campaigns in Dacia, so detailed that they may have been based on Trajan's own war diaries.

3 Roman Forum

In the centre of the Forum *(see pp20–21)* stands a humble ruined structure where fresh flowers are placed year-round. This is the foundation of the Temple to Julius Caesar, built by Augustus in the 1st century BC. The flowers indicate the exact spot of Caesar's cremation.

4 The Pantheon

People originally approached this ancient temple *(see pp18–19)* to all the gods by a steep staircase, but the street level has risen since the 2nd century. The present temple was built by Hadrian, after the ancient 1st-century BC temple burned down.

5 Palatine Hill

Most European languages derive their word for palace from the name of this hill *(see pp22–3)*. All-important in the history of early Rome, first as its birthplace, then as the site of its leaders' homes, it is now ideal for a romantic stroll.

6 Pyramid of Caius Cestius

In the late 1st century BC, spurred by Cleopatra's fame, all things Egyptian were fashionable in Rome. Cestius built this pyramid *(see p126)* as a tomb. It took 330 days to build and is his only claim to fame.

Trajan's Column

7 Column of Marcus Aurelius

A 2nd-century AD commemoration of conquests along the Danube, this colossus *(see p98)* stands 30 m (100 ft) high and consists of 28 marble drums. The 20 spiral reliefs chronicle war scenes. A statue of the emperor and his wife once stood on top of the column, but it was replaced by one of St Paul in 1589.

8 Baths of Caracalla

The most popular spa *(see p125)* of ancient Rome, the baths included exercise areas, hot and cold pools, social lounges, art centres, brothels and libraries. Incredibly, access to the *terme* was free. Today, the complex hosts Rome's most important opera festival.

The historic Baths of Caracalla

9 Crypta Balbi

In the 1980s, a private Roman theatre dating back to 13 BC was discovered here *(see pp64–5)*. By the 3rd century the area had gone downhill, with a lime kiln, glass factory and apartment blocks for workers. The museum brings to life all these stages, and there are regular tours around the excavations.

10 Palazzo Valentini

The polychrome marble walls and mosaic floors are reconstructed using clever technology as visitors walk through the ruins of a private spa complex at these patrician villas *(see p64)*, discovered in 2007. Another itinerary in the exhibition focuses on a newly excavated part of Trajan's Forum, and includes animations of scenes from Trajan's Column.

TOP 10 ROMAN EMPERORS

Emperor Constantine

1 Augustus
The first and most brilliant emperor (31 BC–AD 14) brought a reign of peace after 17 years of civil war.

2 Nero
The most notorious for his excesses, Nero (54–68) fancied himself a great singer and showman.

3 Vespasian
This emperor (69–79) ended civil war and the Jewish revolt, and started construction of the Colosseum.

4 Trajan
One of the most just rulers and successful generals, Trajan (98–117) pushed the Roman Empire to its furthest reaches.

5 Hadrian
A great builder and traveller, Hadrian (117–38) revived Greek ideals, including the fashion of growing a beard.

6 Marcus Aurelius
The closest Rome came to having a philosopher-king of the Platonic ideal (161–80).

7 Septimius Severus
Brought order after civil war, promoted cultural life and left an important architectural legacy (193–211).

8 Diocletian
Diocletian (284–305) set up a governing system of multiple emperors. A virulent persecutor of the Christians.

9 Constantine
Constantine (306–37) established Christianity as the state religion and moved the capital to Constantinople.

10 Romulus Augustulus
The last of the emperors (475–6), his deposition by German warrior Odoacer marked the fall of the Roman Empire.

Early Christian Churches

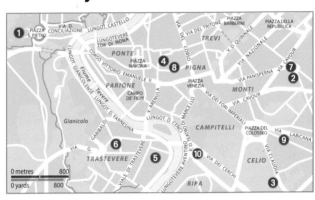

1 St Peter's Basilica

Should the opportunity arise, don't miss seeing the basilica's (see pp16–17) cavernous interior when all the lights are on – only then can you fully appreciate this giant jewel box of colour.

2 Santa Prassede

Santa Prassede (see p132) was founded in the 9th century by Pope Paschal II on the legendary site of a *titulus*, a private house where Christians worshipped in secret during the persecutions of the first and second centuries. The choir and the Chapel of St Zeno were decorated by Byzantine mosaic artists.

Santa Prassede

3 Santa Maria in Domnica

MAP E5 ■ Piazza della Navicella
■ 06 7720 2685 ■ Closed to visitors;
call for latest details ■ www.santa
mariaindomnica.it

Nicknamed Santa Maria della Navicella after the stone boat in the fountain outside – likely to be a votive offering by Roman sailors to the goddess Isis – the first church on this site was probably built over a disused Roman fire station, which Christians used for secret worship. Covering the apse are superb 9th-century mosaics, the figures lifelike and fluid – look at the different expressions of the angels, the wind stirring their drapery, or the sheep licking the gowns of the Apostles as they walk in a meadow. The church is closed due to a construction site located near the main entrance.

4 The Pantheon

According to legend, in the 7th century, demons attacked Christians as they walked past the Pantheon (see pp18–19), and permission was granted to convert this temple to all gods into a church. It is still a church, dedicated to the Madonna and all martyrs.

5 Santa Cecilia in Trastevere

This church (see p144) stands over the steam room or *caldarium* in which, according to legend, St Cecilia was locked for three days to suffocate to death for having tried to give her husband and his brother Christian burials. One story is that she sang throughout her imprisonment – the reason she is now the patron saint of music. In 1599, her tomb was opened and her perfectly preserved body briefly revealed before it disintegrated on contact with the air. Stefano Maderno made sketches, which he used for his haunting sculpture *The Martyrdom of Saint Cecilia*.

6 Santa Maria in Trastevere

Probably Rome's oldest church (see p143), this is certainly one of the most intimate and charming. Dating from the time of Pope Calixtus I (AD 217–222), it was an early centre of Marian devotion and is Rome's only medieval church that has not been altered by either decay or enthusiastic Baroque renovators.

7 Santa Maria Maggiore

One of the city's greatest basilicas (see p131), this dates from the 5th century, as do its earliest mosaics, full of Byzantine splendour. The 16th-century Capella Sistina rare marbles were "quarried", in typical papal fashion, by destroying an ancient wonder – the Palatine's Septizonium, a tower built in AD 203 by Septimius Severus.

Façade of the Santa Maria Maggiore

8 Santa Maria sopra Minerva

Built in 1280 on the ruins of a temple dedicated to Minerva, Roman goddess of wisdom. In the 16th century it (see p97) was

Santa Maria sopra Minerva

the headquarters of the Inquisition in Rome – Galileo was tried for heresy in the adjoining convent.

9 San Clemente

A double decker-church (see p131) above a Roman temple, San Clemente offers visitors a touch of Roman time travel. At street level is a 12th-century church with medieval mosaics, Cosmati-work pavements and choir enclosures and Renaissance frescoes by Massaccio and Masolino. Below is a 4th-century church with traces of frescoes, and below that a series of Roman foundations and a Mithras temple, where initiation rites and ritual feasts took place.

10 Santa Maria in Cosmedin

This wonderfully atmospheric church (see p108) has some of the city's finest Cosmati work (geometric mosaics made of coloured marble fragments reclaimed from ancient buildings) on its pavements, choir enclosure, and a twisting Paschal candlestick. A glass case holds the flower-crowned skull of St Valentine.

🔟 Renaissance and Baroque Churches

Interior of Santa Maria del Popolo

1 Santa Maria del Popolo

Legend says that on this spot, where a great oak grew, Nero died and was buried. The site *(see pp38–9)* was thought cursed, but in 1099, in a vision, Pope Paschal II was told by the Virgin to fell the oak, dig up Nero's bones and build a chapel.

2 Sant'Agostino

This church *(see p90)* a 15th-century marble statue, the *Madonna del Parto*, inspired by Roman goddess Juno and surrounded by gifts from those whose wish for a child has been granted. Across the aisle, the realism of Caravaggio's *Madonna di Loreto* caused a scandal when it was unveiled in 1603 – the pilgrims' feet are filthy and even the Madonna has dirty toenails.

3 Santa Maria della Pace

One of the most fashionable churches *(see p90)* in Renaissance Rome, Santa Maria was frequented by the beau monde. Fiammetta, courtesan lover of Cesare Borgia, donated property to the church, and banker Agostino Chigi commissioned a chapel which was decorated by Raphael with Sibyls, best seen from a window of the Bramante cloisters behind the church.

4 San Luigi dei Francesi

The great attraction here *(see p89)* is Caravaggio's trio of huge paintings *(see p57)*. The central oil on canvas, *St Matthew and the Angel*, is the second version. The first was rejected by the church because the saint was shown with dirty feet – and, some say, because of the overly familiar young angel.

5 Tempietto

MAP C5 ■ Piazza San Pietro in Montorio ■ 06 581 2806 ■ Open 10am–6pm Tue–Sun

Rome's most quintessentially Renaissance building, the Tempietto is a perfectly circular Doric temple built by Bramante in 1501 on the site where St Peter was thought to have been crucified.

The 16th-century Tempietto

Frescoes at Sant'Ignazio di Loyola

6 Sant'Ignazio di Loyola

Construction of Sant'Ignazio di Loyola *(see p98)* began in 1626, when the Catholic church was reeling from the blow dealt by Protestantism. The Jesuits who commissioned it were quite wary of appearing too wealthy – hence the austere façade. By the late 17th century, when the interior was decorated, they were more confident, and commissioned stunning illusionistic frescoes marking the triumphs of Jesuit missionaries.

7 Sant'Andrea al Quirinale

Created in a theatrical style by Bernini and completed in 1670, this church *(see p139)* is an oval shape, with the main entrance located on its short axis – on entering, your eyes hit the high altar, where sculpted angels appear to be positioning a painting of St Andrew crucified on his diagonal cross. Above, a statue of the saint floats on a cloud towards heaven, as if he has just slipped through the broken pediment below.

8 Sant'Ivo

Borromini was a restlessly inventive architect, fascinated with intricate geometry. Sant'Ivo *(see p89)* took over 20 years to build, spanning the reigns of three popes, and each has their family emblem included in the decor: bees for Barberini Pope Urban VIII, doves for Pamphilj Pope Innocent X, and star-topped blancmange – actually a mountain – for Chigi Pope Alexander VI.

9 San Carlo alle Quattro Fontane

Designed by Bernini's arch rival Borromini, San Carlo alle Quattro Fontane *(see p139)* consists of an octagonal courtyard and oval building, and an ingenious geometrically coffered dome, constructed to create the illusion that it is higher than it really is.

10 Santa Maria della Vittoria

Caked with gold and stucco, this is one of Rome's most lavishly decorated churches *(see p137)*. It holds Bernini's notorious statue, *Ecstasy of St Teresa*, showing the saint in the throes of what is possibly the art world's most famous orgasm.

🔟 Museums and Galleries

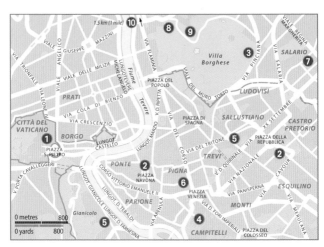

Venus,
Vatican
Museums

1 Vatican Museums
Occupying papal palaces dating from the 13th century onwards, these galleries (see pp12–15) include the Graeco-Roman antiquities, four Raphael Rooms the Etruscan Museum, the Collection of Modern Religious Art, the Sistine Chapel and the Picture Gallery.

2 Museo Nazionale Romano
Founded in 1889, this museum's (see pp34–7) holdings include archaeological finds and antiquities unearthed since 1870, plus pre-existing collections. The works are distributed between the Baths of Diocletian, nearby Palazzo Massimo, Palazzo Altemps, and the Crypta Balbi.

3 Galleria Borghese
A tribute to the unbridled power of favoured papal nephews in the 1600s, this pleasure-palace (see pp24–5), its restored gardens and priceless art collections comprise one of Rome's most gorgeous sights.

4 Musei Capitolini
The glorious square (see pp28–31), designed by Michelangelo, is home to papal art collections that are smaller than the Vatican's, but equally invaluable.

5 Galleria Nazionale d'Arte Antica
This state art collection is divided between two noble family residences, Palazzo Barberini (see p137) and Galleria Corsini (see p146). The first boasts the Gran Salone, with its dazzling illusionistic ceiling by Pietro da Cortona, along with works by Filippo Lippi, El Greco, Holbein and Caravaggio. The second houses a Fra Angelico triptych, and paintings by Rubens, Van Dyck and Caravaggio.

6 Galleria Doria Pamphilj
This aristocratic family's palace (see p97) is filled with masterpieces by such painters as Raphael, Titian and Velázquez, whose portrait of the Pamphilj pope is famous for its psychological depth. This exhibit is accompanied by an audio-guide

The grandiose Galleria Doria Pamphilj

narrated by the present-day Prince Jonathan Doria Pamphilj (in English) that gives rare insight into the history of the collection.

7 MACRO

MAP F1 ■ **Via Nizza 138**
■ 06 0608 ■ Open noon–7pm Tue–Fri (from 10am Sat & Sun)

One of two branches of the Museo d'Arte Contemporanea Roma (the other is in Testaccio, see p127). The building, originally a Peroni beer factory, is an imaginative triumph, with an aerial, glass-floored courtyard and reactive lighting systems. Although there is a permanent collection, the style is that of a contemporary gallery, with an ever-changing series of exhibitions and installations.

8 Villa Giulia

The building (see p117) itself is a 16th-century country retreat designed for Pope Julius III by Vignola. Since 1889, it has housed the state collection of pre-Roman art, including Etruscan artifacts and relics of the Latins and other tribes. The prize Etruscan work is the 6th-century BC Sarcophagus of the Spouses, a large terracotta showing a serenely smiling couple.

9 Galleria Nazionale d'Arte Moderna

The *belle époque* home to this collection (see p118) offers sculptures by Canova and an exhaustive view of 19th-century Italian and European painting. There is also an eclectic selection of modern works, including pieces by artists such as Rodin, Cézanne, Modigliani, Van Gogh, Monet, Klimt and Jackson Pollock.

10 MAXXI

Set in a futuristic concrete building, MAXXI (see pp156–7) hosts a rich season of frequently changing thematic exhibitions of contemporary art, photography and architecture. Short art films and videos are screened for free in a small cinema. The building alone is worth a visit, featuring a gravity-defying overhang, carbon-fibre lighting and freestanding stairways and walkways that look like something straight out of a sci-fi movie.

The award-winning futuristic architecture of MAXXI

🔟 Artistic Masterpieces

1 Caravaggio's Deposition

Caravaggio strove to outdo Michelangelo's *Pietà* by making his Mary old and tired *(see p13)*. Rather than a slender slip of a Christ, Caravaggio's muscular Jesus is so heavy (emphasized by a diagonal composition) that Nicodemus struggles with his legs and John's grasp opens Christ's wound.

2 Raphael's Transfiguration

Raphael's masterpiece *(see p12)* and his final work was found, almost finished, in his studio when he died. A pinnacle of his talent as a synthesist,

Raphael's *Transfiguration*

mixing Perugino's clarity, Leonardo's composition, and Michelangelo's colour palette and twisting figures.

3 Michelangelo's Pietà

The Renaissance is known for naturalism, but Michelangelo warped this for artistic effect. Here *(see p16)*, Mary is too young, her dead son, achingly thin and small, laid

Michelangelo's *Pietà*

across her voluminous lap. Hearing the work being attributed to better known sculptors, the artist crept into the chapel of St Peter's one night and carved his name in the band across the Virgin's chest.

4 Raphael's School of Athens

When Raphael first cast his contemporary artists as Classical thinkers in this imaginary setting, one was missing. After he saw the Sistine ceiling Michelangelo was painting down the hall, Raphael added the troubled genius, sulking on the steps, as Heraclitus *(see p12)*.

5 Michelangelo's Sistine Chapel

Although he considered himself a sculptor first, Michelangelo

Detail from the frescoes of the Sistine Chapel

managed to turn this almost-flat ceiling *(see pp14–15)* into a soaring vault peopled with Old Testament prophets and *ignudi* (nude men). He did it virtually alone, firing all of his assistants save one to help him grind pigments.

6 Bernini's Apollo and Daphne

Rarely has marble captured flowing, almost liquid movement so gracefully. Bernini freezes time, windblown hair and cloak, in the instant the fleeing nymph is wrapped in bark and leaves, transformed into a laurel by her sympathetic river god father *(see p24)*.

Bernini's *Apollo and Daphne*

7 Caravaggio's Calling of St Matthew

Caravaggio uses strong *chiaroscuro* techniques here *(see p89)*. As a naturalistic shaft of light spills from Christ to his chosen chronicler, St Matthew, who is sitting at a table with four other men, Caravaggio captures the precise moment of Matthew's conversion from tax collector to Evangelist.

8 Leonardo da Vinci's St Jerome

Barely sketched out, yet compelling for its anatomical precision and compositional experimentation *(see p13)*. Jerome forms a spiral that starts in the mountains, runs across the cave entrance and lion's curve, up the saint's outstretched right arm, then wraps along his left arm and hand into the centre.

9 Michelangelo's Moses

This wall monument *(see p131)* is a pale shadow of the elaborate tomb for Julius II that Michelangelo first envisaged and for which he carved this figure. Some claim there is a self-portrait in the beard and what are commonly thought to be horns may have been an attempt to create a radiating light effect.

10 Bernini's Ecstasy of St Teresa

The saint here *(see p137)* is being pierced by a smirking angel's lance, and is Bernini at his theatrical best. He sets this religious ecstasy on a stage flanked by opera boxes from which members of the commissioning Cornaro family look on.

🔟 Writers in Rome

Johann Wolfgang von Goethe, German writer and statesman

1 Goethe
The first Grand Tourist, German author Johann Wolfgang von Goethe (1749–1832) rented rooms on the Corso, now a museum dedicated to his life, between 1786 and 1788 *(see p118)*. His book *Italian Journey* laid the blueprint for later tourists who came to Italy to complete their education.

2 John Keats
The English Romantic poet (1795–1821) came to Rome in 1820 for the antiquities and Italian lifestyle – and to bolster his ailing health, which nevertheless failed. Keats died at age 25 of tuberculosis in an apartment that over-looked the Spanish Steps *(see p115)*.

3 Henry James
The New York author (1843–1916) spent half his life in Europe. Rome features in his novels *Daisy Miller* and *Portrait of a Lady*, and in the essay "A Roman Holiday" in

his travelogue *Italian Hours*. In an 1869 letter he proclaimed "At last – for the first time – I live! It beats everything: it leaves the Rome of your fancy – your education – nowhere."

4 Nathaniel Hawthorne
During his Italian sojourn from 1857 to 1859, the American man of letters (1804–64) was so moved by an ancient sculpture in the Capitoline museums he crafted his final novel *The Marble Faun* around it.

5 Alberto Moravia
One of Italy's top modern authors (1907–90), Moravia wrote about Rome in *Racconti Romani*, *La Romana*, *La Ciociara*, *Gli Indifferenti* and *La Noia*, most of which have been translated many times.

Mark Twain

6 Mark Twain
The American writer (1835–1910) spent little time in the Eternal City during his Grand Tour in 1867, but his satirical

impressions in *The Innocents Abroad* have become among the most quoted and memorable of any visitor.

7 Edward Gibbon

When English parliamentarian Gibbon (1737–94) stood in the Forum for the first time in 1764, he was struck by how "…each memorable spot where Romulus stood, or Tully spoke, or Caesar fell, was at once present to my eye." He resolved to write the history of Rome, and in 1788 finished his seminal work, *The Decline and Fall of the Roman Empire*.

8 Gore Vidal

The prolific American writer (1925–2012) was a resident of Rome and Ravello, south of Naples, for decades. His Roman experiences informed such books as *The Judgment of Paris*, *Julian* and his memoir *Palimpsest*.

Romantic poet Lord Byron

9 Lord Byron

The ultimate Romantic poet (1788–1824), Lord Byron spent years in Italy in the company of the Shelleys and other friends, and based a large part of *Childe Harold's Pilgrimage* and *Don Juan* on his experiences here.

10 Mary Shelley

The English author (1797–1851) lived in Rome on and off with her husband, the poet Percy Bysshe Shelley (1792–1822). It was here that Mary completed her Gothic masterpiece *Frankenstein*, while Percy penned *The Cenci* about the scandal of Roman patrician Beatrice Cenci.

TOP 10 CLASSICAL WRITERS IN ROME

1 Plautus
Formulaic comedies of errors by Plautus (250–184 BC) influenced Shakespeare.

2 Caesar
General, dictator and writer (100–44 BC). *De Bello Gallico* describes his campaigns in Gaul (France), *The Civil War* his fight against Pompey.

3 Cicero
Great orator and staunch republican (106–43 BC). His speeches grant insight into Roman political life.

4 Petronius
Petronius (70–130) parodied Roman life in *Satiricon*.

5 Ovid
Greatest Roman Classical poet (43 BC–AD 17). His *Metamorphoses* codified many Roman myths, but *Ars Amatoria* detailed how to entice women and got him exiled.

6 Tacitus
Tacitus (55–117) wrote *Annals and Histories* covering Rome's early Imperial history; *Life of Agricola* his father-in-law's governorship of Britain.

7 Juvenal
Romans invented satire; Juvenal (60–130) perfected the form in his poems.

8 Pliny the Younger
The letters *(Epistulae)* of Pliny (61–113) give us a glimpse of imperial society.

9 Suetonius
The historian Suetonius (70–125) wrote *The Lives of the Caesars*.

10 Virgil
Poet and propagandist (70–19 BC). His epic *The Aeneid* tied Rome's foundation to the Trojan War.

Virgil

📠10 Villas and Palaces

Fresco at Villa Farnesina

1 Villa Farnesina

A little gem, Villa Farnesina *(see p143)* is decorated by some of the greatest artists of the Renaissance, including Raphael. The loggias are now glassed in to protect the precious frescoes, but they were originally open, embodying the ideal of blending indoor and outdoor spaces – a concept borrowed from ancient Roman villa designers.

2 Palazzi del Campidoglio

When Emperor Charles V visited Rome in 1536, Pope Paul III was so embarrassed at the Capitoline Hill's *(see p107)* state that he enlisted Michelangelo's help. Work started 10 years later, but Michelangelo died long before its completion. True to his design, however, are the double flight of steps for the Palazzo Senatorio, the addition of Palazzo Nuovo, the fine façades and placement of ancient sculptures.

3 Palazzo Barberini

When Maffeo Barberini became Pope Urban VIII in 1623, he decided to build a family palace *(see p137)* on the (then) edge of town. Architect Carlo Maderno designed it as an outsize country villa with three floors of arcades. Bernini added the square staircase on the left; Borromini the spiral staircase on the right.

4 Villa Torlonia

Via Nomentana 70 ▪ Open 9am–7pm Tue–Sun ▪ www.museivillatorlonia.it

Created in the 19th century for a wealthy banker, Prince Giovanni Torlonia, this aristocratic estate sprang to fame in the 1920s when it was rented out to Mussolini. He lived here until he was ousted in 1943. The park is open to the public, and there are several small museums, including the original Technotown *(see p70)*.

5 Palazzo Farnese

Considered the Renaissance palace *par excellence*, Palazzo Farnese *(see p110)* reflects the genius of Antonio da Sangallo the Younger and Michelangelo. Home to one of Rome's most unscrupulous families, it was commissioned in 1517 by Alessandro Farnese, later Pope Paul III.

6 Galleria Doria Pamphilj

Occupying an entire block of Via del Corso, this vast palazzo *(see p97)* is still owned by the Doria

The elegant Galleria Doria Pamphilj

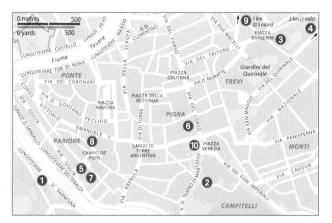

Pamphilj family. In 1940, it was stormed by Nazi troops, but the labyrinthine layout allowed the family to escape. The palace, and its superb art collection – including the *Portrait of Innocent X* by Velázquez and *Rest on the Flight into Egypt* by Caravaggio – are open to the public.

7 Palazzo Spada

Built around 1550 for a wealthy cardinal, the architect unknown, this palace *(see p110)* houses an art gallery and has one of the most ornate Renaissance façades in Rome, featuring reliefs that evoke the city's glorious past. However, the courtyard is the masterpiece, with its figures of the 12 Olympian gods.

8 Palazzo della Cancelleria

One of the loveliest palaces *(see p110)* from the Early Renaissance (late 1400s) – the purity of Palazzo della Cancelleria's façade and courtyard is unparalleled. Several monuments were pillaged to provide the marble and the 44 portico columns inside.

9 Villa Giulia

Intended for hedonistic pleasure, this was a perfect papal retreat where Pope Julius III could indulge his tastes for young boys and Classical statuary. Designed by

Decorated passage, Villa Giulia

Vignola, Ammannati and Vasari, this 16th-century marvel *(see pp40–41)* is all loggias, fountains and gardens.

10 Palazzo Venezia

Built (1455–64) for the Venetian cardinal Pietro Barbo, Rome's first great Renaissance palace *(see p110)* is attributed to two Florentine architects, Alberti and Maiano. Admire the palm court with its 18th-century fountain from the museum café. Piazza Venezia is the de facto centre of Rome and converging point of traffic that is conducted with balletic brio by a white-gloved policeman.

🔟 Squares and Fountains

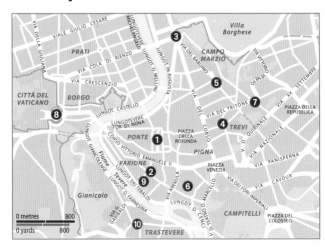

1 Piazza Navona

The elongated oval of Rome's loveliest square (see p89) hints that it is built atop Domitian's ancient stadium (see p92). This pedestrian paradise is filled with cafés, street artists and splashing fountains. Bernini created the central Fountain of Four Rivers, and added the Moor figure to the most southerly of the piazza's other fountains, constantly altered from the 16th to 19th centuries.

2 Campo de' Fiori

This "field of flowers" (see p107) bursts with colour during the morning market, and again after dark when its pubs and bars make it a centre of Roman nightlife. The dour hooded statue overlooking all is in honour of Giordano Bruno, a theologian who was burned at the stake here for his progressive heresies in 1600 during the Counter-Reformation.

3 Piazza del Popolo

Architect Giuseppe Valadier expanded this site (see p116) of festivals and public executions into an elegant Neo-Classical piazza in 1811–23, adding four Egyptian-style lion fountains to the base of one of Rome's oldest obelisks. The 1200 BC Rameses II monolith was originally brought to the Circus Maximus by Emperor Augustus, then placed here by Pope Sixtus V.

4 Trevi Fountain

Tradition holds that if you throw coins into this 1732 Nicola Salvi fountain (see p115), you ensure a return to Rome. Ingeniously grafted on to the back of a palazzo (even the window-sills mutate into rough rocks), the Trevi marks the end of the Acqua

Trevi Fountain

Vergine aqueduct, built by Agrippa in 19 BC from a spring miraculously discovered by a virgin.

The lovely Piazza di Spagna

⑤ Piazza di Spagna
Overlooked by shuttered russet, cream and mustard palazzi, Piazza di Spagna (see p115) attracts visitors from all over the world. The piazza has been at the heart of tourist and expatriate Rome since the 18th century, when artists, musicians and writers ranging from Keats, Shelley and Byron to Goethe, Liszt and Wagner flocked to the city. Visitors can arrive here early in the day to avoid the crowds.

⑥ Fontana delle Tartarughe
Giacomo della Porta designed this delightful fountain (see p109) between 1581 and 1584. The turtles (tartarughe) struggling up over the lip, however, were added in 1658, perhaps by Bernini.

⑦ Piazza Barberini
This busy piazza (see p138) is centred on Bernini's Triton Fountain (1642–3), the merman spouting water from a conch shell. Commissioned by Pope Urban VIII, it features large bees – his family symbol – on its base. There are more chubby Barberini bees, poised as if to take a sip of water, on the other Bernini fountain across the piazza.

⑧ Piazza San Pietro
Bernini's immense colonnade, 196 m (640 ft) across, encircles the piazza (see p16). Its perfect ellipse is confirmed by the optical illusion of disappearing columns viewed by standing at one of the focus points – marble discs set between the central 1st-century BC obelisk, carved in Egypt for a Roman Prefect, and the two fountains: Bernini's on the left, Fontana's on the right.

⑨ Piazza Farnese
MAP K4
The elegant Piazza Farnese is dominated by two fountains incorporating giant granite bath tubs from the Baths of Caracalla. Overlooking the piazza is Palazzo Farnese, whose ceilings, frescoed by Annibale Caracci, are illuminated every night so that they can be seen through the unshuttered windows.

Fountains at the Piazza Farnese

⑩ Piazza Santa Maria in Trastevere
MAP K6
Lining this square are cafés, bars, shops and a 17th-century palazzo abutting a medieval church (see p143), its mosaics romantically floodlit at night. A fountain fitted with shells by Carlo Fontana (1682) atop a pedestal of stairs serves as benches for backpackers to strum guitars and tourists to eat ice cream.

🔟 Underground Sights

San Clemente church

1 San Clemente
The many layers of this church (see p131) reveal the changing ideals of Rome in various eras. Over 2,000 years old, San Clemente is a three-tiered church whose foundations rest on an ancient Roman Mithraic temple, above which there is a 4th-century basilica with traces of frescoes. On ground level, the present-day church dates to the 12th century and has stunning mosaics.

2 Appian Way Catacombs
Underground cemeteries outside the city walls were created in accordance with the laws of the time, not as a response to suppression. San Sebastiano has some well-preserved stucco, while San Callisto's walls have early Christian art. Domitilla is Rome's largest and oldest catacomb network, and the only one to still contain bones. Frescoes of both Classical and Christian scenes can be seen in its passages, including one of the earliest images of Christ as the Good Shepherd. Many of its 1st- and 2nd-century chambers have no Christian connection; several religions practised burial of this sort (see p156).

3 Under the Colosseum
In the late 19th century, excavations revealed a network of tunnels, shafts and corridors (see p26). Wild animals were kept here in cages before being winched up to the arena, and released through a trapdoor. Archers stood by in case any of the beasts escaped.

4 Palazzo Valentini
MAP P3 ▪ Via IV Novembre 119/A ▪ 10am–7pm Wed–Mon ▪ Adm ▪ www.palazzovalentini.it
Below Palazzo Valentini (see p49) were found not only Roman villas but also layers of detritus. Archaeologists concluded that the site was a Renaissance rubbish dump. A section has been replicated, using original finds – shells and bones – useful indicators about the Renaissance diet.

5 Vatican Grottoes
The famous Red Wall behind which St Peter (see p17) was supposedly buried was discovered under the Vatican in the 1940s.

Fresco, Crypta Balbi

6 Crypta Balbi
MAP M4 ▪ Via delle Botteghe Oscure 31 ▪ Open 11am–6pm Tue–Sun ▪ Adm ▪ www.coopculture.it
A jumble of excavations from several eras, Crypta Balbi (see p109) includes a piece of 13 BC *crypta* (porticoed

courtyard) attached to a destroyed theatre. The museum has didactic panels and several medieval frescoes.

7 Mamertine Prison

This was Rome's ancient central lockdown (see p27) (built 7th–6th century BC). Among its celebrity inmates were Vercigetorix, a rebel Celtic chieftain, and St Peter, who left an impression of his face where guards reportedly slammed him against a wall.

8 Roman Houses under Santi Giovanni e Paolo

MAP E5 ■ Clivo di Scauro/Piazza SS Giovanni e Paolo ■ 06 3996 7755 (call for reservations) ■ Open 10am–4pm Wed–Mon) ■ Adm ■ www.coopculture.it

The houses under this church (see p133) belonged to two Constantinian officials, who were put to death under emperor Julian in AD 362 for refusing to worship pagan gods. The buildings include a frescoed nymphaeum dating from the 1st to 4th centuries.

9 Santa Maria della Concezione

MAP E2 ■ Via Veneto 27 ■ Open 7am–1pm, 3–6pm daily ■ Adm

Among the tenets of the Capuchin Order is the necessity of confronting the reality of death, the reason why the Capuchin catacombs below this church contain the skulls and bones of thousands of dead monks, wired together into crowns of thorns and sacred hearts. At the entrance a sign reads "What you are, we used to be; what we are, you will be".

10 Mithraeum under Santa Prisca

MAP D5 ■ Via di Santa Prisca 13 ■ 06 3996 7700 ■ Open 2nd & 4th Sat of the month, 10am for individuals, 11am & noon for groups (by reservation only) ■ Adm

This 3rd-century AD shrine to Mithraism was popular among soldiers and the lower classes while Christianity was gaining status with the patricians.

TOP 10 VISTAS

Roman Forum

1 Roman Forum from Campidoglio
MAP P5
Walk around the right side of Palazzo Senatorio for a postcard panorama – floodlit at night.

2 Il Vittoriano
Climb the so-called "Wedding Cake" (or take the lift) for vistas over the Imperial Fora (see p110).

3 Gianicolo
The Eternal City (see p145) is laid out at your feet from a lover's lane perch across the Tiber.

4 The Spanish Steps
Views spill down the steps (see p115) to the tourist-filled piazza.

5 Musei Capitolini Café
A bird's-eye sweep over the archaeological park at Rome's heart can be seen from here (see p28).

6 St Peter's Dome
St Peter's Colonnade and Castel Sant'Angelo can be seen from Michelangelo's Dome (see p16).

7 Knights of Malta Keyhole
St Peter's Dome is perfectly framed through a gate keyhole in this garden (see p126).

8 Castel Sant'Angelo Ramparts
Lazy Tiber River vistas with the Ponte Sant'Angelo (see p145) directly underneath.

9 Pincio
Valadier carefully designed this view from his gardens, across Piazza del Popolo (see p116) to St Peter's.

10 Villa Mellini
MAP B1
A different panorama, near Rome's observatory above Piazzale Clodio, taking in the city and hills beyond from the northwest.

TOP10 Green Spaces

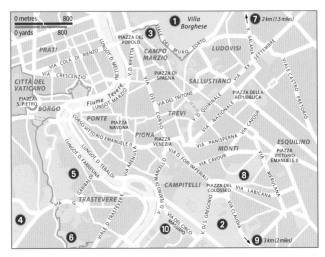

1 Villa Borghese

Extensive, elegant and full of shady glades and beautiful fountains, this is a great park (see p117) for a stroll, a picnic or a jog. You can also go boating on the artificial lake, and rent a bicycle or in-line skates.

Villa Celimontana

2 Villa Celimontana

MAP E5 ■ **Piazza della Navicella 12** ■ **Open dawn–dusk daily**

Picnics have been a tradition here since 1552, when the Mattei family gave pilgrims a simple meal during the Visit of the Seven Churches begun by Filippo Neri. Lovely dinner-concerts are held here in summer.

3 Pincio

The traditional time to enjoy the most famous panorama of Rome is at sunset. Other charms at these terraced gardens (see p117) – a walkers' favourite – include the water clock, the busts of various notables and an Egyptian-style obelisk Emperor Hadrian erected on the tomb of his beloved Antinous.

4 Villa Doria Pamphilj

This is Rome's largest green area (see p146), extending from the Gianicolo along the ancient Via Aurelia. It's a terrific place for a run and offers a course of exercise posts. Its hills are adorned with villas, fountains, lakes and orangeries and are perfect for strolls, or you can enjoy a picnic under the umbrella pines.

5 Orto Botanico

The graceful botanical gardens (see p146) and grounds of Galleria Corsini provide one of the most enjoyable places to while away an hour or two and breathe in air richly perfumed by more than 7,000 plant species that thrive here. The gardens, which now belong to the University of Rome, include indigenous and exotic varieties, grouped according to ecosystems.

(6) Villa Sciarra
MAP C5 ▪ Via Calandrelli
▪ Open dawn–dusk daily

This small park is replete with fountains, gazebos, ponds, loggias and statuary. There are leafy lanes for walking and lawns for relaxing and enjoying a picnic. It's a good place for children, too.

(7) Villa Ada
MAP E1 ▪ Via Salaria 265
▪ Open dawn–dusk daily

This huge public park, originally the hunting reserve of King Vittorio Emanuele III, has rolling lawns, serene waters and copses. It's worth the trip out if you need an antidote to the fumes and noise of the city. On summer nights the lake at the northern end of the park hosts food stalls and concerts.

(8) Parco del Colle Oppio
MAP E4 ▪ Via Labicana

After hours of walking around the Forum and the Colosseum in the high summer heat, these green slopes can be a welcome sight. Most of the Colle Oppio park is actually the roof of Nero's Golden House *(see p133)*, and you can see skylight structures for its rooms. If you haven't had enough of sightseeing, you can also examine the massive remains of the Baths of Trajan scattered about the area.

(9) Parco della Caffarella
Via della Caffarella
▪ www.caffarella.it

Combining farmland and wilderness with abundant wildlife, these fields and meadows are dotted with the remains of Roman temples. There is also a large children's playground.

Fountain, Parco Savello, Aventine

(10) Aventine
MAP D5 ▪ Via del Circo Massimo

One of the seven hills of Rome, the Aventine is lush, leafy and little-trafficked. With romantic *fin de siècle* villas set among public gardens, it is a haven from city chaos. The roses of the Roseto Comunale are in flower in May and June; up the hill is Parco Savello, also known as the Giardino degli Aranci, planted with orange trees and offering magnificent views.

The charming Parco del Colle Oppio

🔟 Off the Beaten Track

Fontana delle Rane, Piazza Mincio

1 Quartiere Coppedè
Between Via Salaria and Via Tagliamento

A bijou neighbourhood of elaborate Art Nouveau palazzi and villas designed by Gino Coppedè. This is architecture at its most fanciful and eclectic, inspired by Assyria, ancient Greece and Gothic fairytale. The Fontana delle Rane in Piazza Mincio leapt to fame when the Beatles jumped in after playing a gig nearby.

2 Museo delle Anime del Purgatorio
MAP L1 ■ Lungotevere Prati 12 ■ 06 6880 6517 ■ Open 7:30–11am & 4:30–7:30pm daily

The neo-Gothic church of Sacro Cuore del Suffragio hosts Rome's most arcane museum. After a church fire in 1897, priest Victor Jouet became convinced that certain scorch marks showed the face of a soul in purgatory, and started collecting objects he believed were proof of the dead trying to contact the living. The spookiest examples on display are the handprints burned onto surfaces.

3 Villa Poniatowski
Via di Villa Giulia 34 ■ 06 322 6571 ■ Open Fri 3–6pm ■ Adm ■ www.museoetru.it

The restored frescoed rooms of this villa house Etruscan archaeological finds. Highlights are a tomb carved from a tree trunk, fine gold jewellery and decorated make-up containers.

4 San Teodoro
MAP P6 ■ Via di San Teodoro 7 ■ Open 9:30am–12:30pm Sun–Fri

This circular 6th-century Greek Orthodox church is one of Rome's hidden treasures. St Theodore was martyred on this spot, and the church was built into the ruins of a grain warehouse that stood here. The apse mosaic showing Christ seated on an orb is original.

5 Auditorium of Maecenas
MAP F4 ■ Largo Leopardi 2 ■ 06 0608 ■ Guided tours by appt only (call the day before)

A bon viveur and patron of the arts, Maecenas was famous at the time of Emperor Augustus for his lavish parties. This space is thought to

have been a summer dining room. The walls retain traces of exquisite *trompe l'oeil* windows with views of gardens, flowers and birds.

6 Museo delle Mura
MAP F6 ■ Via di Porta San Sebastiano 18 ■ Open 9am–2pm Tue–Sun ■ www.museodelle muraroma.it

Porta San Sebastiano is the most impressive surviving gate in the Aurelian Walls. It now houses a small museum *(see p157)* containing prints and models that illustrate the history of the walls.

Remains of the Theatre of Pompey

A fresco at the Catacombs of Priscilla

7 Catacombs of Priscilla
Via Salaria 430 ■ 06 4542 8493 ■ Open for tours only, call ahead to reserve ■ Adm ■ www.catacombe priscilla.com

Few people visit the Catacombs of Priscilla, which date back to the 1st century AD. Benedictine nuns take visitors on fascinating tours that include the tombs of over 40,000 Christians and the earliest known image of the Madonna and Child.

8 Theatre of Pompey
MAP L4 ■ Da Pancrazio: Piazza del Biscione 92 ■ Open 12:30–2:30pm & 7:30–11pm Thu–Tue

A hint of Pompey's 61–55 BC theatre is evident in the medieval curve of Largo del Pollaro. Its fabric is now visible only in the ancient travertine corridors of the downstairs rooms of the Da Pancrazio restaurant.

9 Santa Costanza's Mausoleum
MAP J3 ■ Via Nomentana 349 ■ 06 8620 5456 ■ Open 7:30am–noon & 3–7:30pm daily ■ Adm

Initially built as a mausoleum for emperor Julian's wife Helena, this 4th-century church has some of Rome's well-preserved early-Christian mosaics, arranged on the circular ceiling of the building. The church is now mainly used for weddings and special ceremonies.

10 Cinecittà si Mostra
Via Tuscolana 1055 ■ 06 722 931 ■ Open 10am–6pm Wed–Mon, guided tours only (at 11:30am Sat and Sun in English) ■ Adm ■ cinecittasimostra.it

Step behind the scenes at Italy's legendary film studio. Tours of film sets take in a Broadway created by director Martin Scorsese's 2002 *Gangs of New York* and an ancient Rome made of polystyrene built for the television series *Rome*, but also used for other shows including *Doctor Who*.

Cinecittà si Mostra

🔟 Children's Attractions

Visitors engaging with exhibits at the interactive children's museum Explora

1 Explora

MAP C1 ■ Via Flaminia 80-86 ■ 06 361 3776 ■ Children must be accompanied ■ 1-hour 45-minute visits 10am (except in Aug), noon, 3pm, 5pm Tue–Sun ■ Booking recommended ■ Adm ■ www.mdbr.it

Youngsters can interact with life-size dioramas and models, which give a child's eye view of the world. There's a popular create-your-own TV show.

2 Villa Borghese

Scipione Borghese's private Renaissance park *(see p117)* and the adjacent 19th-century Pincio gardens, with statues and fountains, are a joy to explore, especially on two wheels. There are bike rental stands scattered throughout the park. You can also rent paddle boats for the little lake or take the kids to the park's small funfair.

3 MAXXI

Futuristic MAXXI *(see p156)*, designed by Iraqi architect Zaha Hadid, is a fabulous building for children to explore, with its illuminated stairways, suspended walkways, and floors that curve up to meet the walls without a joint. Exhibitions are presented in a way that children will find stimulating and exploration is made fun with one of the museum's interactive guides.

4 Bioparco

MAP E1 ■ Piazzale del Giardino Zoologico 1 ■ Open Apr–Oct: 9:30am–6pm Mon-Fri (to 7pm Sat & Sun); Nov–Mar: 9:30am–5pm daily ■ Adm ■ www.bioparco.it

Rome's once run-down zoo has been overhauled to become a pretty "biological garden" in a corner of Villa Borghese park.

Children's train at the Bioparco

5 Technotown

MAP F2 ■ Via Lazzaro Spallanzani 1a ■ 06 0608 ■ Open 9:30am–7pm Tue–Sun ■ Adm ■ www.technotown.it

Occupying a 20th-century house in the lush Villa Torlonia *(see p60)* gardens, Technotown is a multimedia playhouse for kids, with educational and fun interactive exhibits including robotics, special effects and 3D photography.

6 Time Elevator

MAP D3–4 ▪ Via dei Santi Apostoli 20 ▪ 06 6992 1823 ▪ Open 10:30am–8:15pm daily ▪ www.time-elevator.it ▪ Adm

The panoramic movies shown here come complete with surround-sound, flight simulator and 5D technology. Not advisable for those suffering from motion sickness.

7 Casina di Raffaello

MAP D2 ▪ Via della Casina di Raffaello (Villa Borghese) ▪ 06 0608 ▪ Open 10am–3:30pm Tue–Fri, 10am–8pm Sat & Sun ▪ www.casina diraffaello.it ▪ Adm

This city-run playhouse for kids aged 3–10 years offers educational toys and games, a toy library, a theatre and a bookshop, plus weekly events and workshops. Park entrance free.

8 Castel Sant'Angelo

Little visitors will enjoy spending a few hours at Castel Sant'Angelo (see p144) with its winding passageways, hidden lookouts, dungeons and moat. The castle has had many uses over the years, and the museum's extensive collection of weapons and artworks that illustrate the millennia-long history make this an interesting trip for adults too.

9 Cooking Classes

Eataly (see p129) regularly organizes Italian cooking classes for children. A few classes offered here are adjusted for English-speaking children.

Traditional puppets, Gianicolo

10 Puppet Shows on the Gianicolo

MAP B4 ▪ Teatro di Pulcinella, Gianicolo ▪ Shows at 10:30, check days

You can appreciate Punch and Judy without understanding Italian (the pugilistic characters are native to Italy). This is the last of the old puppet kiosks that once peppered Rome's public parks, offering appealing shows for free.

TOP 10 Roman Dishes

1 Saltimbocca
This savoury veal dish is so good they call it "jumps-in-the-mouth". A veal escalope is layered with sage leaves and prosciutto then sautéed in white wine.

2 Bucatini all'Amatriciana
Named after Amatrice, the northern Lazio town high in the Abruzzi mountains where it originated. The sauce consists of tomatoes mixed with Italian bacon – *guanciale* (pork cheek) or *pancetta* (pork belly) – laced with chilli pepper and liberally dusted with grated Pecorino romano cheese. The classic pasta accompaniment are *bucatini* (thick, hollow spaghetti). The original *amatriciana bianca* version (before tomatoes, an American food, entered Italian cuisine) adds parsley and butter.

Ox-tail stew at Coda alla Vaccinara

4 Coda alla Vaccinara
Oxtail braised in celery and tomato broth. Like *pajata*, this is a product of trying to make something out of the *quinto quarto* (the unusable "fifth fourth" of the day's butchering), which was part of the take-home pay of 19th-century slaughterhouse workers. Checchino dal 1887 *(see p129)*, the restaurant that created this delicacy, is one of Rome's finest.

5 Carciofi alla Giudia
Artichokes, flattened then fried. This typical Roman Jewish dish is often accompanied by fried courgette (zucchini) flowers stuffed with mozzarella cheese and anchovies.

6 Spaghetti alla Carbonara
Piping hot pasta is mixed with a raw egg, grated Parmesan and black pepper so that the eggy mixture cooks with the heat of the pasta. It is then tossed with pieces of *pancetta* (bacon). One of several

Carciofi alla Romana

3 Carciofi alla Romana
Tender Italian artichokes, often laced with garlic and mint, are braised in a mixture of olive oil and water.

Spaghetti alla Carbonara

stories has it that the recipe was born out of US army rations after World War II, but no one seems to have proven or discarded the theory.

7 Pajata

It may sound revolting but it's actually delicious: suckling calf intestines boiled with its mother's milk still clotted inside. Usually the intestines are chopped, coated with a tomato sauce and served over pasta.

8 Abbacchio Scottadito

Roasted Roman spring lamb, so succulent the name claims you'll "burn your fingers" in your haste to eat it. When *abbacchio* (lamb) is unavailable, once the spring slaughter is over, they switch to less tender *agnello* (young mutton).

A bowl of gnocchi in sauce

9 Gnocchi

Dense and bite-sized potato and flour dumplings, gnocchi originated in Northern Italy but have infiltrated nearly every regional cuisine. Rome's version of the dish is made with semolina and/or corn flour, doused in butter and parmesan and oven-baked. The original gnocchi are served much more frequently, however. Try them with tomato sauce, gorgonzola cheese or simply *burro e salvia* (with butter and sage).

10 Cacio e Pepe

Sometimes the simplest dishes are the best. Perfectly *al dente* ("with a bite") spaghetti is tossed hot with cracked black pepper and grated Pecorino romano (a local sharp, aged sheep's milk cheese rather similar to Parmesan).

TOP 10 WINES AND LIQUEURS

1 Frascati
Lazio's only high profile wine, a dry, fruity, not always perfect white from the hills south of Rome.

2 Castelli Romani
Cousin to Frascati from the neighbouring hill towns and also made with Trebbiano grapes.

3 Colli Albani
Another Trebbiano-based white from the slopes of Lazio's dormant volcano.

4 Grappa
The most powerful of Italy's *digestivi* (drunk after a meal), this is quite a harsh-tasting liqueur.

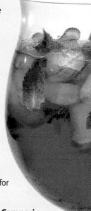

A glass of grappa

5 Est! Est! Est!
A bishop's taste-tester, sampling this sweet white in a northern Lazio lakeside village, excitedly ran to the door and scribbled *"Est! Est! Est!"* (Latin for "This is it!").

6 Torre Ercolana
One of Lazio's unsung reds, made from Cabernet and Cesanese grapes.

7 Chianti
This old favourite from over the border in Tuscany is one of the most common reds you'll find in Rome's bars and restaurants.

8 Lacrima Christi
"Tears of Christ", a white wine from the slopes of the infamous Mount Vesuvius near Pompeii *(see p158)*.

9 Orvieto Classico
Dry white from southern Umbria – so good that the Renaissance artist Signorelli once accepted it as payment.

10 Campari
A bitter red apéritif, best diluted in soda water, or lemonade for a sweet drink.

Campari

🔟 Restaurants

1 La Pergola

Universally recognized as Rome's finest restaurant, La Pergola (see p153) is also the one where top chef Heinz Beck has been awarded three Michelin stars for his extraordinary, innovative Mediterranean dishes. Perched atop Monte Mario hill, the restaurant offers stunning views of St Peter's and the entire city skyline. The wine cellar is among Europe's most prestigious.

2 Imàgo

Housed on the sixth floor of the Hassler hotel (see p170), this restaurant (see p123) has panoramic views of Rome from the top of the Spanish steps. Chef Francesco Apreda won his first Michelin star here for his creative Italian fusion cuisine.

3 Il Pagliaccio

An exclusive, understated and tiny restaurant in the centro storico, Il Pagliaccio (see p95) has two

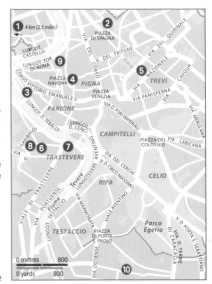

Intimate setting at Il Pagliaccio

Michelin stars for its inventive and refined contemporary Italian fusion food. Book well in advance as it can only seat 28 diners.

4 La Rosetta

This sophisticated restaurant (see p103) is run by renowned chef Massimo Riccioli who personally hand-picks the ingredients. The seafood arrives daily from nearby harbours, and the bread and desserts are prepared in-house by the maître pâtissier. The gourmet offerings include fish tapas, rock lobster with artichokes and spaghetti with calamari, and a four-course tasting menu.

5 Open Colonna

Housed in the rooftop conservatory of Palazzo della Esposizioni, Antonio Colonna's restaurant (see p141) has the advantage of being particularly affordable at lunchtime with a stellar all-you-can-eat buffet at only €30. It offers great service and amazing views.

The chic modern decor of Glass Hostaria

6 Glass Hostaria

Exquisite, intelligent fusion food, partnered with cutting-edge, contemporary chic decor, have won chef Cristina Bowerman a Michelin star in the heart of Trastevere. Glass Hostaria *(see p153)* combines Italian dishes and fine-dining with flavours from all over the world. The inventive menu changes seasonally. Despite the minimalist interior, the ambience is warm and friendly.

7 Osteria La Gensola

This wonderful family-run Sicilian restaurant *(see p153)* has a well-balanced menu with a focus on fish and seafood, which is freshly caught and cooked to perfection. The restaurant has a good selection of meat dishes and offers a surprisingly original take on traditional Roman cuisine. The atmosphere is intimate, with attentive and friendly service.

8 Antica Pesa

Many Hollywood names have dined here *(see p153)*, as attested to by the pictures at the entrance. A classy ambience, contemporary frescoes and a lovely garden act as the perfect backdrop for the high-quality Roman cuisine at this well-established restaurant dating back from 1922. Meals are served in a leafy courtyard in warm weather. There is an extensive but pricey wine list.

9 Il Convivio

The elegant feel of this restaurant *(see p95)* is reflected in its classic dishes, all prepared only with certified local and organic ingredients that meet the highest standards. The three brothers who run this establishment have made it their mission to celebrate Italian cuisine by offering a creative menu based on traditional recipes, earning the restaurant a well-deserved Michelin star. It also has an impressive wine cellar.

People eating at Eataly

10 Eataly

Sponsored by Slow Food, Rome's Eataly *(see p129)* is the flagship for this chain of gastronomic emporia (also at Piazza della Repubblica 41). Everything from sustainable fish and Gragnano pasta to Alpine ice cream is on offer. Every month a different Roman osteria is hosted on the second floor.

TOP 10 Osterias, Trattorias and Pizzerias

1 Felice
This Testaccio trattoria *(see p129)* is famous for two things – grumpy owners and excellent, utterly traditional Roman food centering on meat and offal – given its proximity to the one-time slaughterhouse. Classics are *tonnarelli cacio e pepe*, lamb baked with potatoes, *carciofi alla romana* and offal cooked in a variety of ways. Advance booking is recommended.

2 Roscioli
MAP L4 ■ Via dei Giubbonari 21–5 ■ 06 687 5287 ■ Closed Sun ■ €€

This casual and very popular *osteria*-deli-wine bar is run by the family who make some of the best bread and pizza in Rome *(see p112)*. Come for a snack or a full meal – the spaghetti carbonara is particularly recommended.

Deli products on sale at Roscioli

3 Da Giovanni
This good-value trattoria *(see p152)* has a lovely atmosphere and serves up simple pasta dishes and legume soups. An ideal spot for lunch after visiting the Vatican and St Peter's, it encapsulates utter period authenticity – decor, food and staff could all belong to the 1950s.

People eating at La Gatta Mangiona

4 La Gatta Mangiona
Via Federico Ozanam 30/32 ■ 06 534 6702 ■ Open 7:45–11:30pm Tue–Sun ■ €

Head to this simple spot for one of the best pizzas in Rome. High-crust Neapolitan-style pizzas are made from specially selected flours and slow-rise pizza dough. Expect all the classics, as well as innovative combinations.

5 Sora Margherita
This tiny, no-frills *osteria (see p113)* has a cult following. The dishes here are made in the Roman-Jewish tradition: menu highlights include an excellent *cacio e pepe*; stuffed, deep-fried courgette flowers; and anchovies baked with endive. The inside space is cosy, with vintage posters decorating the walls. Credit cards are not accepted.

Margherita pizza

6 Casa Bleve

Run by Anacleto Bleve, one of Rome's most respected foodies and a pioneer in the rigorous sourcing of ingredients from local, artisanal producers, this osteria *(see p95)* in a 16th-century palazzo has won multiple national awards. Try the *sfizi di Casa Bleve*, a visual and olfactory feast of innovative antipasti, such as pumpkin flower stuffed with pistacio and ricotta. Ask if they have *burrata*, a creamier variant of mozzarella that is flown in several times a week from Puglia and served with a rich fig jam. The wine list offers a great selection.

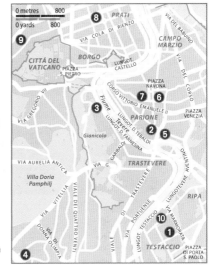

7 Mastrociccia Osteria Bistrot

This small restaurant *(see p 95)* near Piazza Navona serves traditional local dishes, but the real focus here is on meat. Try the tagliata with rocket and Parmesan or popular Roman meat dishes such as *coda alla vaccinara* (oxtail in tomato sauce) or meatballs. There is also a patio and a wide selection of wine and beer.

8 La Pratolina

Busy and buzzy, this is the perfect place for dinner *(see p152)* after a day of exploring the Vatican Museums. Here, oval-shaped, slow-risen pizzas are baked in a lava-stone wood-burning oven. Our top tip? Order the delicious Genovese, which is garnished with mozzarella di bufala, pesto, Pachino tomatoes and ham.

9 Pizzarium Bonci

MAP A2 ■ **Via della Meloria 43** ■ **06 3974 5416** ■ **Open 11am–10:30pm Mon–Sat** ■ **€**

Esteemed pizza-maker Gabriele Bonci is known as "the Michelangelo of pizza" and his restaurant serves the best *pizza a taglio* (pizza by the slice) in Rome. Toppings range from the classic margherita to ricotta, black pepper and courgette. The *suppli* (croquette-type antipasti) are also delicious, and there is a range of regional beers and drinks.

10 Da Remo

Scrocchiarella (crispy thin crust) Roman-style pizzas with all the classic toppings are served at this ebullient Testaccio pizzeria *(see p129)*. It is also a great choice for families with children as there is a playground in the piazza.

Chefs at work at Da Remo

🔟 Cafés and Gelaterie

The cosy interiors of the 18th-century Antico Caffè Greco

1 Antico Caffè Greco

Rome's 1760 answer to all the famed literary cafés of Paris. Just off the Spanish Steps on the busiest shopping street in town, it is an elegant holdover (see p122) from yesteryear, its tiny tables tucked into a series of genteel, cosy rooms plastered with photos, prints and other memorabilia from the 19th-century Grand Tour era. The A-list of past customers runs from Goethe and Wagner to Byron and Casanova.

2 Caffè Sant'Eustachio

Rome's most coveted *cappuccini* come from behind a chrome-plated shield that hides the coffee machine from view so no one can discover the owner's secret formula. All that is known is that the water comes from an ancient aqueduct and the brew is pre-sweetened. Always crowded (see p102).

3 San Crispino

MAP P2 ■ Via della Panetteria 42

Navigate the glut of inferior ice cream parlours infesting the Trevi neighbourhood to reach this elegantly simple little *gelateria*. The signature ice cream contains honey but there are other velvety varieties made with fresh fruit or nuts and sinful delights laced with liqueurs.

4 Tre Scalini

This café's (see p94) claim to fame is Rome's most decadent *tartufo* (truffle) ice cream ball, which is almost always packaged in other outlets. Dark chocolate shavings cover the outer layer of chocolate ice cream, with a heart of fudge and cherries.

5 Giolitti

This 19th-century café (see p102) is the best known of Rome's *gelaterie*. Touristy but excellent.

6 Café Doney

Still the top café (see p140) on the famous Via Veneto, but long past its prime as the heartbeat of Rome's 1950s heyday (along with the now-defunct rival Café de Paris

Rome's iconic Caffè Sant'Eustachio

across the road) – when celebrities in sunglasses hobnobbed with starlets at outdoor tables under the magnolias. The lifestyle was documented in – and in part created by – Fellini's seminal film *La Dolce Vita*, whose shutterbug character Paparazzo lent a name to his profession of bloodhound photographers.

Gelato

7 La Tazza d'Oro

Here *(see p102)* only top quality Brazilian beans go into the coffee. There's nothing fancy in this unassuming place and no touristy gimmicks (despite being just off the Pantheon's piazza). Just a long,

Local favourite, La Tazza d'Oro

undulating bar counter where regulars enjoy a *espresso* that, amazingly, manages to be both among the best and the cheapest in Rome.

8 Gelarmony
MAP C2 ■ Via Marcantonio Colonna 34

The ingredients at this hugely popular ice cream parlour come directly from Sicily. More than 60 flavours are available, and the presentation is second to none. Their pistachio flavour is especially good.

9 Grom

Artisanal, organic *gelato* made with top-quality local ingredients is on offer here *(see p102)*. The company has its own organic farm where they grow the fruit they use. Expect long queues.

10 Caffè Rosati

The older, more left-wing of Piazza del Popolo's rival cafés (the other is Caffè Canova), this *(see p122)* was founded by two of the Rosati brothers (a third continued to manage the family's original Via Veneto café). It sports 1922 Art Nouveau decor and its patrons park their newest Ferrari or Lotus convertibles out front.

🔟 Shopping Streets

1 Piazza di Spagna
This is Rome's prime designer shopping area, with Fendi, Versace and Ferrè on Via Borgognona; Gucci, Bulgari, Prada, Hermès, Ferragamo, Trussardi and Valentino on Via Condotti (see p120); Chanel and Tiffany & Co on elegant Via del Babuino; and Fendi, Missoni and Krizia on the piazza itself. Babuino and Via Margutta also have some superb art, antique and furniture shops – don't miss nos. 45, 86 and 109 on Margutta.

2 Monti
MAP R4

Lying behind the Imperial Fora, Monti is Rome at its most hip, with vintage clothes shops and an eclectic selection of jewellery and home accessories by upcoming designers. Head to Via dei Serpenti and Via Leonina.

3 Via del Corso
MAP N1–N3

Up and down Rome's central axis street that bisects the north from the south, more commonly known as the Corso, you'll find the entire range of shopping options, including stylish clothes, handbags, shoes, music and stationery. The prime shopping arena here is the Art Nouveau Galleria Alberto Sordi.

Galleria Alberto Sordi shopping arcade

Vintage store, Via dei Coronari

4 Via dei Coronari
Named for the rosary makers and sellers that used to line the way when it was on the main pilgrimage route to St Peter's, this street (see p92) now has a reputation for antiques. Prices, however, are usually inflated and most pieces are imported.

5 Via del Governo Vecchio
Running behind Piazza Navona, this street has long been known for its vintage clothes shops, now joined by one-off shops devoted to new designers.

6 Trastevere

Reflecting the area's *(see p142)* changing demographics, jewellery, book, food and boho clothes shops now rub shoulders with niche designers. Piazza San Cosimato has a small, bustling daily produce market and Porta Portese a vibrant Sunday morning flea market.

7 Via Appia Nuova

A popular shopping street in the San Giovanni district, Via Appia Nuova has high-end boutiques such as Leam *(see p134)*.

8 Via Cola di Rienzo

Less crowded than Via del Corso, this is the best street in the city for those looking for mid-range clothing. Castroni is an excellent shop to go to when looking for hard-to-find international and traditional food items.

Via Cola di Rienzo

9 Via Nazionale
MAP R2

The shops lining this busy major thoroughfare that runs from Termini Station to Piazza Venezia include such brand names as Desigual, G Star and Furla.

10 Campo de' Fiori

Central Rome's bustling fruit and veg market sets the tone for this area *(see p107)*, which is known for its fantastic food shops, both traditional and innovative. Via Giubbonari is lined with affordable clothes shops, while Via dei Pellegrini and Via dei Ballauri have several chic stores.

TOP 10 MARKETS

Flea market, Porta Portese

1 Porta Portese
MAP C5 ▪ Via Ippolito Nievo
Mammoth flea market with genuine and fake antiques, memorabilia, plants, clothing and more. Sunday morning.

2 Campo de' Fiori
MAP L4
Fruit, vegetable and fish market in an authentic medieval square.

3 Via Mamiani
MAP F4
Rome's largest market selling the freshest meat and fish. Monday to Saturday mornings.

4 Via Sannio
Vintage clothing and designer fakes *(see p134)*. Weekday mornings and Saturday.

5 Antique Print Market
MAP M1 ▪ Largo della Fontanella di Borghese
Antique and reproduction prints. Monday to Saturday mornings.

6 Testaccio Market
MAP D6
Lavish displays of nature's bounty. Monday to Saturday mornings.

7 Via Trionfale Flower Market
MAP B2
Fresh cut flowers and all sorts of plants at bargain prices. Tuesday morning.

8 Borghetto Flaminio
MAP D1 ▪ Piazza della Marina 32 ▪ Adm
A flea market in a former bus depot. Every Sunday, September to July.

9 Piazza San Cosimato
MAP C5
Trastevere's lively fruit and vegetable market. Monday to Saturday mornings.

10 Quattro Coronati
MAP E4
Off-beat produce market. Monday to Saturday mornings.

⬛10 Rome for Free

Sphere Within a Sphere by Arnaldo Pomodoro, Vatican Museum

① Museums for Free
State and city museums are free for under 18s. All state museums, including archaeological sites such as the Roman Forum and the Colosseum, are free for all visitors on the first Sunday of every month. The Vatican Museums are free on the last Sunday of the month.

② Free Medieval-Style Lie Detection Service
The *Bocca della Verità* – made famous by Gregory Peck and Audrey Hepburn in *Roman Holiday* – is in the narthex of Santa Maria in Cosmedin *(see p108)*. It was believed that if someone told a lie while their hand was in the mouth, it would be bitten off.

③ Free City Views
MAP D5 ■ Parco Savello, Piazza Pietro D'Illiria
The orange garden on top of the Aventine hill offers a fabulous city views from under the orange trees. It's also a great place for a picnic, followed by a walk to the famous Knight of Malta keyhole, through which you can admire a perfectly framed view of Saint Peter's Dome.

Bocca della Verità

④ World's Best Preserved Roman Temple
The Pantheon *(see pp18–19)* is the only one of Rome's ancient monuments to which entry is free. The ancient temple was converted to a church in the Byzantine era.

⑤ Mussolini's Muscle Men
Stadio dei Marmi, encircled by 60 travertine muscle-bound athletes, was built by Mussolini *(see p157)*. in the hope of bringing the Olympics to Rome. Now an icon of Fascist kitsch, it is free and open to the public

⑥ The Caravaggio Trail
There are six magnificent Caravaggio canvasses that can be seen for free in the churches of San Luigi dei Francesi *(see p89)*, Sant'Agostino *(see p90)* and Santa Maria del Popolo *(see pp38–9)*.

⑦ Michelangelo for Free
Admire Michelangelo masterpieces for free at San Pietro in Vincoli *(see p131)* and Santa Maria sopra Minerva. The latter has Michelangelo's *Risen Christ (see p97)*, while his muscle-bound *Moses* was created for

San Pietro and is still there. It does cost 50c to switch the lights on, but there are usually plenty of other people around to take care of that.

8 Byzantine Splendour

Admire magnificent, jewel-like Byzantine mosaics at Santa Maria in Domnica (see p50) and Santa Prassede (see p132), although you'll need to wait for others to put money in the slot to turn the lights on.

9 St Peter's

Access to the Basilica (see pp16–17), Necropolis and Grottoes of St Peter is free, but to make the experience special – and avoid the queues that begin to build up from around 9am – go early, before breakfast, when usually the only other people there will be nuns, monks, priests and pilgrims.

10 Contemporary Architecture

Although an entrance fee is charged for the exhibitions at MAXXI (see pp156–7), the museum has free video presentations and large parts of this stunning building can be enjoyed for free of charge. MACRO (see pp54–5) also has free entry and a gorgeous roof terrace.

Intertwining walkways at MAXXI

TOP 10 BUDGET TIPS

Good-value bakery food

1 Rome is full of marvellous bakeries and delicatessens offering fabulous food for a fraction of the prices charged in cafés and restaurants.

2 At restaurants and trattorias, order the house wine – it is served by the quarter, half or litre and is vastly cheaper than bottled wine.

3 To save money when self catering, avoid the centro storico delis and mini-supermarkets. Instead shop at neighbourhood markets such as Piazza Vittorio or Testaccio.

4 Look out for aperitivo "happy hours", where customers pay a set price for a drink and are served a variety of small dishes.

5 The Roma Pass is valid for 2 or 3 days and includes free public transport, free entry to two museums, and discounted entry at many others.

6 Once you have a Roma Pass, plan ahead to select the most expensive museums as your free choices.

7 All churches can be visited for free, but do have a few coins handy as some of the art can only be viewed by turning on a light. This usually costs either 50 cents or a euro.

8 Several museums (including the Museo Nazionale Romano) have multiple sites for which the same ticket is valid.

9 You can visit state museums for free on the last Sunday of every month.

10 Organize your days to make the most of public transport passes, which are available for 1, 2, 3 and 7 days.

⏏️⏏️ Cultural Festivals

Rome's Birthday celebrations

1 Rome's Birthday

Every 21 April there's a gala civic observance in the Piazza del Campidoglio, in celebration of Rome's traditional founding in 753 BC (see p46). Music, fireworks, costumed processions and a speech by the mayor mark the event, and the Musei Capitolini (see pp28–9) are free of charge.

2 May Day Concert
MAP F5 ▪ Piazza S Giovanni ▪ 1 May

Held in front of the Basilica of San Giovanni in Laterano (see p131), this is a vast, free event, boasting a line-up of top Italian popstars and the occasional international luminary. It's in celebration of socialist Italy's "Day of the Worker", when just about everything shuts down.

3 International Horse Show
MAP E1 ▪ Piazza di Siena, Villa Borghese ▪ Last week May

Villa Borghese's annual splash-out for the equestrian classes, with international showjumping in a garden setting. Much of the park is closed off for the event and parties.

4 Summer Opera Festivals

The Rome Opera Company offers its usual summer programme in the Baths of Caracalla (see p125), with other opera programmes all over the city, and workshops to make opera accessible to all. Singers come from around the globe.

5 Festa dell'Unità

Put on by the PD, the former Communist Party, this lively evening event features music, films, dancing, games and more. The venue changes every year, as do the dates, but it's usually held in a central park from mid-June to late July.

6 ¡Fiesta! and Rock in Roma
Parco Rosati, Via delle Tre Fontane; Ippodromo delle Capannelle, Via Appia Nuova 1245 ▪ Metro Colli Albani then bus ▪ Mid-Jun–mid-Aug ▪ www.fiestafestival.it, www.rockinroma.com

The converted racetrack of Capannelle hosts Rock in Roma, bringing world-renowned rock stars to the outdoor stage, while ¡Fiesta! at Parco Rosati celebrates Latin American culture in all its forms.

7 Isola Tiberina
Isola Tiberina, Lungotevere de' Cenci

Seasonal bars and cafés pop-up on Tiber Island and along the river banks every summer. There's also

Pop-up cafés and bars, Lungotevere

live music, a market and an outdoor film festival (including English-language screenings).

⑧ Roma Summer Festival
Viale Pietro de Coubertin
30 ▪ 06 802 41281 ▪ www.auditorium.com

The annual summer concert series brings big international names in pop, jazz and folk music to Auditorium Parco della Musica's outdoor arena.

Performance, Luglio Suona Bene

⑨ RomaEuropa Festival
End Sep–early Dec
▪ www.romaeuropa.net

A fast-growing performing arts festival with a pronounced emphasis on the provocative, held every autumn in various superlative venues, including the French Academy, Palazzo Farnese and the Spanish Academy. All kinds of music, dance and theatre, including several international artists.

⑩ Rome Film Fest
October ▪ www.romacinemafest.it

The Rome Film Fest is Rome's answer to the Venice film festival. Hosted by the Auditorium Parco della Musica complex, the fest organizes film premieres and gala events starring Italian and international movie celebrities. Many of the screenings are open to the public, but it is advisable to book ahead.

TOP 10 RELIGIOUS FESTIVALS

Pentecost at the Pantheon

1 Epiphany
6 Jan
Friendly witches land in Piazza Navona to give free candy to children.

2 Carnival
Late Jan–Feb
Dressing up, parties and pranks.

3 Easter Week
Mar/Apr
Good Friday Procession of the Cross at the Colosseum and Easter Sunday blessing from the balcony of St Peter's.

4 Pentecost
MAP M3 ▪ Whitsunday
Rose petals shower down through the Pantheon's oculus (see p18), followed by pageantry.

5 Feast of Sts Peter and Paul
MAP D6 ▪ 28–29 Jun ▪ Piazza S Paolo and Via Ostiense
Fireworks and partying to celebrate the founders of the Catholic Church.

6 Madonna della Neve
5 Aug
Commemorating a papal vision of an August snowfall in the 4th century.

7 All Souls' Day
1 Nov
Romans visit the graves of loved ones.

8 Christmas Market
MAP L3 ▪ 1 Dec–6 Jan ▪ Piazza Navona
Sugar candy, nativity figurines and all the Christmas trimmings.

9 Christmas Eve Midnight Mass
24 Dec
Most churches celebrate Jesus's birth, but tickets are required to attend St Peter's Basilica.

10 "Urbi et Orbi"
25 Dec
The noontime Christmas Day blessing by the pope from St Peter's balcony.

Rome
Area by Area

The Spanish Steps at dusk

TOP 10 Around Piazza Navona

This is Baroque Rome in all its glory, with curvaceous architecture and elaborate fountains by the era's two greatest architects, Bernini and Borromini, and churches filled with works by Caravaggio and Rubens. The street

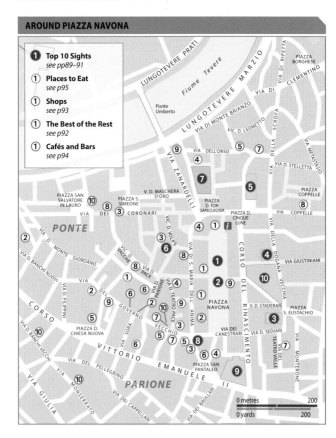

The Ganges, Four Rivers Fountain

plan was overhauled by 16th- to 18th-century popes, although ancient Rome peeks through in the curve of Palazzo Massimo alle Colonne and the shape of Piazza Navona. This is also a district of craftsmen and antiques restorers, and more recently, a centre of Roman nightlife.

AROUND PIAZZA NAVONA

1 Top 10 Sights
see pp89–91

1 Places to Eat
see p95

1 Shops
see p93

1 The Best of the Rest
see p92

1 Cafés and Bars
see p94

PIAZZA BORGHESE
LUNGOTEVERE PRATI
Fiume Tevere
VIA DI RIPETTA
VIA DI CLEMENTINO
LUNGOTEVERE MARZIO
Ponte Umberto
VIA DI MONTE BRIANZO
VIA DI LEONETTO
VIC. D. LEONETTO
VIA DELLA SCROFA
VIA METASTASIO
VIA DELL'ORSO
VIA D. STELLETTA
PIAZZA COPPELLE
VIA ZANARDELLI
V. D. MASCHERA D'ORO
PIAZZA D. TOR SANGUIGNA
PIAZZA D. CINQUE LUNE
VIA COPPELLE
PIAZZA SAN SALVATORE IN LAURO
PIAZZA S. SIMEONE
VIA DEI CORONARI
VIC. D. VOLPE
VIA DI S. MARIA DELL'
VIA DELLA DOGANA VECCHIA
PONTE
VIA D. MONTE GIORDANO
VIC. D. VACCHE
VIA D. PACE
VIA GIUSTINIANI
VIA D. BANCHI NUOVI
VIA DELLA PACE
VIA D. PARIONE
CORSO DEL RINASCIMENTO
PIAZZA NAVONA
V. D. STADERARI
PIAZZA S. EUSTACHIO
VIA D. FILIPPINI
VIA DEL GOVERNO
VIA D. TEATRO PACE
VIA D. ANIMA
VIA SORA
VIA D. TEATRO VALLE
MONTERONE
CORSO
VIA D. BANCHI VECCHI
PIAZZA D. CHIESA NUOVA
VIA DEL TEATRO VECCHIO
VIA DEI CANESTRARI
VIA D. SEDIARI
VITTORIO EMANUELE II
PIAZZA SAN PANTALEO
VIA GIULIA
VIA MONSERRATO
PARIONE
VIA DEL PELLEGRINO
VIA DEI CAPPELLARI
VIA DEI BAULLARI

0 metres	200
0 yards	200

Fountain, Piazza Navona

most gorgeous courtyard. The double arcade is closed at the far end by Sant'Ivo's façade, an intricate Borromini interplay of concave and convex curves. The crowning glory is the spiralling ellipse of the dome. The interior, however, is somewhat disappointing despite its Pietro da Cortona altarpiece. When the courtyard is closed, you can see the dome from Piazza Sant'Eustachio.

 San Luigi dei Francesi
MAP L2 ■ Piazza S Luigi dei Francesi 5 ■ 06 688 271 ■ Open 9:30am–12:45pm & 2:30–6:30pm Mon–Fri, 9:30am–12:15pm & 2:30–6:30pm Sat, 11:30am–12:45pm & 2:30–6:30pm Sun

France's national church in Rome has some damaged Domenichino frescoes (1616–17) in the second chapel on the right, but everyone makes a beeline for the last chapel on the left, housing three large Caravaggio works. His plebeian, naturalistic approach often ran foul of Counter-Reformation tastes. In a "first draft" version of the *Inspiration of St Matthew*, called *St Matthew and the Angel*, the angel guided the hand of a rough labourer-type saint; the commissioners made the artist replace it with this more courtly one *(see p52)*. Underlying sketches in the *Martyrdom of St Matthew* and the *Calling of St Matthew (see p57)* show how Caravaggio was moving from symbolism to realism.

① Piazza Navona
MAP L3

One of Rome's loveliest pedestrian squares *(see p62)* is studded with fountains and lined with palaces, the church of Sant'Agnese, and classy cafés such as Tre Scalini *(see p94)*.

② Four Rivers Fountain
MAP L3 ■ Piazza Navona

The statues ringing Bernini's theatrical 1651 centrepiece symbolize four rivers representing the continents: the Ganges (Asia, relaxing), Danube (Europe, turning to steady the obelisk), Rio de la Plata (the Americas, bald and reeling), and the Nile (Africa, whose head is hidden since the river's source was then unknown). The obelisk, balancing over a sculptural void, is a Roman-era fake, its Egyptian granite carved with the hieroglyphic names of Vespasian, Titus and Domitian.

③ Sant'Ivo
MAP L3 ■ Corso del Rinascimento 40 ■ Open 9am–noon Sun; closed Jul & Aug

Giacomo della Porta's Renaissance façade for the 1303 Palazzo della Sapienza, the original seat of the university of Rome, hides the city's

The nave of San Luigi dei Francesi

5 Sant'Agostino
MAP L2 ■ Piazza di Sant'Agostino 80 ■ Open 7:30am–noon & 4:30–7:30pm daily

Raphael frescoed the prophet Isaiah (1512) on the third pillar on the right, and Jacopo Sansovino provided the pregnant and venerated *Madonna del Parto*, but Sant'Agostino's pride and joy is Caravaggio's *Madonna di Loreto* (1603–6). The master's strict realism balked at the tradition of depicting Mary riding atop her miraculous flying house (which landed in Loreto). The house is merely suggested by a travertine doorway and flaking stucco wall where Mary, supporting her overly large Christ child, is venerated by a pair of scandalously scruffy pilgrims.

6 Santa Maria della Pace
MAP L2 ■ Arco della Pace 5 ■ Open 9:30am–6:30pm daily

Baccio Pontelli rebuilt this church for Pope Sixtus IV in 1480–84, but the lovely and surprising façade (1656–7), its curved portico squeezed into a tiny piazza, is a Baroque masterpiece by Pietro da Cortona. Raphael's first chapel on the right is frescoed with *Sibyls* (1514), which was influenced by the then recent unveiling of the Sistine Chapel ceiling *(see pp14–15)*. Peruzzi decorated the chapel across the aisle and Bramante's first job

in Rome was designing a cloister based on ancient examples. It now hosts frequent concerts.

A frescoed gallery at Palazzo Altemps

7 Palazzo Altemps
This beautiful 15th-century palace was overhauled in 1585 by Martino Longhi, who is probably also responsible for the stucco and travertine courtyard (previously attributed to Antonio da Sangallo the Younger or Peruzzi). Its series of elegant rooms now provide an excellent home to one wing of the Museo Nazionale Romano *(see pp34–7)*, its frescoed galleries filled with ancient sculptures.

8 Pasquino
MAP L3 ■ Piazza Pasquino

That this faceless and armless statue was part of "Menelaus with the body of Patroclus" (a Roman copy of a Hellenistic group) is almost irrelevant. Since this worn fragment took up its post here in 1501, it has been Rome's most vocal "Talking Statue".

Pasquino, **Piazza Pasquino**

⑨ Palazzo Massimo alle Colonne

MAP L3 ▪ Corso Vittorio Emanuele II 141 ▪ Open 7am–1pm 16 Mar only

This masterpiece of Baldassare Peruzzi *(see p60)*, built in 1532, marks the transition of Roman architecture from the High Renaissance of Bramante and Sangallo into the theatrical experiments of Mannerism that would lead up to the Baroque. The façade is curved for a reason; Peruzzi honoured Neo-Classical precepts so much he wanted to preserve the arc of the Odeon of Domitian, a small theatre incorporated into the south end of the emperor's stadium.

⑩ Palazzo Madama

MAP L3 ▪ Piazza Madama 11 ▪ 06 6706 2177 ▪ Visits by appointment only

Based around the 16th-century Medici Pope Leo X's Renaissance palace, the Baroque façade of unpointed brick and bold marble window frames was added in the 17th century. Since 1870 it's been the seat of Italy's Senate, so public admission is obviously limited.

Grand interiors of Palazzo Madama

A MORNING AROUND PIAZZA NAVONA

▶ MORNING

Start in the courtyard of the Sapienza, marvelling at the remarkable façade of **Sant'Ivo** *(see p89)*. Head around the church's right side and out the back exit on to Via della Dogana Vecchia. If you need a morning pick-me-up, turn left and then right into **Piazza Sant'Eustachio** *(see p100)* if the namesake church is open, pop in for a look around the early 18th-century interior. In the elongated piazza to the left are fine views of Sant'Ivo's dome and two great cafés to choose from, La Tazza d'Oro and Sant'Eustachio.

Return to Via della Dogana Vecchia and turn right to visit the Caravaggio works inside **San Luigi dei Francesi** *(see p89)*. Continue up the street to Via delle Coppelle and turn left for more works of art by Caravaggio at **Sant'Agostino**. Continue into Piazza delle Cinque Lune and walk a few yards to the left down Corso del Rinascimento, then relax from the sightseeing with a stroll amid the street performers and splashing fountains of **Piazza Navona** *(see p89)*.

Enjoy a bruschetta at **Baguetteria del Fico** *(see p94)* before heading around the corner to **Palazzo Altemps**, now home to a wing of the Museo Nazionale Romano and full of Classical statuary. Spend a good hour admiring the works of art. Try a *tartufo* ice cream or a full lunch at the wonderful **Tre Scalini** *(see p94)*, before ending the morning window-shopping along the antiques of **Via dei Coronari** *(see p92)*.

See map on p88 ←

The Best of the Rest

1 Sant'Agnese in Agone

MAP L3 ▪ Piazza Navona ▪ Open 9am–1pm & 3–7pm Mon–Fri, 9am–1pm & 3–8pm Sat, Sun & hols

This church was built in honour of a young girl whose hair miraculously grew to cover her nakedness after she was stripped in a brothel. Borromini's façade combines concave and convex shapes.

2 Palazzo Pamphilj

MAP L3 ▪ Piazza Navona 14 ▪ Open for guided tours only (to book call 06 683 981)

This 17th-century palace was commissioned by Pope Innocent X and has a wonderful Pietro da Cortona fresco upstairs.

3 Via dei Coronari

MAP K2

Lined with antiques shops, this street *(see p80)* is at its torch-flickering best during the May and October antiques fairs.

4 Santa Maria dell'Anima

MAP L2 ▪ Via di Santa Maria dell' Anima 66 ▪ Open 9am–12:45pm & 3–7pm daily, except Wed am

Highlights in this breathtaking church include a Giulio Romano altarpiece and Peruzzi's Hadrian VI tomb (1523).

5 Chiesa Nuova

MAP K3 ▪ Piazza della Chiesa Nuova/Via del Governo Vecchio 134 ▪ Open 6:45am–noon & 5–7:45pm (to 8pm on Sun)

Pietro da Cortona painted the dome and apse, and Rubens painted three sanctuary canvases for this church.

6 Palazzo Braschi

MAP L3 ▪ Piazza San Pantaleo 10 ▪ 06 0608 ▪ Open 10am–7pm Tue–Sun (reservation recommended) ▪ Adm

The last papal family palace was built in 1791–1811 by Cosimo Morelli. Inside is a museum dedicated to Roman history.

7 Sant'Antonio dei Portoghesi

MAP L2 ▪ Via dei Portoghesi 2 ▪ Open 8:30am–1pm & 3–6pm Mon–Fri, 8:30am–noon & 3–6pm Sat, 9am–noon & 4–7:30pm Sun

A Baroque gem of a church. Out front is the Torre della Scimmia, a rare remnant of medieval Rome.

8 Domitian's Stadium

MAP L3 ▪ Via di Tor Sanguigna 13 ▪ Open 10am–7pm daily ▪ Adm ▪ www.stadio domiziano.com

The outline of this AD 86 stadium is echoed in Piazza Navona, built on top of its remains.

9 Museo Napoleonico

MAP L2 ▪ Piazza di Ponte Umberto I ▪ Open 10am–6pm Tue–Sun (by appt only) ▪ Adm

This collection of paintings, furnishings and *objets d'art* once belonged to the Bonaparte clan.

10 San Salvatore in Lauro

MAP K2 ▪ Piazza S Salvatore in Lauro 15 ▪ Open 9am–noon & 4–7pm daily

This church houses da Cortona's *Adoration of the Shepherds* (1630).

Santa Maria dell'Anima

Shops

1 Al Sogno
MAP L2 ▪ Piazza Navona 53

Enjoy a nostalgic trip browsing dolls, doll's houses, life-size teddy bears and wooden toys. Although hard for children to resist, staff disapprove of them touching anything.

Dolls on display at Al Sogno

2 Murano Max
MAP L3 ▪ Via dei Banchi Nuovi 6

A large selection of blown-glass vases, tableware and jewelry from Murano are available in a variety of colours at this shop.

3 SBU Store
MAP L3 ▪ Via di San Pantaleo 68–9

A former draper's shop on the ground floor of a historic building is now one of Rome's most fashionable menswear stores selling everything from casual jeans to formal suits.

4 Antica Cappelleria Troncarelli
MAP L2 ▪ Via della Cuccagna 15

This tiny hat shop is older than the Italian nation – it opened in 1857, and has changed little over the years. It offers a range of stylish models for men and women.

5 Massimo Maria Melis
MAP L2 ▪ Via dell'Orso 57

A film costume designer turned goldsmith, Massimo Melis creates breathtaking jewellery inspired by Roman and Etruscan designs, often incorporating ancient stones, seals and coins.

6 Cinzia Vintage
MAP K3 ▪ Via del Governo Vecchio 45

A historic second-hand shop on Via del Governo, Cinzia Vintage sells everything from old Levis to the occasional brand name.

7 Altro-quando
MAP L3 ▪ Via del Governo Vecchio 82-83

This photography and art bookshop doubles as an event venue and a movie theatre. They also sell magnets, posters and fun gadgets.

8 Kouki Bazar
MAP K2 ▪ Via dei Coronari 190

Buy bags of beads at this Aladdin's cave, or make your own selection and have it strung while you wait.

9 Nicotra di San Giacomo
MAP C3 ▪ Via del Governo Vecchio 128

The elegant and unique jewellery at this shop is handcrafted by artisans and combines Italian tradition with contemporary fashion.

10 Delfina Delettrez
MAP C3 ▪ Via di Monserrato 24A

Descendant of the Fendi family, this jewellery designer makes wearable art that often appears in fashion magazines such as *Vogue*.

See map on p88 ←

Cafés and Bars

Diners at the famous Tre Scalini

1 ## Tre Scalini
MAP L3 ■ Piazza Navona 28
This historic café (see p78), right on Piazza Navona, is renowned for its delectable chocolate homemade *tartufo* ice cream ball.

2 ## Abbey Theatre Irish Pub
MAP K3 ■ Via del Governo Vecchio 51–53
Removed from the hubbub of the nightlife core nearby, this cosy Irish-themed pub serves Guinness and an Irish and Italian all-day food menu.

3 ## Bistrot Chiostro del Bramante
MAP K3 ■ Arco della Pace 5
A modern museum café with outdoor tables overlooking the Baroque cloister. Stop by for a cup of coffee or to enjoy one of the tasty salads.

4 ## La Botticella
MAP C3 ■ Via di Tor Millina 32
This lively spot is popular among locals for its delicious craft beers, traditional Roman dishes and its friendly atmosphere. Its ambience evokes the feeling of visiting Rome in the bygone days.

5 ## Two Sizes – Tiramisu
MAP K3 ■ Via del Governo Vecchio 88
Specializing in tiramisu, this small dessert bar serves the sweet treat in two sizes and five different flavours – coffee, strawberry, peanut butter, caramel and pistachio.

6 ## Baguetteria del Fico
MAP K3 ■ Via della Fossa 12
A café serving gourmet sandwiches and baguettes, best accompanied by a glass of red wine or a spritz. If you're here for lunch, try the classic bruschetta or the bestselling mortadella with pistachio sandwiches.

7 ## Enoteca Il Piccolo
MAP K3 ■ Via del Governo Vecchio 74
A small wine bar with a personal touch, the friendly Enoteca il Piccolo is a great choice for wine with tasty homemade snacks and salads, and *vin brulè* (mulled wine) in winter.

8 ## Bar del Fico
MAP K3 ■ Piazza del Fico 26
Large *aperitivo* (happy-hour) buffets, delicious cocktails and a marvellous Sunday brunch are served at this popular bar-cum-restaurant.

9 ## Caffè Domiziano
MAP L2 ■ Piazza Navona 88
Service is slightly slow but this café features one of the most beautiful views in Rome, with a wide terrace directly on Piazza Navona.

10 ## Mimì e Cocò
MAP C3 ■ Via del Governo Vecchio 73
An intimate wine bar with dim lighting, serving cheese and meat platters accompanied by great wines.

Places to Eat

PRICE CATEGORIES

For a three-course meal for one with half a bottle of wine (or equivalent meal), taxes and extra charges.

€ under €40   €€ €40–60   €€€ over €60

1 Da Francesco
MAP K2–K3 ▪ Piazza del Fico 29 ▪ 06 686 4009 ▪ €

Popular with tourists, this has an excellent appetiser buffet offering hand-cut prosciutto, fresh seafood salads and many vegetarian options. It also has great pizza and pasta.

2 Da Tonino
MAP K3 ▪ Via del Governo Vecchio 18–19 ▪ 333 587 0779 ▪ Closed Sun ▪ €

Massive portions of pasta, and mains ranging from traditional veal stew to lamb with crisp roast potatoes, are served at this cheerful trattoria.

3 Mastrociccia Osteria Bistrot
MAP L3 ▪ Via del Governo Vecchio 76 ▪ 06 8666 1806 ▪ €

A traditional trattoria serving all the staples, including meatballs in tomato sauce and Roman pizzas.

4 Il Convivio
MAP L2 ▪ Vicolo dei Soldati 31 ▪ 06 686 9432 ▪ Closed Sun ▪ €€€

Located in the historic centre, Il Convivio (see p75) offers seasonal cuisine based on Italian traditions.

5 Cul de Sac
MAP L3 ▪ Piazza Paquino 73 ▪ 06 6880 1094 ▪ €

One of Rome's oldest wine bars has a wide range of labels. It's a bit of a squeeze, but it's a better option than most bars in nearby Piazza Navona.

6 Pizzeria La Montecarlo
MAP K3 ▪ Vicolo Savelli 13 ▪ 06 686 1877 ▪ Closed Mon ▪ €

The offspring of Baffetto's owners run this joint. It has less ambience than its famous parent, Pizzeria da Baffetto in Via del Governo Vecchio, but benefits from shorter queues.

7 Casa Bleve
MAP L3 ▪ Via de Teatro Valle 48 ▪ 06 686 5970 ▪ Closed Sun ▪ €€€

Anacleto Bleve sources the freshest ingredients from small producers to create dishes at this osteria (see p76).

8 Casa Coppelle
MAP M2 ▪ Piazza delle Coppelle 49 ▪ 06 6889 1707 ▪ €€

This relaxed, contemporary restaurant serves French and Roman food, such as caramelised artichoke tarte tatin, and fabulous gorgonzola and pear risotto.

Cosy interior of Lo Zozzone

9 Lo Zozzone
MAP L3 ▪ Via Teatro della Pace 32 ▪ 06 6880 8575 ▪ €

The wonderful Lo Zozzone serves slices of crisp pizza bianca (with a base of olive oil and salt), filled with any combination from the deli counter. Eat on the terrace or take away.

10 Il Pagliaccio
MAP J3 ▪ Via dei Banchi Vecchi 129a ▪ 06 6880 9595 ▪ Closed Sun, Mon & Tue L ▪ €€€

This restaurant (see p75) serves Mediterranean dishes in a modern dining room, offering various tasting menus and à la carte specialities.

See map on p88 ←

🔟 Around the Pantheon

During the Roman Empire the Tiber Bend area was a military training ground called the Campo Marzio. After the fall of Rome, this riverside district was all but forgotten until the Baroque boom gave the area's palaces their distinctive look. Mussolini cleaned up the quarter in the 1920s and 1930s to bring out its ancient character, adding Fascist buildings complete with self-aggrandizing bas-reliefs.

Detail, Piazza della Rotonda

AROUND THE PANTHEON

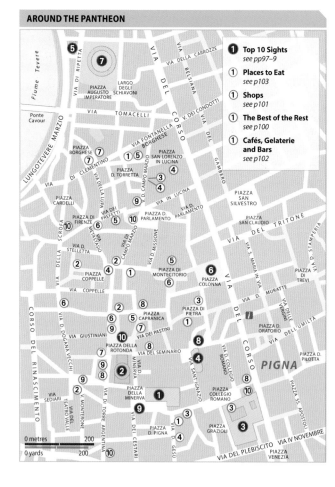

- **1** Top 10 Sights
  see pp97–9
- **1** Places to Eat
  see p103
- **1** Shops
  see p101
- **1** The Best of the Rest
  see p100
- **1** Cafés, Gelaterie and Bars
  see p102

PIGNA

0 metres 200
0 yards 200

The Pantheon, fronted by the Fontana del Pantheon and obelisk of Rameses II

① Santa Maria sopra Minerva

MAP M3 ■ Piazza della Minerva 42 ■ Open 11am–1pm & 3–7pm daily

Only truly Gothic church in Rome (see p51), as the name suggests, above a temple to Minerva. Michelangelo's *Risen Christ* (1514–21), to the left of the main altar, is a muscular rendition of the Saviour so shockingly nude that church officials added the bronze wisp of drapery. Filippino Lippi frescoed the last chapel on the right; the lower scene on the right wall includes portraits of young Giovanni and Giulio de' Medici (known as Popes Leo X and Clement VII), who are buried in tombs by Antonio Sangallo the Younger, in the apse, with Fra Angelico and (most of) St Catherine of Siena.

② The Pantheon

"Simple, erect, severe, austere, sublime" – even Lord Byron struggled to find adequate words to describe this marvel (see pp18–19) of Roman architecture, the only ancient Roman temple to survive virtually intact through the millennia.

③ Galleria Doria Pamphilj

MAP N3 ■ Via del Corso 305 ■ Open 10am–7pm Mon–Thu, 10am–8pm Sat & Sun (by appt only) ■ Adm ■ www.doriapamphilj.it

The best of the private collection galleries (see p55) in Rome. In addition to paintings by Rubens, Correggio, Tintoretto, Carracci and Brueghel, star works include Caravaggio's *Mary Magdalene*, *Rest on the Flight into Egypt*, and *Young St John the Baptist* (a copy he made of his Capitoline version), Titian's *Salome with the Head of John the Baptist* and Bernini's bust of Pope Innocent.

Santa Maria sopra Minerva

Interior of Sant'Ignazio di Loyola

4 Sant'Ignazio di Loyola
MAP N3 ■ Piazza di S Ignazio ■ Open 9am–8pm daily, also 8pm–midnight Fri–Sun

When the Jesuits' new Baroque church was finished, it still lacked a dome. Master of *trompe l'oeil* Andrea Pozzo used the technique in 1685 to create the illusion of an airy dome on the flat ceiling over the church's crossing; stand on the yellow marble disc for the full effect, then walk directly under the "dome" to see how skewed the painting actually is. Pozzo also painted the nave vault with the lovely *Glory of Sant'Ignazio*.

RECYCLED TEMPLES

Romans are ingenious recyclers. The Pantheon became a church, Hadrian's Temple a stock exchange. Santa Maria sopra Minerva was built atop a temple to Minerva; San Clemente on one to Mithras. In the 11th century, the walls of San Lorenzo in Miranda in the Forum and San Nicola in Carcere on Via Teatro di Marcello were both grafted onto temple columns.

---

5 Ara Pacis Museum
MAP D2 ■ Lungotevere in Augusta ■ 06 0608 ■ Open 9:30am–7:30pm daily ■ Adm ■ www.arapacis.it

Augustus Caesar built this "Altar of Peace" between 13 BC and 9 BC to celebrate the famed *pax romana* (Roman peace) he instituted – largely by subjugating most of Western Europe, the Levant and North Africa. Fragments of the altar were excavated over several centuries, and in the 1920s Mussolini placed the reconstituted Ara Pacis by Augustus's Mausoleum. The altar is now housed in a Richard Meier-designed museum, the first modern structure to be built in the centre of Rome in more than 70 years.

6 Column of Marcus Aurelius
MAP N2 ■ Piazza Colonna

Trajan's Column was such a success *(see p26)* that this one was erected to honour Marcus Aurelius in AD 180–93. The reliefs celebrate his battles against the Germans (169–73) on the bottom and the Sarmatians (174–6) on the top. In 1588, Pope Sixtus V replaced the statues of the emperor and his wife with that of St Paul.

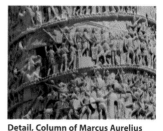

Detail, Column of Marcus Aurelius

7 Augustus's Mausoleum
MAP D2 ■ Piazza Augusto Imperatore

Augustus built this grand imperial tomb in 27 BC, his ashes later joined by those of emperors Tiberius and Nerva, and worthies such as Agrippa and Marcellus. Barbarian invaders later made off with the urns and locals mined its travertine facing for their palaces. The ancient rotunda has served time as a circus for bear-baiting, fortress, hanging garden and concert hall. In the 1920s its crown was restored to the ancient style, covered with grass and cypress, and Mussolini laid out the Fascist piazza around it. Visitors are permitted to view the mausoleum only from the outside.

Ruins, Augustus's Mausoleum

8 Piazza di Sant'Ignazio
MAP M2

Francesco Raguzzini laid out this masterpiece of Baroque urban design for the Jesuits in 1727–8, creating a piazza carefully planned right down to the ornate iron balconies and matching dusty pink plaster walls.

9 Bernini's Elephant Obelisk
MAP M3 ■ Piazza della Minerva

An example of Bernini's fun-loving side. This baby elephant, carved to the master's designs in 1667 by Ercole Ferrata, carries a miniature 6th-century BC Egyptian obelisk on its back. It is a playful reference to Hannibal's war elephants, which carried siege towers across the Alps to attack the Romans in 218 BC.

10 Piazza della Rotonda
MAP M3

This piazza hosted a busy daily market until 1847; some of the Pantheon's portico columns still bear holes from the stall posts once set into them. The square is now filled with cafés and visitors, ranged around Giacomo della Porta's 1575 fountain, which has a tiny Egyptian obelisk dedicated to Rameses II.

A WALK AROUND THE PANTHEON

▶ Start with a cappuccino at **Caffè Sant'Eustachio** *(see p102)*. Follow Salita de' Crescenzi to **Piazza della Rotonda** and the stunning beauty of the **Pantheon** *(see pp18–19)*. Head down to Piazza della Minerva to admire Bernini's Elephant Obelisk and **Santa Maria sopra Minerva** *(see p97)*.

Via S Caterina da Siena becomes Via Pie' di Marmo (look right to see the famous ancient marble foot). The street meets the piazza in front of **Galleria Doria Pamphilj** *(see p97)*. After paying homage to the works inside, take a coffee break at the elegant **Caffè Doria** *(see p102)*. Then head out the east end of the piazza to Via Lata, then on to the Corso to **Santa Maria in Via Lata** *(see p100)*. Turn left up the Corso to the Baroque Piazza di Sant'Ignazio for Rome's best *trompe l'oeil* frescoes in **Sant'Ignazio di Loyola**. Work your way past the square's mini palaces onto Piazza di Pietra. An alley leads to the **Column of Marcus Aurelius**. Lunch with politicians and lobbyists from the nearby Parliament at reliable and deeply traditional **Da Gino al Parlamento** *(see p103)* or head to **Giolitti** *(see p102)* for ice cream.

Walk west on Via del Leone into Piazza Borghese, home to an antiques print market and the **Palazzo Borghese** *(see p100)*. Two blocks north you'll come to Piazza Augusto Imperatore, where this walk ends after you've visited its churches, **Augustus's Mausoleum** and ■ the **Ara Pacis Museum**.

See map on p96 ←

The Best of the Rest

Visitor's at Hadrian's Temple

1 Hadrian's Temple
MAP M2 ■ **Piazza di Pietra 9A**
■ **Access inside for cultural events only**
Eleven huge columns still stand from a Temple to Hadrian built in AD 145 by his adoptive son, Antoninus Pius.

2 Santa Maria Maddalena
MAP M2 ■ **Piazza della Maddalena 53** ■ **Open 7am–noon & 5–8pm Mon–Fri, 9:30am–noon & 5–8pm Sat & Sun**
The 1735 façade of this church by Giuseppe Sardi is Rome's best monument to the Rococo movement.

3 Piè di Marmo
MAP N3 ■ **Via S Stefano del Cacco, Via del Piè di Marmo**
This large, marble foot belonged to an unidentified ancient statue, thought to be around 26 ft (8 m) high.

4 San Lorenzo in Lucina
MAP M2 ■ **Piazza S Lorenzo in Lucina 16A** ■ **Open 8am–8pm daily**
Founded in the 5th century, this church was overhauled in 1090–1118. Guido Reni painted the Crucifixion altarpiece, while Bernini designed the second chapel on the right.

5 Palazzo di Montecitorio
MAP M1 ■ **Piazza di Montecitorio 33** ■ **06 676 01** ■ **Currently closed to the public**
Bernini's palace houses the Chamber of Deputies. The south façade is the 17th-century original; the north is Art Nouveau.

6 Piazza di Montecitorio
MAP M1
The square's obelisk was once part of the Augustus's giant sundial, which used to be flanked by the Ara Pacis (see p98).

7 Palazzo Borghese
MAP M1 ■ **Via Borghese & Via di Ripetta** ■ **Access to outside only**
The oddly shaped "harpsichord of Rome", begun by Vignola in 1560, was finished with a Tiber terrace by Flaminio Ponzio.

8 Fontanella del Facchino
MAP N3 ■ **Via Lata**
This small 16th-century wall fountain is fashioned as a water-seller whose barrel forever spouts fresh water.

9 Piazza Sant'Eustachio
MAP M3
The lovely Piazza Sant'Eustachio is home to two cafés competing for the title of Rome's best cappuccino, as well as an 1196 bell tower, and an excellent view of Sant'Ivo (see p89).

10 Santa Maria in Via Lata
MAP N3 ■ **Via del Corso 306** ■ **Open 5–10:30pm daily (from 6pm in summer)**
Pietro da Cortona designed this church's façade (1660) and Bernini designed the high altar (1639–43). Its frescoes can now be seen in the Crypta Balbi (see p64). The church is also famous for its fascinating underground crypt. Book ahead.

Santa Maria in Via Lata

Shops

Art supplies at Ditta G. Poggi

1 Ditta G. Poggi
MAP M3 ■ Via del Gesù 74

One of Rome's most famous art supplies stores, sells everything from oil paints and sketchbooks to pencils and charcoal.

2 Davide Cenci
MAP M2 ■ Via di Campo Marzio 1–8

Founded in 1926, Davide Cenci is a men's and women's clothes boutique. Their own classic but highly fashionable line is sold alongside international labels such as Ralph Lauren, Church's, Brooks Brothers, Fay, Burberry and Giorgio Armani.

3 Campo Marzio
MAP M2 ■ Via di Campo Marzio 41

Accessories and luxury writing instruments here include silver-plated fountain pens and calligraphy sets; exquisite, vividly coloured leather notebooks; leather iPad and phone covers; and leather computer cases, briefcases and hand luggage.

4 Vittorio Bagagli
MAP M2 ■ Via di Campo Marzio 42

Purveyor of fine houseware since 1855, this store sells design-led Alessi kitchen gadgets, Pavoni coffee machines and Solimene pottery.

5 Michele di Loco
MAP M1 ■ Via del Leone 7

Exquisite men's and women's shoes and boots by a carefully selected clique of niche designers are sold here. There is also a branch at Via de Baullari 22, near Campo de' Fiori.

6 Mercato dell'Antiquariato
MAP M1 ■ Piazza Borghese

This lovely antiquarian market consists of about 17 stalls specializing in antique prints and books.

7 Città del Sole
MAP L1 ■ Via della Scrofa 65

Part of an Italian chain of classy toy stores with the very best in educational playthings, this shop places an emphasis on innovative design and natural materials.

8 Manufactus
MAP M3 ■ Via della Rotonda 15

A traditional bookbindery and stationery trove. This shop offers notebooks, leather bags, wallets and a plethora of all-Italian gifts.

9 Campomarzio70
MAP M2 ■ Via di Campo Marzio 70

A luxurious perfume shop carrying the finest Italian brands and sophisticated cosmetic treatments. It also stocks handmade fragrances.

10 Container 16
MAP L1 ■ Via della Scrofa 16

This concept store sells a curated selection of Italian design objects for the home. Items on offer include contemporary tablecloths and stylish kitchenware.

See map on p96

Cafés, Gelaterie and Bars

1 Giolitti
MAP M2 ■ Via degli Uffici del Vicario 40

This 19th-century landmark café *(see p78)* is widely regarded as serving Rome's best ice cream.

Tables outside Giolitti

2 Caffè Sant'Eustachio
MAP M3 ■ Piazza Sant'Eustachio 82

Another best – this café *(see p78)* is renowned for serving the best cappuccino in Rome. Their technique is a closely guarded secret.

3 Caffè Doria
MAP N3 ■ Galleria Doria Pamphilj, enter on Via della Gatta 1A

With the atmosphere of an English tea room, this elegant café has coffees and pastries, light lunches, afternoon tea, and evening drinks with nibbles.

4 Grom
MAP M2 ■ Via della Maddalena 30A

This 100 per cent organic ice cream chain *(see p79)* has classic recipes.

5 Achilli al Parlamento
MAP M1 ■ Via dei Prefetti 15

Popular with politicos from the nearby parliament buildings, this wine bar is atmospheric and stylish.

6 San Crispino
MAP M2 ■ Piazza della Maddalena 3

San Crispino has been making artisan gelato from pure organic ingredients since the early 1990s. It has several branches around town, and the ice creams, sorbets and meringues are as good as ever.

7 La Tazza d'Oro
MAP M2 ■ Via degli Orfani 84

A die-hard locals' joint, La Tazza d'Oro *(see p79)* has been serving what devotees swear is Rome's best coffee since 1946.

8 Enoteca Capranica
MAP M2 ■ Piazza Capranica 104

This wine bar-cum-restaurant is just the place for a quick *aperitivo* (happy hour buffet) or a more leisurely alfresco lunch. The bottle-lined interior shows that this is a serious wine bar with a well-stocked cellar and a great choice.

9 Cremeria Monteforte
MAP M3 ■ Via della Rotonda 22 ■ Closed Dec & Jan

Despite its touristy location, this gelateria *(see p19)* guarded by a wooden Pinocchio doorman serves the best *fragola* (strawberry) ice cream in town, as well as innovative flavours such as orange chocolate.

10 Pascucci Frullati Bar
MAP M4 ■ Via di Torre Argentina 20

This bar has the frothiest milk shakes and smoothies in Rome. They come in all flavours and in any combination.

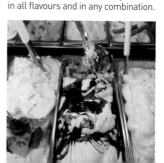

Italian gelato on sale

Places to Eat

PRICE CATEGORIES

For a three-course meal for one with half a bottle of wine (or equivalent meal), taxes and extra charges.

€ under €40 €€ €40–60 €€€ over €60

1 Matricianella
MAP M1 ■ Via del Leone 3–4 ■ 06 683 2100 ■ Closed Sun ■ €€

Try the *carciofi alla giudia* (Jewish-style crispy fried artichokes), *fritto vegetale* (lightly-battered fried vegetables) and *saltimbocca* (veal rolled up with prosciutto and sage), at this quintessential Roman trattoria in the *centro storico*.

2 Il Bacaro
MAP L2 ■ Via degli Spagnoli 27 ■ 06 687 2554 ■ €€

Il Bacaro's decor is contemporary inside, but the vine-clad terrace outside has the feel of old Rome. The menu has traditional dishes from across Italy. Booking is essential.

3 Osteria dell'Ingegno
MAP N2 ■ Piazza di Pietra 45 ■ 06 678 0662 ■ €

This popular wine bar serves huge meat and cheese platters.

4 Trattoria Enoteca Corsi
MAP M4 ■ Via del Gesù 88 ■ 06 679 0821 ■ Closed Sat D & Sun ■ €

As well as a huge wine selection, this popular restaurant offers traditional dishes at affordable prices. Check the blackboard for the daily specials.

5 Clemente alla Maddalena
MAP M2 ■ Piazza della Maddalena ■ 06 683 3633 ■ €€

Excellent Italian cuisine is served at this elegant restaurant.

6 Obicà
MAP M1 ■ Via dei Prefetti 26A ■ 06 683 2630 ■ €

This café-restaurant specializes in dishes containing very high-quality buffalo mozzarella.

7 Armando al Pantheon
MAP M3 ■ Salita dei Crescenzi 31 ■ 06 6880 3034 ■ Closed Sat D & Sun ■ €€

Roman classics as well as lighter dishes are served at this long-standing, friendly family-run trattoria.

Diners at Armando al Pantheon

8 Taverna del Seminario
MAP M3 ■ Via del Seminario 105 ■ 06 8110 9909 ■ €

Typical Italian food and great house Chianti are offered at this place, all for a reasonable price.

9 La Rosetta
MAP M2 ■ Via della Rosetta 8/9 ■ 06 686 1002 ■ €€€

Tuna tartare and lobster pasta are a real treat, as is the variety of other shellfish and seafood dishes featured on the menu at this fish restaurant and oyster bar founded in 1966.

10 Da Gino al Parlamento
MAP M1 ■ Vicolo Rosini 4 ■ 06 687 3434 ■ Closed Sun ■ €€

Largely unchanged since opening in 1963 and popular with politicians, this restaurant with *trompe l'oeil* frescoes has Roman classics such as *tonnarelli cacio e pepe* (pasta with cheese and black pepper). Book ahead.

See map on p96

TOP 10 Campo de' Fiori to the Capitoline

This area is where Caesar was assassinated, but it is also home to the glory of Capitoline Hill. In ancient times, this district was full of important public monuments, but when the papacy moved to France and Rome was close to extinction, it was here that the remaining citizens lived in squalor. With the return of the popes, commerce flourished and the area revived. Today, this typical Roman neighbourhood bears clear signs of its long history.

Musei Capitolini

CAMPO DE' FIORI TO THE CAPITOLINE

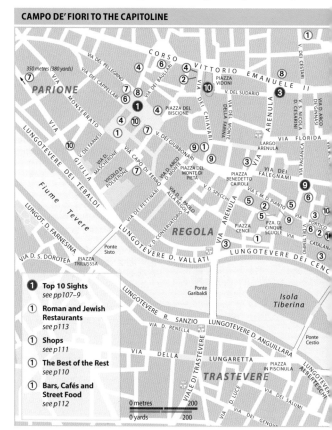

① **Top 10 Sights**
see pp107–9

① **Roman and Jewish Restaurants**
see p113

① **Shops**
see p111

① **The Best of the Rest**
see p110

① **Bars, Cafés and Street Food**
see p112

Previous pages The vast dome of the Pantheon

1 Campo de' Fiori
MAP L4

The "Field of Flowers" *(see p62)* occupies what was, in ancient times, the open space in front of the Theatre of Pompey. Since the Middle Ages, it has been one of Rome's liveliest areas, a backdrop for princes and pilgrims alike. It was also the locus of the Inquisition's executions, as attested to by the statue of Giordano Bruno, burned here in the Jubilee celebrations of 1600.

2 Capitoline Hill
MAP N5

Everything in Rome is built on top of something else. The Capitoline *(see pp28–9)* was originally two peaks: the Arx, with the Temple of Juno, and the Cavo, with the Temple of Jupiter, now mostly occupied by the Palazzo dei Conservatori *(see pp30–31)*. The huge Tabularium (Record Office) was built between them in 78 BC, thus forming one hill, called the Capitol; and over that the Palazzo Senatorio was built in the 12th century.

The ruins of Capitoline Hill

3 Largo di Torre Argentina
MAP M4

The ruins of four Republican temples (one dating back to the 4th century BC) were uncovered here in 1925. To the west is the 18th-century Teatro Argentina, with its inscription to the Muses. Many 19th-century operas debuted here, including Rossini's *Barber of Seville*. It was a flop on its first night, but only because his enemy, Pauline Bonaparte, had hired a gaggle of hecklers to disrupt it.

4 Theatre of Marcellus
MAP N5 ■ Via del Portico d'Ottavia 29 ■ Open daily 9am–7pm (9am–8pm in winter)

One of three ancient theatres in this district, the Theatre of Marcellus dates back to 23 BC, and was probably the most frequented of all Imperial theatres in Ancient Rome until the Colosseum captured the public's favour. The lower archways once housed picturesque medieval shops. To the right stand three columns and a frieze fragment that belonged to a Temple of Apollo, also from the 1st century BC.

The vibrant, ornamented ceiling of Chiesa del Gesù

⑤ Santa Maria in Cosmedin
MAP N6 ■ Piazza della Bocca della Verità 18 ■ Open 9am–7pm Sat & Sun ■ www.cosmedin.org

Originally a bread distribution centre, the site became a church in the 6th century and, 200 years later, the focus of Rome's Greek exile community. The Greek title "in Cosmedin" means "decorated". Little remains of the earliest ornamentation; most of it is from the 12th and 13th centuries, although there is a graceful altar screen characteristic of Eastern Orthodox churches. The most popular element is the *Bocca della Verità* (Mouth of Truth), an ancient cistern cover. Legend has it that the mouth snaps shut on the hands of liars.

⑥ Foro Boario
MAP N6

The name refers to the ancient cattle market that once existed here. Now the area is a little park with two small 2nd-century BC temples and an Arch of Janus. Dating from the reign of Constantine or later, the arch is unprepossessing, but the temples are amazingly well preserved. The rectangular Temple of Portunus, god of rivers and ports, was converted in the 9th century into a church dedicated to St Mary the Egyptian, a prostitute who became a desert hermit. The pretty, circular shrine is a Temple of Hercules Victor.

⑦ Chiesa del Gesù
MAP N4 ■ Piazza del Gesù ■ Open 7am–12:30pm & 4–7:30pm daily

This prototype Counter-Reformation church, enormous and ornate, was meant to proclaim the pre-eminence of the Jesuit faith. The façade is elegant, but the interior is dazzling – first impressions are of vibrant gold, bathed in sunlight, and the vision of angels and saints being pulled into heaven through a miraculous hole in the roof. The tomb of Ignatius, the order's founder, is adorned with the world's largest chunk of lapis lazuli.

⑧ Santa Maria in Aracoeli
MAP N4 ■ Scala dell'Arce Capitolina 14 ■ Open 9:30am–5:30pm daily (9am–6:30pm in summer)

This 6th-century church stands on the site of the ancient Temple of

---

THE JEWS IN ROME

Since the 2nd century BC, Jews have been a significant presence in Rome. They thrived throughout the Middle Ages, until, in 1556, Pope Paul IV confined them to the squalid Ghetto here, on the bank of the Tiber, where they remained until 1870. Sixty years later they again suffered deadly persecution under the Fascists, but today Roman Jews number about 14,000 and are an integral part of civic life.

Juno Moneta (Juno the Sentinel), which was also the Roman mint – and the origin of the word "money". Legend says you can win the lottery by climbing on your knees up the 14th-century front steps – but what you will definitely gain is a fine view. The nave's columns come from older structures; the third one on the left is inscribed "a cubiculo Augustorum" ("from the emperor's bedroom").

⑨ Fontana delle Tartarughe

MAP M5 ▪ Piazza Mattei

The "Fountain of the Tortoises" (see p63) is the work of three artists. It was designed by Giacomo della Porta for the Mattei family. Taddeo Landini added the bronze boys. Later, an unknown artist added the tortoises that gave the fountain its name.

The restored Fontana delle Tartarughe

⑩ Sant'Andrea della Valle

MAP L4 ▪ Piazza Sant'Andrea della Valle ▪ Open 3–7:30pm Mon–Sat, 8:30am–7pm Sun

Why has one of the most impressive 17th-century Baroque churches been left with an asymmetrical façade? Only one angel supports the upper tier. Upon its completion, when Pope Alexander VII dared to criticize the work, sculptor Cosimo Fancelli refused to produce a second angel, saying "If he wants another he can make it himself!". Many come to see the setting of Act I of Puccini's *Tosca*, but the church also has Rome's second-largest dome and some wonderful Domenichino frescoes.

ROMAN CULTURE, LAYER UPON LAYER

▶ This walk is designed to last 2 to 4 hours. It's best to start in the morning. Starting with the **Theatre of Marcellus** (see p107), notice the soaring buttresses that support the palace, added in the 16th century. Heading round the next corner, in the 17th-century **Santa Maria in Campitelli** (see p110) use binoculars to espy the oak leaves depicted in the altar's tiny icon. Continuing west, as you approach the **Fontana delle Tartarughe**, listen for the sound of splashing water echoing off the medieval walls. To the north, the **Crypta Balbi Museum** (see pp64–5) has fascinating displays about the neighbourhood's history. One block north is the awe-inspiring **Chiesa del Gesù**.

For one of the best cappuccino-cornetto combinations in town, stop off at **Bar del Cappuccino** (Via Arenula 50).

At **Sant'Andrea della Valle** look up at the unusual barrel-vaulted ceiling. Then head south to Via di Grotta Pinta for the remains of the **Theatre of Pompey** (see p69). A block northwest, in the piazza of the **Palazzo Farnese** (see p110), admire the twin fountains, composed of stone tubs from the Baths of Caracalla. Walk across **Campo de' Fiori** (see p107) to **Palazzo della Cancelleria** (see p110) to contemplate its Renaissance perfection.

End with a luxurious meal at **Ar Galletto** (Piazza Farnese 104) or grab some lunch on the go at **Antico Forno Roscioli** (Via dei Chiavari 34).

See map on pp106–7 ←

The Best of the Rest

1 Palazzo Farnese
MAP K4 ■ Piazza Farnese
67 ■ 06 686 011 ■ Open for guided
tours only (Mon & Wed 3, 4 & 5pm,
Fri 3 & 4pm); book online
at least one week ahead
■ www.visite-palazzofarnese.it
One of Rome's largest palaces (see
p60) features art by Michelangelo, like
the wonderful cornice. Book ahead.

2 Il Vittoriano
MAP N4 ■ Piazza Venezia
■ Open 9:30am–7:30pm daily
(last entry 6:45pm)
The motifs on this monument to
Victor Emmanuel II inspired its
nickname, "The Wedding Cake".

**3 Synagogue and Jewish
Museum**
MAP M5 ■ Lungotevere dei Cenci
■ 06 6840 0661 ■ Museum: open
10am–6pm Sun–Thu (to 5pm in
winter); 10am–4pm Fri (9am–2pm in
winter); closed on Jewish hols
Dating from 1904, this synagogue is
also home to the city's Jewish museum.

4 Palazzo della Cancelleria
MAP L4 ■ Piazza della
Cancelleria 1 ■ Open for group guided
tours only Sat 9am–noon ■ Adm
Once the Papal Chancellery, this
lovely Renaissance structure (see
p61) has an unparalleled courtyard.

Entrance of Palazzo della Cancelleria

5 Portico d'Ottavia
MAP M5
Built in honour of Octavia, Augustus's
sister, this was an entrance to the
Circus Flaminius. You can view
the ruins and archaeological digs
from scaffolding.

6 Museo Barracco
MAP L4 ■ Corso Vittorio
Emanuele II 168 ■ 06 0608 ■ Open
10am–4pm Tue–Sun (1–7pm summer)
■ www.museobarracco.it
This palazzo has a small but
important collection of ancient
sculpture and some ceramics.

7 Galleria Spada
MAP L5 ■ Piazza Capo di
Ferro 13 ■ 06 687 4896 ■ Open
8:30am–7:30pm Wed–Mon ■ Adm
(free first Sun of the month)
The Palazzo Spada (see p61) houses
a fine collection of Baroque paintings
amassed in the 17th century by
Bernardino and Virginio Spada.
Don't miss Borromini's incredible
perspective gallery.

8 Palazzo Venezia
MAP N4 ■ Via del Plebiscito
118 ■ 06 678 0131 ■ Open 9:30am–
6:30pm ■ Adm (free first
Sun of the month)
Pope Paul II used to watch carnival
horse races from the balcony here
(see p61) in the 15th century; it's
also where Mussolini shouted his
Fascist harangues.

**9 Santa Maria in
Campitelli**
MAP N5 ■ Piazza Campitelli 9
■ Open 7am–7pm daily
One of the most lavish tabernacles
in Rome can be found in this church.

10 Via Giulia
MAP K4
This fashionable street was laid
out by Bramante in the early
16th century and is lined with
elegant palazzi.

Shops

1 Calzoleria Petrocchi
MAP M3 ▪ Vicolo delle Ceste 29 ▪ Open on weekends by appt only

Bruno Ridolfi keeps alive the high fashion, made-to-measure cobbler traditions of his uncle Tito Petrocchi, who shod glamorous stars in the 1950s and 1960s *dolce vita* heyday.

2 Beppe e I Suoi Formaggi
MAP M5 ▪ Via di Santa Maria del Pianto 9A/11

This shop has cheeses created by Beppe in Piemonte, along with salami, hams, preserves, olive oil, bread and wine sourced from Italian artisans. Buy to take home, or stay for a lunch of choice produce with a glass of wine.

3 Cartolerie Internazionali
MAP D4 ▪ Via Arenula 85

An array of art supplies, pens, gift ideas, photo albums and greeting cards is sold at this stationery shop.

Fahrenheit 451

4 Fahrenheit 451
MAP L4 ▪ Campo de' Fiori 44

Cinema, art and photography books fill this shop from floor to ceiling.

5 Boccione Limentani
MAP M5 ▪ Via del Portico d'Ottavia

Known simply as the kosher bakery, this neighbourhood institution offers *biscotti*, *pizze* and three kinds of *crostate* (tarts) – ricotta and cherry, ricotta and chocolate and almond paste and cherry. There's always a queue here.

Inside Alimentari Ruggeri

6 Alimentari Ruggeri
MAP L4 ▪ Campo de' Fiori 1

This fabulous deli has a dizzying selection of cheeses, cured meats and many food souvenirs.

7 Acqua Madre Hammam
MAP M5 ▪ Via di S Ambrogio 17 ▪ Closed Mon

Recharge your batteries with a visit to this luxury *hammam*. There's a sauna and Turkish bath, plus a wide choice of body treatments.

8 Feltrinelli
MAP M4 ▪ Largo di Torre Argentina, 5/A

A large bookstore with an extensive selection of English-language books, as well as a range of board games, music and gadgets.

9 104 Pandemonium
MAP L4 ▪ Via dei Giubbonari 104

This boutique carries a selection of the latest fashion trends and is a popular store among locals.

10 Leone Limentani
MAP M5 ▪ Via del Portico d'Ottavia 47

The best-known Italian brands in kitchen design and utensils are sold in this vast warehouse-like space.

See map on pp106–7

Bars, Cafés and Street Food

(1) Antico Forno Roscioli
MAP L4 ▪ Via dei Chiavari 34
▪ 06 686 4045 ▪ Open 7am–7:30pm
Mon–Sat; closed Sat in Jul & Aug

Pizza, *rustici* (small puff pastries with a filling), focaccia and hot dishes are served fresh from the oven. The classic is *pizza bianca* (pizza with olive oil and salt).

(2) Origano Campo dei Fiori
MAP L4 ▪ Largo Chiavari 83/84

A bistrot with many vegan options, including artichoke *carpaccio* and vegan tiramisu, as well as fish dishes like swordfish spaghetti.

(3) Bar del Cappuccino
MAP L5 ▪ Via Arenula 50
▪ 06 6880 6042 ▪ Closed Sun

This unassuming, friendly bar serves some of the best cappuccinos in town, with decorated foam on request.

(4) Pandivino - Street Food
MAP L4 ▪ Piazza del Paradiso 39
▪ Closed Tue

A cosy and friendly tapas bar that infuses Italian and Spanish flavours.

(5) Antica Norcineria Viola
MAP L4 ▪ Campo de' Fiori 43
▪ 06 6880 6114 ▪ Closed Aug

Viola specializes in Umbrian ham and salami, which are considered to be the best in Italy.

Fresh breads at Forno Campo de' Fiori

(6) Forno Campo de' Fiori
MAP K4 ▪ Campo de' Fiori 22
▪ 06 6880 6662

Run by a branch of the Roscioli family, this bakery specializes in *pizza bianca*, *pizza rosso* (with a tomato sauce) and *crostate* (tarts).

(7) Bar Giulia
MAP J3 ▪ Via Giulia 84
▪ 06 686 1310 ▪ Closed Sun

This simple snack bar serves good sandwiches. The barman prepares great cappuccinos with fancy foam designs.

(8) Fonzies The Burger House
MAP M5 ▪ Via Santa Maria del Pianto 13

Great burgers and Jewish-Roman meat specialties such as *straccetti* and meatballs. Certified kosher.

(9) Dar Filettaro a Santa Barbara
MAP L4 ▪ Largo dei Librari 88
▪ 06 686 4018 ▪ Closed Sun

This tiny place is a Roman food institution selling crisp, deep-fried salt cod. Perfect for a quick lunch.

(10) Taba Café
MAP L4 ▪ Campo de' Fiori 13/14

A relaxed café and bar with retro decor, it is great for an aperitivo with a buffet or a cheese platter with a glass of wine.

Meat section of Antica Norcineria Viola

Roman and Jewish Restaurants

PRICE CATEGORIES

For a three-course meal for one with half a bottle of wine (or equivalent meal), taxes and extra charges.

€ under €40   €€ €40–60   €€€ over €60

1 Piperno

MAP M5 ▪ Monte de'Cenci 9 ▪ 06 6880 6629 ▪ Closed Sun D, Mon ▪ €€

Roman-Jewish cuisine is at its finest at Piperno, located in a beautiful quiet piazza. Traditional dishes include *carciofi alla giudia* (Jewish-style fried artichokes). Booking is a must.

Crispy fried artichokes

2 BellaCarne Kosher Grill

MAP M5 ▪ Via del Portico d'Ottavia 51 ▪ 06 683 3104 ▪ Closed Fri D, Sat L ▪ €€

Using only kosher ingredients, this restaurant serves traditional meat recipes with a creative twist.

3 La Taverna del Ghetto

MAP N5 ▪ Via Portico d'Ottavia 7 ▪ 06 6880 9771 ▪ Closed Fri D, Sat L ▪ €€

Enjoy kosher cooking in the medieval dining rooms, or outside on the piazza. Grilled fish is the speciality.

4 Ar Galletto

MAP K4 ▪ Piazza Farnese 104 ▪ 06 686 1714 ▪ Closed 1 week Aug ▪ €€

This hearty trattoria with a pleasant terrace serves traditional Roman food.

5 Sora Margherita

MAP M4 ▪ Piazza delle Cinque Scole 30 ▪ 06 687 4216 ▪ Closed Sun D, Wed, Fri & Sat L, Thu ▪ €€

Enjoy wonderful, hearty Roman-Jewish delicacies at this small *osteria*. There is no sign – look for the red streamers in the doorway.

6 Ba'Ghetto

MAP M5 ▪ Via del Portico d'Ottavia 57 ▪ 06 6889 2868 ▪ Closed Fri D, Sat L ▪ €€

Jewish certified kosher dishes from Rome and Northern Africa are served at this modern trattoria.

7 Osteria da Fortunata

MAP K4 ▪ Via del Pellegrino 11 ▪ 06 60667291 ▪ €

A traditional Roman trattoria specializing in delicious fresh pasta, such as *carbonara* and *amatriciana*. Try the fried courgette flowers with anchovies.

8 Da Giggetto

MAP M5 ▪ Via del Portico d'Ottavia 21A–22 ▪ 06 686 1105 ▪ Closed Mon ▪ €€

This busy eatery is next to the Portico d'Ottavia *(see p110)*. It serves an exquisite version of *carciofi alla giudia* along with hearty pasta and sustaining meat and offal stews.

9 Sheva

MAP M5 ▪ Via Santa Maria del Pianto 1B ▪ 06 9259 7940 ▪ €

Jewish specialities here include kosher dried meat and saffron, risotto with pumpkin and chestnut and pasta with courgette.

10 Nonna Betta

MAP M5 ▪ Via del Portico d'Ottavia 16 ▪ 06 6880 6263 ▪ Closed Tue ▪ €

This kosher-style restaurant's long menu features Rome's favourite Jewish specialities, from famous fried artichokes to anchovies with endive and a variety of pastas.

See map on pp106–7

🔟 The Spanish Steps and Villa Borghese

Detail, Trevi Fountain

Here is Rome at its most elegant, laid out under 16th-century papal urban planning schemes. Baroque popes redeveloped the area around the Corso, now called the Tridente after the three streets exiting Piazza del Popolo. The district exudes theatricality and stylishness, with Rome's most fashionable *passeggiata* unfolding down the length of Via del Corso.

THE SPANISH STEPS AND VILLA BORGHESE

1 Galleria Borghese

Worth seeing for its setting alone, this gallery *(see pp24–5)* is home to Rome's best collection of early Bernini sculptures.

2 The Spanish Steps and Piazza di Spagna
MAP D2

This elegant, off-centre sweep of a staircase is Rome's most beloved Rococo monument. Although it is at its most memorable in May, when it is covered in azaleas, it is littered with people drinking in *la dolce vita* all year round. Francesco De Sanctis designed the steps in 1723–6 for

Spanish Steps and Piazza di Spagna

King Louis XV, and their true name in Italian is Scalinata della Trinità dei Monti, after the church at the top *(see p116)*. Hourglass-shaped Piazza di Spagna, named after the Spanish Embassy nearby, is centred on Bernini's Barcaccia fountain. Bernini's father, Pietro, possibly helped train his son in making this tongue-in-cheek 1629 fountain of a sinking boat. The design ingeniously solved the problem of low water pressure by having a boat sprouting leaks rather than the more usual jets and sprays.

3 Santa Maria del Popolo

This spectacular church *(see pp38–9)* offers a priceless lesson in Renaissance and Baroque art, architecture and sculpture.

4 Trevi Fountain
MAP P2 ■ Piazza di Trevi

Anita Ekberg bathed in it in *La Dolce Vita*; *Three Coins in a Fountain* taught us to throw coins in it over our shoulder to ensure a return visit (healthier than the original tradition of drinking the water for luck) – thanks to the movies, Trevi is one of Rome's most familiar sights. The right relief shows a virgin discovering the spring from which Agrippa built the aqueduct that still feeds the fountain. Salvi's Baroque confection is grafted onto a Classical triumphal arch.

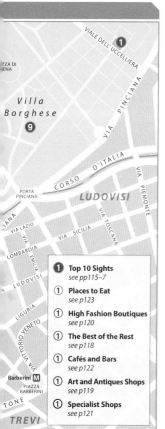

Keats-Shelley Memorial
MAP D2 ▪ Piazza di Spagna 26 ▪ 06 678 4235 ▪ Open 10am–1pm & 2–6pm Mon–Sat ▪ Adm ▪ www.keats-shelley-house.org

The apartment overlooking the Spanish Steps, in which John Keats died in 1821, has been turned into a modest museum about the Romantic British poets (see pp58–9) who lived in Rome. Documents, letters, copies of publications and Keats' death mask are on display. Joseph Severn cradled Keats' head as he died; his resultant sketch *Keats on his Deathbed* is also exhibited.

Trinità dei Monti
MAP D2 ▪ Piazza Trinità dei Monti ▪ Open 10:15am–8pm (from noon on Wed, from 9am on Sun)

Crowning the French-commissioned Spanish Steps, this church was originally part of a convent founded by Louis XII in 1503. The twin-towered

Interior of Trinità dei Monti

façade (1584) is by Giacomo della Porta; the double staircase outside (1587) is by Domenico Fontana. The Baroque interior has three chapels. Daniele da Volterra frescoed the third chapel on the right and painted the *Assumption* altarpiece (which depicts his teacher Michelangelo on the far right); he also painted the *Deposition* in the second chapel on the left.

The grounds of Villa Medici

Villa Medici
MAP D2 ▪ Viale Trinità dei Monti 1 ▪ Open 10am–7pm Tue–Sun (booking recommended); guided tours only for the gardens and apartments ▪ Adm ▪ www.villamedici.it

Built in 1540, this villa was used as a prison for those who fell foul of the Inquisition – its most famous inmate was Galileo. Now home to the French Academy, it is used for concerts and exhibitions. Highlights are the Stanza degli Uccelli, frescoed with flowers and birds, and the Niobidi, ancient Greek art showing the massacre of Niobe and her 14 children.

Piazza del Popolo
MAP D2

Rome's elegant public living room (see p62) started as a trapezoidal piazza in 1538. In 1589, Sixtus V had Domenico Fontana build a fountain crowned with a 3,200-year-old obelisk – the 25-m (82-ft) megalith, honouring Ramses II, was originally brought to Rome from Heliopolis by Augustus. Napoleon's man in Rome hired Giuseppe Valadier to overhaul the piazza to its current Neo-Classical look in 1811–23, a giant oval that heads up the steep slope of the Pincio via a winding road.

9 Villa Borghese
MAP D2 ■ Entrances on Piazza Flaminio, Piazza del Popolo, Via Trinità dei Monti and Corso Italia

One of Rome's largest green spaces (see p66), this is made up of public park, landscaped gardens, statuary, fountains, groves, pavilions and a water clock. There are also four museums: ancient Etruscan artifacts at Villa Giulia (see pp40–41), Renaissance and Baroque art at Galleria Borghese (see pp24–5), modern art at Galleria Nazionale d'Arte Moderna (see p55), and the Museo Carlo Bilotti (see p118) has contemporary works by Giorgio de Chirico (1888–1978). In 1608 Cardinal Scipione Borghese turned these vast family lands just outside the Aurelian Walls into a private pleasure park, opened to the public in 1901. In 1809–14, Giuseppe Valadier turned the adjacent space within the city walls into the Pincio gardens, a favourite passeggiata destination containing an elaborate tea house and an obelisk.

Lake and pavilion, Villa Borghese

10 Villa Giulia
MAP D1 ■ Piazzale di Villa Giulia 9 ■ Open 9am–8pm Tue–Sun ■ Adm (free first Sun of the month)

Italy's top Etruscan collection (see pp40–41), celebrating the peninsula's first great civilization, which flourished from the 8th to the 3rd centuries BC, is contained here.

AN AFTERNOON ROMAN PASSEGGIATA

▶ Begin in **Piazza SS Apostoli** to see its namesake church (see p118) and the 2nd-century AD relief of an Imperial eagle against the portico's right wall. Continue straight across Via dell'Umiltà and through the elaborate iron, glass, and frescoed 1880s pedestrian passage. Turn right on Via di Muratte to get to the beautiful **Trevi Fountain** (see p115). Three coins tossed backwards over your shoulder should ensure a return trip to Rome. Leave the square on Via del Lavatore and turn left on Via della Panetteria for some of Rome's best gelato at **San Crispino** (see p78).

Turn right up Via del Tritone and left on Via Francesco Crispi for the Galleria d'Arte Moderna at No.24 to admire some contemporary art. Walk down Via Capo le Case and right on Via dei Due Macelli into **Piazza di Spagna** and the **Spanish Steps** (see p115). Spend as long as you like window-shopping along the grid of streets west of the piazza, but try to finish up by 5pm so you can work your way north – weaving between Via del Babuino and Via Margutta to see the art and antiques shops (see p119) – to **Piazza del Popolo**.

Pause for a cappuccino at **Caffè Canova** (see p122). Visit **Santa Maria del Popolo** (see pp38–9) to admire its Caravaggios, Raphaels and Berninis. Stop at **Santa Maria in Montesanto** (see p118) around 7pm for the Gregorian chant, then get a pizza at **Il Brillo Parlante** (Via della Fontanella 12), always ⏸ popular with locals and visitors.

See map on pp114–15 ⬅

The Best of the Rest

1 Via dei Condotti
MAP D2

The "Fifth Avenue" of Rome is lined with chic shops and top designer fashion and haute couture boutiques.

2 Galleria Nazionale d'Arte Moderna
MAP D1 ■ Viale delle Belle Arti 131 ■ 06 322 981 ■ Open 9am–7pm Tue–Sun ■ Adm (free first Sun of the month)

The national modern art museum covers 19th- and 20th-century works of mostly Italian art but there are also some pieces by international artists.

3 Museo Carlo Bilotti
MAP D2 ■ Viale Fiorello la Guardia (Villa Borghese) ■ Open 1–7pm Tue–Fri (10am–4pm in winter), 10am–7pm Sat & Sun ■ Adm

This small art museum includes works by Giorgio de Chirico, Gino Severini and Andy Warhol.

4 SS Ambrogio e Carlo al Corso
MAP N1 ■ Via del Corso 437 ■ Open 7am–7pm daily

Pietro da Cortona designed the tribune, cupola and stuccoes of this Roman Baroque church in 1669.

5 Canova's Studio
MAP D2 ■ Via del Babuino 150a ■ Open 8am–midnight daily

The artist's studio walls are embedded with fragments of statuary.

6 Galleria Colonna
MAP N2 ■ Via della Pilotta 17 ■ Open 9am–1:15pm Sat or by appt (06 678 4350) ■ Closed Aug ■ Adm

This gallery features work by Tintoretto, Lotto and Veronese in a lavish Baroque palace.

7 Porta del Popolo
MAP D2 ■ Piazza del Popolo

Architect Nanni di Baccio Bigio used the Arch of Titus as the model for this gateway in the 16th century.

8 Casa di Goethe
MAP D2 ■ Via del Corso 18 ■ Open 10am–6pm daily (tours: on request) ■ Adm

German author Goethe (see p58) lived here from 1786 to 1788; his letters are on display.

9 Santi Apostoli
MAP N2 ■ Piazza dei S Apostoli 51 ■ Open 7am–noon & 4–7pm

Built in the 6th century, this basilica was restructured in 1702–8. It has a trompe-l'oeil vault above the altar.

10 Santa Maria dei Miracoli and Santa Maria in Montesanto
MAP D2 ■ Miracoli: Via del Corso 528; open 7am–12:30pm & 4–7:30pm daily ■ Montesanto: Via del Babuino 198; open 5:30–8pm Mon–Fri, 11am–1:30pm Sun

Carlo Fontana built these late 17th-century "twin" churches, although Bernini is said to have guided him in the decoration of the more elaborate Montesanto.

Façade of the Santa Maria dei Miracoli

Art and Antiques Shops

Rugs inside Danon

1 Danon
MAP D2 ■ Via Margutta 36–7

Danon is a leading, long-established dealer of antique Oriental rugs.

2 Benucci
MAP D2 ■ Via del Babuino 150C

The presitigious Benucci gallery specialises in museum-quality 17th- and 18th-century art and antique furniture, as well as some modern and contemporary pieces.

3 Erica Ravenna Fiorentini
MAP D2 ■ Via della Reginella 3

This large art gallery showcases leading Italian contemporary artists. It hosts exhibitions and events throughout the year.

4 Paolo Antonacci Antichitá
MAP D2 ■ Via Alibert 16/a

Specializing in painting and furnishings from the period between the late 18th century to the first half of the 20th century, this antique dealer also organizes contemporary art shows.

5 Alberto di Castro
MAP D2 ■ Piazza di Spagna 5

Etchings, lithographs and other prints from the 1660s to the 1920s are on sale in this lovely shop.

6 Art Gallery W Apolloni
MAP D2 ■ Via Margutta 53B

This gallery sells curated collections of antique paintings and sculptures. It is located on the ground floor of a former art studio where Picasso once produced work.

7 Galleria Valentina Moncada
MAP D2 ■ Via Margutta 54

This is one of Italy's most important contemporary art galleries. Trained in New York, Moncada is an internationally recognized curator and talent scout who discovered Chen Zhen and was the first to exhibit Tony Cragg in Italy. She has worked with artists ranging from Anish Kapoor and Damien Hirst to Gillian Wearing and Rachel Whiteread.

8 Monogramma Arte Contemporanea
MAP D2 ■ Via Margutta 102

Exhibitions at this contemporary art gallery aim to present Italian artists to an international audience.

9 Dantebus Margutta
MAP D2 ■ Via Margutta 38/A

A gallery that promotes and sells contemporary art and photography, as well as art books and objects.

10 Il Marmoraro
MAP D2 ■ Via Margutta 53B

Pieces of marble are engraved with various inscriptions by the owner of this small shop.

Marble slabs at Il Marmoraro

See map on pp114–15

High Fashion Boutiques

1 **Laura Biagiotti**
MAP D2 ▪ Via Belsiana 57

This is one of the largest fashion houses in Italy, making couture for women since 1972 and for men since 1987. The late Biagiotti earned the moniker "Queen of Cashmere" for her use of soft wool.

2 **Ferragamo**
MAP D2 ▪ Via dei Condotti 65

The shoemaker to the stars during Hollywood's Golden Age of the 1950s hasn't lost its touch, but it now mass-produces styles rather than creating unique works.

3 **Gucci**
MAP D2 ▪ Via dei Condotti 8

The Florentine saddle-maker turned his leather-working skills into one of Italy's early fashion successes. This flagship store has top-notch bags, shoes and other accessories.

4 **Valentino**
MAP D2 ▪ Piazza di Spagna 38

The *prêt-à-porter* collection of this native Roman designer in the top echelon of fashion since Jackie Kennedy and Audrey Hepburn donned his clothes in the 1960s.

5 **Prada**
MAP D2 ▪ Via dei Condotti 92

This Milan fashion house with minimalist, slightly retro clothing is the most highly priced of the top Italian designers.

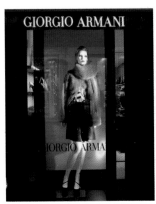
Mannequin at Giorgio Armani

6 **Giorgio Armani**
MAP D2 ▪ Via dei Condotti 77

One of Italy's top designers offers luxury womenswear, menswear and accessories. The Emporio Armani branch at Via del Babuino 140 sells the designer's couture line at lower prices. The lowest-end line, Armani Jeans, is at Via del Babuino 70A.

7 **Gianni Versace**
MAP D2 ▪ Piazza di Spagna 12

The house of the late fashion designer never compromises the clothing's flamboyant cuts and use of colour.

8 **Fausto Santini**
MAP D2 ▪ Via Frattina 120

Beautiful and elegant men's and women's shoes and bags of supreme quality are available here.

9 **Fendi**
MAP D2 ▪ Largo Goldoni 420

Founded by Adele and Edoardo Fendi and nurtured by their five daughters, this Roman fashion empire reigns over Italy's rage for furs.

10 **Boutique Alberta Ferretti**
MAP D2 ▪ Via Condotti 34

The well-cut women's clothing here is feminine yet powerful and modern.

Shop windows at Prada

Specialist Shops

1 Flos Store
MAP D2 ■ Via del Babuino 85

This minimalist shop sells contemporary lamps and lighting solutions. Peruse the stands for a new light made by one of Italy's most celebrated designers.

2 PRO FVMVM
MAP D2 ■ Via di Ripetta 248

The fragrances created by this Roman luxury perfumery include Alba, Acqua Viva and Confetto. Be prepared to empty your wallet.

3 Buccone
MAP D2 ■ Via di Ripetta 19–20

A vast selection of wines at excellent prices are available at this historic wine shop. Homemade pasta, honey and jam are sold here as well.

Wines and speciality foods, Buccone

4 Tessuti Totti
MAP D2 ■ Via del Babuino 93

This shop offers luxurious Italian fabrics, including Genovese velvet, elegant curtains and printed textiles.

5 Venchi Cioccolato e Gelato
MAP N2 ■ Via del Corso 335

A famous chocolate shop that sells excellent bars, pralines, torroni and

Inside Venchi Cioccolato e Gelato

other refined Italian products and gifts. While you shop, have a scoop of the delicious ice cream.

6 c.u.c.i.n.a.
MAP D2 ■ Via Mario de' Fiori 65

The motto of this shop, which carries superb minimalist kitchenware, translates as "How a kitchen inspires new appetites".

7 Fabriano Boutique
MAP D2 ■ Via del Babuino 173

This luxury stationery shop carries Italian-made product lines for the office and school, all manufactured to the highest quality.

8 Modigliani
MAP D3 ■ Via Frattina 56

Exquisite Tuscan handmade ceramics and select home accessories including cutlery and flatware can be found at this design studio located near the Spanish Steps.

9 Vertecchi
MAP D2 ■ Via della Croce 70

The queen of Rome's stationery stores, Vertecchi has hundreds of types of pens (the fancier ones are sold next door at No. 72), a large selection of notebooks, as well as the very best in art supplies.

10 Quetzalcoatl
MAP D2 ■ Via delle Carrozze 26

Taking the name of Aztec deity Quetzalcoatl – who the Aztecs believed gifted cacao seeds to mankind – this chocolatier offers elaborately presented, exquisitely crafted chocolates.

See map on pp114–15

Cafés and Bars

1 Enoteca Antica
MAP D2 ▪ Via della Croce 76b

Delicious antipasti and wine by the glass are served in this old-fashioned lively establishment.

2 Antica Birreria Peroni
MAP N3 ▪ Via San Marcello 19

This beer hall from 1906 is sponsored by Italy's premier brewery. It serves delicious Roman cuisine and offers fantastic value for money.

3 Antico Caffè Greco
MAP D2 ▪ Via Condotti 86

Rome's premier literary café *(see p78)* since 1760, Antico Caffè Greco is best known for being frequented by 19th-century English Romantic poets.

4 Stravinskij Bar
MAP D2 ▪ Via del Babuino 9

Impeccably prepared dry martinis, a classy atmosphere and the enchanting garden of the Hotel de Russie *(see p170)* make this one of the most exclusive bars in town. Light Mediterranean dishes are served for lunch.

5 Crystal Bar
MAP D2 ▪ Via Margutta 56 (inside Hotel Art)

A contemporary yet intimate bar and restaurant inside the Hotel Art. There is a creative menu and abundant aperitivo buffets.

6 Ciampini al Café du Jardin
MAP D2 ▪ Piazza Trinità dei Monti ▪ Closed Nov–Feb

Enjoy a drink while watching the sunset at this enchanting café.

7 Caffè Rosati
MAP D2 ▪ Piazza del Popolo 4–5

Art Nouveau rival to the formerly right-wing Canova across the piazza, this café *(see p79)* has long been the haunt of left-wing intellectuals.

8 Caffè Canova
MAP D2 ▪ Piazza del Popolo 16–17

The previously right-wing bastion in the long-standing Piazza del Popolo café war, this place has cheaper espresso and better ice cream (but the Rosati is more stylish).

9 Ginger Sapori e Salute
MAP N1 ▪ Via Borgognona 45–46

Aimed at the health-conscious, Ginger serves salads, vegan dishes, smoothies and inventive mains.

10 Babingtons Tea Rooms
MAP D2 ▪ Piazza di Spagna 23

Opened in 1893 by a Derbyshire lady, this was the expat hub of the later Grand Tour era. It serves pricey tea and dainty British edibles.

Interior of Babingtons Tea Rooms

Places to Eat

Fiaschetteria Beltramme

① Fiaschetteria Beltramme

MAP D2 ▪ Via della Croce 39 ▪ 06 6979 7200 ▪ No credit cards ▪ €

Regulars and tourists sit around communal tables at this ultra-traditional trattoria just down the block from the Spanish Steps.

② Edy

MAP D2 ▪ Vicolo del Babuino 4 ▪ 06 3600 1738 ▪ Closed Sun L ▪ €

Some of the best food and lowest prices in the neighbourhood can be found at Edy. It serves a mix of seafood and Roman dishes. The candle-lit tables out front are a nice touch.

③ Imàgo

MAP D2 ▪ Piazza della Trinità dei Monti 6 ▪ 06 6993 4726 ▪ Closed L ▪ €€€

A classy hotel-restaurant (see p74) serving creative Italian cuisine.

④ Il Margutta Vegetarian

MAP D2 ▪ Via Margutta 118 ▪ 06 3265 0577 ▪ €

Creatively mixing organic ingredients and local produce, the chef at this restaurant presents dishes that are inspired by the art on the walls.

⑤ Pesciolino

MAP D2 ▪ Via Belsiana 30 ▪ 06 6979 7843 ▪ Closed Mon, Tue–Fri L ▪ €€

Fish-based cuisine in a modern setting on a quiet street. Specialties include grilled octopus, shrimps and mussel pasta, as well as different ceviches and raw fish options.

⑥ Babette

MAP D2 ▪ Via Margutta 1d ▪ 06 321 1559 ▪ Closed Mon ▪ €€

Emphasizing on quality ingredients, this lovely restaurant offers nuanced Italian dishes. On warm days, food is served outside, in a gorgeous piazza.

Casina Valadier, offering great views

⑦ Casina Valadier

MAP D2 ▪ Piazza Bucarest ▪ 06 6992 2090 ▪ Closed Mon ▪ €€€

Housed in an 18th-century villa with a splendid view of the city, this elegant restaurant serves gourmet Italian cuisine paired with great wines. It is perfect for special occassions.

⑧ Al 34

MAP D2 ▪ Via Mario de' Fiori 34 ▪ 06 679 5091 ▪ Closed Mon L ▪ €€

Excellently priced menus here feature inventive Italian cooking.

⑨ Hamasei

MAP N1 ▪ Via della Mercede 35/36 ▪ 06 679 2134 ▪ Closed Mon ▪ €€€

This popular, minimalist Japanese restaurant has a sushi bar and also offers more substantial dishes.

⑩ Dal Pollarolo

MAP D2 ▪ Via di Ripetta 4-5 ▪ 06 361 0276 ▪ Closed Fri–Sun D ▪ €

Pasta dishes here include the local *pasta alla checca*, with raw tomatoes, fennel seeds, olives and capers.

See map on pp114–15

🔟 Ancient Rome

This area has always been a study in contrasts. In ancient times, the emperor's palaces were built on the Palatine, not far from the docks where roustabouts heaved goods imported from around the world. Today, the area is again an enclave of smart houses and greenery, studded with hidden art treasures and some of the world's finest ancient monuments and priceless archaeological finds.

Detail, Baths of Caracalla

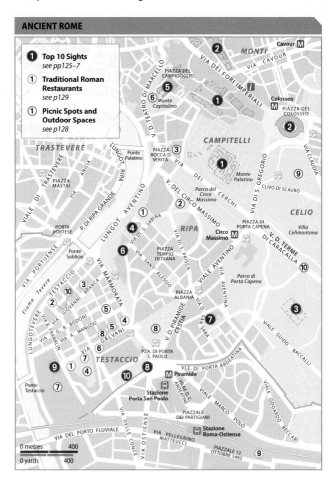

ANCIENT ROME

① **Top 10 Sights**
see pp125–7

① **Traditional Roman Restaurants**
see p129

① **Picnic Spots and Outdoor Spaces**
see p128

1 Roman Forum and Palatine Hill

Once the heart of the Roman empire, these ruins *(see pp20–21)* are an eerie landscape that seems gripped by the ghosts of an ancient civilization.

2 The Colosseum and Imperial Fora

These monuments memorialize Imperial supremacy. The Colosseum *(see pp26–7)* embodies the Romans' passion for brutal entertainment. Trajan's Forum was called a Wonder of the World by contemporaries; the only remnant is Trajan's Column – Roman sculptural art at its peak.

3 Baths of Caracalla

MAP E6 ▪ Via delle Terme di Caracalla 52 ▪ 06 3996 700 ▪ Open 9am–1 hr before sunset Tue–Sun ▪ Adm (free first Sun of the month)

Inaugurated in 217, these luxurious baths were used by up to 2,000 people at a time until 546, when invading Goths destroyed the aqueducts. In general, Roman baths included social centres, art galleries, libraries, brothels and *palestrae* (exercise areas). Bathing involved taking a sweat bath, a steam bath, a cool-down, then a cold plunge. The Farnese family's ancient sculpture collection was found here, including *Hercules*, a signed Greek original. Today, the ruins of individual rooms can be seen.

The elegant nave of Santa Sabina

4 Santa Sabina

MAP D5 ▪ Piazza Pietro d'Illiria 1 ▪ 06 579 401 ▪ Open 7:15am–8pm daily

This church was built over the Temple of Juno Regina in about 425 to honour a martyred Roman matron. In 1936–8 it was restored almost to its original condition, while retaining 9th-century additions such as the Cosmatesque work and the bell tower. Corinthian columns are surmounted by arcades with marble friezes and light filters through the selenite window panes. The doors are 5th-century carved cypress, with 18 panels of biblical scenes, including the earliest known Crucifixion – strangely without any crosses.

5 Musei Capitolini

The original motivation for these museums *(see pp28–31)* was political. When the popes started the first museum here in 1471, it laid claim to Rome's hopes for civic autonomy – the Palazzo dei Conservatori was the seat of hated papal counsellors, who ran the city by "advising" the Senate. Today the museums contain a spectacular collection of art.

The ruins of the Baths of Caracalla

CLASS DIVISIONS AND POWER STRUGGLES

The ceaseless struggle between the governing and the working classes is typified by the history of this area. Romulus on the Palatine versus Remus on the Aventine gave rise to patricians and plebeians respectively. The contrast still exists, between wealthy Aventine and down-to-earth Testaccio.

6 Piazza of the Knights of Malta

MAP D5

Everyone comes here for the famous bronze keyhole view of St Peter's Basilica, ideally framed by an arbour of perfect trees *(see p65)*. However, it's also worth a look for the piazza's wonderful 18th-century decoration by Giambattista Piranesi, otherwise renowned for his powerful engravings of fantasy-antiquity scenes. To honour the ancient order of crusading knights (founded in 1080), the architect chose to adorn the walls with dwarf obelisks and trophy armour, in the ancient style. Originally based on the island of Rhodes, then Malta, the knights are now centred in Rome.

Pyramid of Caius Cestius

7 San Saba

MAP E6 ■ Piazza Gian Lorenzo Bernini 20 ■ www.sansaba.gesuiti.it

Originally a 7th-century oratory for Palestinian monks fleeing their homeland, the present church is a 10th-century renovation with many additions. The portico of the 15th-century loggia houses archaeological fragments. The style of floorplan is Greek, while the interior decoration throughout the structure is mostly Cosmatesque. The greatest oddity is a 13th-century fresco that depicts St Nicholas throwing a bag of gold to three nude women on a bed in order to "save" them from prostitution.

Detail, San Saba

8 Pyramid of Caius Cestius

MAP D6 ■ Piazzale Ostiense ■ 06 3996 7700 ■ By appt only 11am 3rd & 4th Sat & Sun of month ■ Adm

This 12 BC edifice remains an imposing monument to Gaius Cestius Gallus, who was instrumental in quelling the First Jewish-Roman War. It is 36 m (118 ft) high and took 330 days to erect, according to an inscription carved upon it. Unlike Egyptian originals, however, it was built of brick then covered with marble, which was the typically pragmatic Roman way of doing things.

MACRO Testaccio in Testaccio

9 Mattatoio
MAP C6 ■ Piazza Orazio Giustiniani 4 ■ 06 39967500 ■ Open during exhibitions only ■ Adm ■ www.mattatoioroma.it

Originally a working-class quarter that grew up around a slaughter-house, it is now a trendy, arty area. The 19th-century former slaughter-house has been converted into a dynamic contemporary art gallery, Mattatoio, which hosts temporary exhibitions of Italian and international art. Monte Testaccio itself – composed entirely of pottery shards – is home to the city's best nightclubs.

10 Protestant Cemetery
MAP D6 ■ Via Caio Cestio 6 ■ Open 9am–5pm Mon–Sat (to 1pm Sun); closed one week in Aug ■ Donation

Also called the Acattolico (Non-Catholic) Cemetery, people of many faiths have been buried here since 1738. The most famous are the English poets John Keats and P B Shelley *(see pp48–9)*. Until 1870, crosses and refer-ences to salvation were forbidden.

Keats' tombstone

A MORNING PARKLAND STROLL

The parkland on the other side of the Circus Maximus from the Palatine Hill conceals exquisite early churches and other gems. Start on the south side of the Circus Maximus, now a sunken patch of dust and weeds, but once a majestic racecourse until the popes plundered its stones to build their palaces. Head up the hill to the **Roseto Comunale** *(see p67)*. In spring and summer few places in Rome radiate such beauty. Continue along the old wall and enter Parco Savello's **Giardino degli Aranci** *(see p67)* to take in the view from the parapet. Next door is Santa Sabina *(see p125)*. Use a torch and binoculars to scrutinize carved wooden doors and the Crucifixion scene. Stop next at Piranesi's **Piazza of the Knights of Malta** and peer through the celebrated keyhole.

Wind down Via di Sant'Anselmo until Viale Aventino and **San Saba**. Stop to appreciate the notorious St Nicholas fresco on the left wall. In Parco della Resistenza dell'8 Settembre you can get a *gelato* in the park's café and admire the 3rd-century Aurelian Wall *(see p156)*.

Cross over to the lovely **Protestant Cemetery**, pay your respects at the graves of Shelley, Keats and friends, pause to reflect on the splendid **Pyramid of Caius Cestius** and leave your donation in the box as you exit.

A five-minute walk north takes you to **Volpetti**, Rome's premier deli, or to **Taverna Volpetti**, a *tavola calda* (self-service buffet) around the corner from the deli, both great choices for lunch *(see p129)*.

See map on p124 ←

Picnic Spots and Outdoor Spaces

1 Giardino degli Aranci

The orange garden *(see p67)* inside the Parco Savello on the top of the Aventine hills offers not only one of Rome's most gorgeous vistas, but also well kept lawns for picnicking and relaxing under the orange trees.

Beautiful roses at Roseto Comunale

2 Roseto Comunale

Open only for a month around May or June, when the roses are in full bloom. Visitors can admire 10,000 varieties of roses with the Circus Maximus as a backdrop *(see p67)*.

3 Mercato Campagna Amica

MAP P6 ■ Via di S Teodoro, 74

A picturesque organic market where you can stock up on bread, cheese and vegetables. Enjoy your food on the tables outside or pick a spot on the grass in the Circus Maximus for a meal with a side of history.

4 Monte dei Cocci

MAP D6 ■ Via Piazza Orazio Giustiniani

This pile of broken amphorae and ancient Roman pottery in the middle of Testaccio makes for an interesting view. All around it are restaurants offering takeaway meals and benches in the piazza to enjoy them.

5 Piazza Testaccio

MAP D6

For some urban views, get some takeaway from Volpetti *(see p129)* or some cheese from the Testaccio market, and pick a bench on Piazza Testaccio while you watch true Romans go about their daily activities.

6 Scalinata dell'Aracoeli

MAP N4 ■ Piazza d'Aracoeli

The staircase leading up the Aracoeli church is a great place to rest and eat a sandwich in clear view of Piazza Venezia.

7 Città dell'Altra Economia

MAP C6 ■ Largo Dino Frisullo

Housed inside the former abattoir of Testaccio, this big Sunday market is a celebration to local and organic food, offering various outdoor spots to sit and enjoy great bread, spreads and vegetables.

8 Parco della Resistenza dell'VIII Settembre

MAP D6 ■ Viale Manlio Gelsomini

This tranquil park offers shade and benches for a lunch break on a summer day. Get a sandwich at one of the snack bars on Via Marmorata.

9 Parco del Celio

MAP P6 ■ Piazza San Gregorio 1

Slightly off the beaten track, this park was once the vegetable garden of the monastery of San Gregorio. Today, it is a great spot to take a break amid the ruins and the trees.

10 Via delle Terme di Caracalla

MAP E5

This large road is flanked on both sides by green areas where Romans go running or simply relax.

Traditional Roman Restaurants

① Checchino dal 1887
MAP D6 ■ Via di Monte Testaccio 30 ■ 06 574 3816 ■ Closed Mon & Tue ■ €€

Among the great Roman restaurants, this offers offal-based delicacies such as *rigatoni alla pajata* (pasta with calf intestine).

② Agustarello
MAP D6 ■ Via G Branca 98 ■ 06 574 6585 ■ No credit cards ■ €

The Roman-style, rich dishes here include *coda alla vaccinara* (oxtail), *lingua* (tongue) and other rustic fare.

③ Da Remo
MAP D6 ■ Piazza Santa Maria Liberatrice 44 ■ 06 574 6270 ■ Open 7pm–1am Mon–Sat ■ €

This quintessential Roman pizzeria is always packed. It is known for its *scrocchiarella* pizzas, with thin crispy crusts and simple toppings.

④ Taverna Volpetti
MAP D6 ■ Via A Volta 8/10 ■ 06 574 4306 ■ Closed Mon ■ €

Volpetti Più is an upscale self-service *tavola calda* with dishes to eat in or take away. Around the corner, Rome's top deli, Volpetti, is the ideal place to have a lunchtime sandwich.

Deli products at Taverna Volpetti

PRICE CATEGORIES
For a three-course meal for one with half a bottle of wine (or equivalent meal), taxes and extra charges.

€ under €40   €€ €40–60   €€€ over €60

---

⑤ Felice
MAP D6 ■ Via Mastro Giorgio 29 ■ 06 574 6800 ■ Closed Aug ■ €

This simple trattoria is one of the best places in Rome to try traditional *carciofi alla romana* (see p72).

⑥ Osteria Degli Amici
MAP D6 ■ Via Zabaglia 25 ■ 06 578 1466 ■ Closed Tue ■ €

Founded by two gourmet friends, this traditional *osteria* serves Roman specialities in a friendly setting.

⑦ Angelina
MAP D6 ■ Via Galvani 24A ■ 06 5728 3840 ■ €€

The old butcher's tables and tiled walls are testimony of this restaurant's past as a butcher's store, and this is also reflected in the meaty menu.

⑧ Da Oio a Casa Mia
MAP D6 ■ Via Galvani 43–45 ■ 06 578 2680 ■ €

This no-frills trattoria offers classic versions of Roman dishes, with classic pastas and offal on the menu.

⑨ Eataly
MAP D6 ■ Piazzale 12 Ottobre 1492 ■ 800 957800 ■ €/€€€

This four-story "temple of Italian food" (see p75) celebrates local dishes, including quick lunches and sumptuous dinners.

⑩ Trapizzino
MAP D6 ■ Via Giovanni Branca 88 ■ 06 4241 9624 ■ €

Pizza meets sandwich at this popular eatery, resulting in a triangular piece of baked dough filled with Roman staples such as oxtail, tripe or chicken.

See map on p124 ←

🔟 The Esquiline and Lateran

In ancient times the largest of Rome's seven hills was almost entirely an upper-class residential area. The western slope was densely populated and seen as a squalid slum. However, in the 4th century, this zone became central to the growth of Christianity. In supporting it as the official faith, Constantine did not dare step on too many pagan toes, so he set up churches outside town on the sites of holy tombs. Still known today for its religious history, the area has also become a multicultural hub.

Moses, San Pietro in Vincoli

THE ESQUILINE AND LATERAN

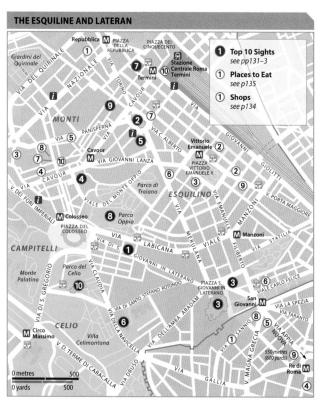

- ① **Top 10 Sights**
  see pp131–3
- ① **Places to Eat**
  see p135
- ① **Shops**
  see p134

0 metres 500
0 yards 500

1 San Clemente
MAP F4 ■ Via di S Giovanni in Laterano 45 ■ 06 774 0021 ■ Open for guided tours only ■ www.basilica sanclemente.com

Architectural layers here *(see p51)* reveal Rome's history, from the 2nd century BC to the 15th century AD.

2 San Giovanni in Laterano and Scala Santa
MAP F5 ■ Piazza di S Giovanni in Laterano ■ Open 7am–6:30pm daily (cloisters 9am–6pm; baptistry 9am–12:30pm, 4–6:30pm; museum 10am–5:30pm); Scala Santa 9am–1pm & 3–6pm daily ■ Adm for cloisters

Founded by Constantine in the 4th century, this is the cathedral of Rome's bishopric. Popes were crowned here until the 19th century. Besides its grandiose Baroque bulk, the church boasts the world's first baptistry and, with its octagonal shape, it became the model for all those to come. A building on the piazza houses the Scala Santa, which are claimed to be the stairs to Pontius Pilate's house that Jesus ascended to face his trial. Tradition says that St Helena, mother of Emperor Constantine, brought them here from Jerusalem.

Devotees climbing the Scala Santa

3 Santa Maria Maggiore
MAP F3 ■ Piazza di S Maria Maggiore ■ Open 7am–6:45pm daily

This basilica *(see p51)* presents a unique blend of architectural styles. The nave and its mosaics are original 5th century; the Cosmatesque work,

Mosaic, Santa Maria Maggiore

apse mosaics and Romanesque bell tower are medieval; the coffered ceiling (made of gold) is from the Renaissance period; and the domes and front and back façades are Baroque. Pope Sixtus V erected the Egyptian obelisk in 1587 as part of his overall town-planning, to provide landmarks for pilgrims. The column in front of the obelisk was taken from the Basilica of Maxentius and Constantine in 1615.

4 San Pietro in Vincoli
MAP R4 ■ Piazza di S Pietro in Vincoli 4A ■ Open 8am–6pm daily

Michelangelo's sculpture *Moses* is the unmissable experience here. Weirdly horned and glaring, the righteously indignant patriarch is about to smash the tablets in outrage at his people's idolatry. This powerful artwork was just one of 40 that the artist planned, but never finished, for the tomb of Pope Julius II *(see p57)*. The original shrine was built in the 4th century to house the chains supposedly used to bind St Peter in prison. It has been rebuilt since then, first in the 8th century and again in the 15th century.

Depictions of angels and saints at Santa Prassede

5 Santa Prassede
MAP F4 ■ Via di S Prassede 9A
■ Open 10am–noon & 4–6pm Mon–Sat, 11am–1pm & 4–6pm Sun

Built in the 9th century over a 2nd- century oratory, the original design of this basilica is still discernible despite restorations. In the central nave, a stone slab covers the well where St Prassede is said to have buried 2,000 martyrs. The apse and the Chapel of St Zeno were decorated with gold-glinting work depicting saints, lambs, palm trees and poppies. There is also a fragment of the column that Christ was said to have been bound to when he was flogged.

6 Santo Stefano Rotondo
MAP F5 ■ Via di S Stefano Rotondo 7 ■ Open 10am–1pm & 2–5pm in winter, 10am–1pm & 3:30–6:30pm in summer

The unusual shape of this church (468–83) may mean it was built over

Exterior of the Santo Stefano Rotondo

ESTABLISHMENT OF THE CHURCH

This area played a central role in early Christianity. Although Constantine himself was not a firm convert, his mother, St Helena, was untiring in her promotion of the new religion. She convinced her son to found the official seat of the Bishop of Rome on the site of the ancient Laterani family villa, which his wife Fausta had inherited.

Nero's round *Macellum Magnum* (meat market). Or perhaps its form was inspired by Jerusalem's Church of the Holy Sepulchre. Recent digs have found a Mithraeum underneath. The structure is a delightful sanctuary, situated far from urban uproar, although 16th-century frescoes by Niccolò Pomarancio depict martyrdoms in sadistic fashion.

7 Palazzo Massimo alle Terme

Housing an extraordinary collection of ancient frescoes, mosaics and sculpture, this branch of the Museo Nazionale Romano *(see pp34–5)* is perhaps the most inspiring, with exhibits contained on four floors and originally dating from the 2nd century BC to the end of the 4th century AD. The late 19th-century building was built by the Massimo family and later served as a Jesuit college.

(8) Domus Aurea
MAP E4 ■ Via della Domus Aurea ■ 06 3996 7700 ■ Open Sat & Sun by appt only

After the great fire of Rome in 64 AD, Nero built a new villa decorated with gold and precious stones, giving the villa its name, which means Golden House. Later emperors, embarrassed by his profligacy, tried to undo as much of it as possible. The Flavians drained Nero's lake to build the Colosseum (see p26), and Trajan built Rome's first great public bathws over the original house. It was only in 1772 that archaeologists started excavations within the Domus Aurea.

(9) Santa Pudenziana
MAP E3 ■ Via Urbana 160 ■ 06 481 4622 ■ Open 9–11:30am & 3–6pm daily

Converted in the 4th century from a Roman bathhouse, Santa Pudenziana is one of the oldest churches in Rome and now serves the Filipino community. Its simple structure differs from the ornate features of Rome's other churches. The main draw here is the 5th-century apse mosaic, depicting an enthroned Christ surrounded by his disciples and two female figures crowning St Peter and St Paul.

(10) Santi Giovanni e Paolo
MAP E5 ■ Piazzale SS Giovanni e Paolo 13 ■ Open 8:30am–noon & 3:30–6pm daily

The home of these 4th-century martyrs is still visible under the 5th-century structure (see p65). Except for the Late Baroque interior, much of the church is medieval. The 45 m (145 ft) bell tower's base is that of the 1st-century Temple of Claudius that once stood here.

Santi Giovanni e Paolo

EXPLORING ROME'S EARLY CHURCHES

▶ **MORNING**

Start with **San Clemente** (see p131), with its fascinating layers. At the lowest level use a torch (flashlight) to appreciate the beautiful fresco of the head of a bearded man. Walk one block over to the Via dei Santi Quattro Coronati to glimpse the produce market (see p81), then turn left and walk up the hill to Santi Quattro Coronati, a little-visited 4th-century church with remarkable frescoes in the chapel (1246). Continue on until you reach **San Giovanni in Laterano** (see p131). The 13th-century Cosmatesque cloisters with gorgeously twisted columns and mosaic inlays will make your visit truly memorable.

Then head across the piazza for a hearty lunch at **Cannavota** (Piazza S Giovanni in Laterano 20) or stop at **Panella** (see p134) on your way to Santa Maria Maggiore.

AFTERNOON

At **Santa Maria Maggiore** (see p131) check out the ancient column in front, then use binoculars inside to examine the 5th-century mosaics lining the upper reaches of the nave. Next, walk over to **Santa Prassede,** where you can take in some of Rome's most radiant Byzantine mosaics and a powerful painting of the Flagellation in the sacristy.

For sustenance after your spiritual journey, walk back past Santa Maria Maggiore and turn right onto via Panisperna to catch the essence of Roman cuisine at ⬤ **La Carbonara** (see p135).

See map on p130 ←

Shops

① **Via Sannio Market**
MAP G5

Despite the influx of cheap, made-in-China clothes and designer fakes, this historic flea market *(see p81)* still sells good-condition second-hand clothes and paraphernalia.

② **Nuovo Mercato Esquilino**
MAP F4 ■ Via Mamiani and Via Principe Amedeo

Rome's most ethnically diverse market has stalls selling Chinese noodles and soya sauce, African and Asian vegetables, halal meat and spices from all over the world.

③ **OVS**
MAP F4 ■ Piazza Vittorio Emanuele 108–12

Clothing at bargain prices and a large range of cosmetics and toiletries is sold at this store This is the largest of several branches in Rome.

④ **Pompi**
MAP G6 ■ Via Albalonga 7/9

Known as "the temple of tiramisu", this bar sells the popular dessert in many different varieties, including the must-try banana and strawberry kinds. It also has cakes, pastries, ice cream and many other goodies.

⑤ **Leam**
MAP G5 ■ Via Appia Nuova 26

Prada and D&G are some of the designer brands that are sold at this extremely trendy and high-end clothing emporium. It also has a huge online store.

Panella delicatessen and café

⑥ **Panella**
MAP F4 ■ Via Merulana 54

A chic contemporary deli-café, Panella has fantastic freshly baked artisan breads, pizzas, savoury pies and salads to eat in or take away, and shelves of upscale grocery products that make great presents.

⑦ **UPIM**
MAP F3 ■ Via Gioberti 64

This trendy and more expensive branch of the mid-range department store chain stocks popular clothing brands and designer homeware.

⑧ **Coin**
MAP G5 ■ Piazzale Appio 7

A contemporary high-end department store, with reasonable prices, Coin sells clothing, accessories and shoes, as well as kitchenware and more general furnishings.

⑨ **L'Artigianino**
MAP G5 ■ Via Appia Nuova 187

Prices for the leather wallets, bags, purses and belts on offer range from €10 to €250. Styles are mostly colourful with classic designs, too.

⑩ **Borri Books**
MAP F3 ■ Inside Termini Station, Plazza dei Cinquecento

This bookshop across three floors has a large English-language section.

Clothing emporium, Leam

Places to Eat

PRICE CATEGORIES
For a three-course meal for one with half
a bottle of wine (or equivalent meal),
taxes and extra charges.

€ under €40   €€ €40–60   €€€ over €60

1 Rosemary – Terra e Sapori
MAP R2 ■ Via Modena 16
■ 06 4891 3645 ■ €

This eco-friendly bistro serves
Italian specialties made with local
seasonal produce. The menu includes
soups, salads, sandwiches, and
homemade cakes and biscuits.

2 Himalaya's Kashmir
MAP F4 ■ Via Principe Amedeo
325-327 ■ 06 446 1072 ■ €

Samosas, tandoori, thali and all
the usual accompaniments feature
at this popular Indian restaurant.

Delicious pasta and platter

3 Osteria I Clementini
MAP Q4 ■ Via di San Giovanni
in Laterano 106 ■ 06 4542 6395 ■ €

This family-run trattoria is known for
its delicious pastas and fish dishes,
including a fabulous tuna steak or a
calamari platter. Their cooked broad-
leaf vegetables are popular in Rome.

4 Taverna Romana
MAP Q4 ■ Via Madonna dei
Monti 79 ■ 06 474 5325 ■ Closed Sun
D, Aug ■ €

Enjoy traditional, inexpensive lunches
and dinners at this popular *taverna*.

Try soupy pasta with *ceci* (chickpeas)
or *fagioli* (beans), *maltagliati* pasta
with fresh ricotta or marvellous
slow-cooked guinea fowl.

5 La Carbonara
MAP R3 ■ Via Panisperma 214
■ 06 482 5176 ■ Closed Sun, Aug ■ €

Organic produce is used in traditional
Roman dishes at this cosy *osteria*.

6 Pinsa e Buoi
MAP G5 ■ Via Carlo Felice 51
■ 06 7720 1760 ■ €

This intimate trattoria serves Roman
staples, including offal dishes,
delicious pasta and *pinsa* pizzas.

7 Daruma Sushi
MAP R4 ■ Via dei Serpenti 1
■ 06 4893 1003 ■ €€

Sushi, sashimi, miso soup and fresh
noodles are on the menu at this lively
Japanese fast-food and takeaway place. It offers a free
delivery service to local hotels.

8 M'indujo
MAP Q4 ■ Via dei
Serpenti 9 ■ 342 659 6917
■ Closed Sun in summer ■ €

Juicy gourmet sandwiches
inspired by Calabrian food
are on offer here, served
with a variety of fries and
each made with the freshest
ingredients. Great value,
open for lunch and dinner.

9 Palazzo del Freddo
MAP G4 ■ Via Principe Eugenio
65 ■ 06 446 4740 ■ Closed Mon ■ €

A historic *gelateria* with an Art Deco
interior, Palazzo del Freddo is famous
for its superb ice creams, *granitas*
and bite-sized *sanpietrini*.

10 La Bottega del Caffè
MAP R4 ■ Piazza Madonna
dei Monti 5 ■ 06 474 1578 ■ €

This bustling bistro and bar is the
life and soul of Monti. Come for
breakfast, a drink or a light meal.

See map on p130

TOP 10 The Quirinal and Via Veneto

The original hill of Rome, the Quirinal was mainly residential in Imperial times, noted for its grand baths and temples. In the Middle Ages, it reverted to open countryside and it wasn't until the 16th century that it again became important, when the crest

Mosaic detail, Baths of Diocletian

of the hill was claimed for the pope's new palace. Following that, important papal families built their large estates all around the area, including the Barberini, the Corsini and the Ludovisi. The Quirinal Palace has passed through many metamorphoses but the biggest change to the area came after 1870. The Ludovisi sold off their huge villa to developers, and Via Veneto and the smart area around it became an instant success with the wealthy classes of the newly unified country. This quarter speaks of elegance and power throughout all its ages.

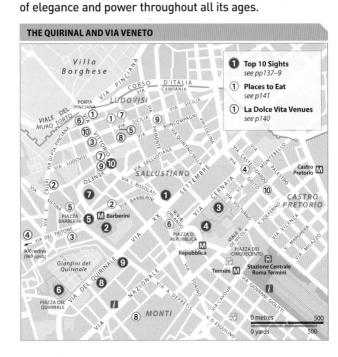

THE QUIRINAL AND VIA VENETO

1 Top 10 Sights
see pp137–9

1 Places to Eat
see p141

1 La Dolce Vita Venues
see p140

1 Santa Maria della Vittoria

MAP E2 ■ **Via XX Settembre 17**
■ **Open 9am–noon & 3:30–6pm daily**

This 17th-century Baroque church has perhaps Rome's most ornate decor, most of it by Bernini. The most indulgent corner is the Cornaro Chapel, home to Bernini's shocking *Ecstasy of St Teresa (see p57)*.

2 Palazzo Barberini

MAP Q1 ■ **Via delle Quattro Fontane 13** ■ **06 481 4591** ■ **Open 10am–6pm Thu–Sun (booking recommended)** ■ **Adm (free first Sun of the month)**

The Barberini sold their palace to the state in 1949 to house part of the National Gallery, which was founded in 1893 with the purchase of the Corsini Palace. Among the famous works is the controversial *La Fornarina*, supposedly Raphael's mistress, probably painted by his pupil Giulio Romano.

3 Baths of Diocletian

MAP F3 ■ **Baths of Diocletian: Viale Enrico de Nicola 79; open 11am–6pm Tue–Sun** ■ **Aula Ottagona: Via Romita, Piazza della Repubblica; open during exhibitions only** ■ **www.coopculture.it**

One of the ancient world's largest *thermae*, these public baths were completed in 306. A large section is now part of the Museo Nazionale Romano *(see pp34–7)* and holds a collection of epigraphs, *stele* and statues. The Aula Ottagona has two 2nd-century BC bronze sculptures which were found hidden in a trench 6 m (20 ft) below the floor of the Temple of the Sun on the Quirinal hillside.

The altar, Santa Maria degli Angeli

4 Santa Maria degli Angeli

MAP F3 ■ **Piazza della Repubblica** ■ **Open 10am–1pm & 4–7pm**

In 1561 the pope commissioned Michelangelo to transform the central hall of Diocletian's Baths, the *frigidarium* (cold plunge room), into a church. The result is this vast, overwhelming space. Even so, the finished church takes up only half of the space of the original baths. Michelangelo had to raise the floor 2 m (6 ft) in order to use the ancient 15 m (50 ft) rose-red granite columns the way he wanted to.

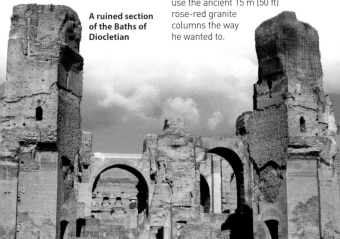

A ruined section of the Baths of Diocletian

POWER AND ELEGANCE

Since the 16th century, the Quirinal Hill has been the elemental expression of temporal power and dominion in Rome: first the popes, then the kings, and now the presidents of the Republic. Since the late 1800s, Via Veneto has complemented that raw clout with the charisma and glamour of great wealth and all that money can buy.

5 Piazza Barberini
MAP Q1

This could be called the piazza of the bees (see p63), the Barberini family symbol (judiciously upgraded from horseflies when their fortunes improved). Both of the piazza's Bernini fountains have large bees carved onto them to let everyone know who sponsored their creation. The central figure of a triton blowing his conch is one of Rome's most appealing and memorable. The other fountain is a simple scallop shell.

Fountain, Piazza Barberini

6 Palazzo del Quirinale
MAP P2 ■ Piazza del Quirinale: 06 39967557; www.quirinale.it; Wed, Fri, Sat, Sun 9:30am–3:30pm (booking compulsory); adm ■ Scuderie del Quirinale: Via XXIV Maggio 16; 02 9289 7722; open during exhibitions only (hours vary); adm; www.scuderiequirinale.it

The Quirinal hill was the enclave of the ancient Sabines in early Rome. Today, it is graced by 5.5-m (18-ft) Roman copies of 5th-century BC Greek originals of the Dioscuri and their prancing horses. The hill's stark, imposing palace, Rome's largest, was built in 1574 as a summer papal residence, to escape the endemic malaria around the Vatican. In 1870 it became the residence of the kings of Italy and, since 1947, Italy's presidents have resided and held official functions here. Across the piazza, the Scuderie del Quirinale is the former stables of the palace, used for horses, carriages and, eventu-ally, motor vehicles until 1938. In the 1990s the building was restored and converted into Rome's prime art exhibition space by the well-known architect Gae Aulenti.

7 Via Veneto
MAP E2

This street boasts a number of *belle époque* grand hotels and pavement cafés. It enjoyed its famous *dolce vita* heyday in the 1950–60s, when movie stars posed here for the paparazzi. Today, the allure is sadly limited for anybody other than tourists, but every visitor to Rome should come at least once to take a stroll of this lovely part of the city.

8 Capuchin Crypt and Museum
MAP E2 ■ Via Veneto 27 ■ Open 9am–7pm daily ■ Adm

A taste for the macabre may be all you need to enjoy this *memento mori*.

Skulls and skeletons, Capuchin Crypt

Fantastically creepy chapels are decorated with mosaics made from the bones of dead monks, a few of whose cowled skeletons remain propped up in bone-built niches.

Interiors of Sant'Andrea al Quirinale

Sant'Andrea al Quirinale
MAP Q2 ▪ Via del Quirinale 29
▪ Open 9am–noon & 3–6pm Tue–Sun
▪ Donation

Built between 1658 and 1670, this was the only construction over which Bernini was able to exercise total artistic control and may represent his architectural peak. The shallow, wide space needed an oval plan, counterpoised the concave curving entrance. The eye is drawn around the elliptical interior, where canonical elements blend with sculptural decoration to produce an elegant harmony. For so small a church, the impact is surprisingly grand.

San Carlo alle Quattro Fontane
MAP R2 ▪ Via del Quirinale 23
▪ Open 10am–1pm Mon–Sat

Borromini's masterpiece appears about as radically freeform as architecture could be in the 17th century. He filled this small space with fluid undulations, which have complex geometrical relationships. He succeeded in blurring the line between architecture and sculpture, resulting in a homogeneous interior topped by an oval dome.

EXPLORING THE QUIRINAL

▶ MORNING

Start on Quirinal Hill (or Monte Cavallo after the horse sculptures). Walk across Piazza del Quirinale to the Scuderie del Quirinale to see an art exhibition. Then walk halfway down Via del Quirinale and find Bernini's architectural tour de force, the church of **Sant'Andrea al Quirinale**. Inside, note the maritime motifs, symbolic of Andrew the fisherman.

Continue on to Borromini's **San Carlo alle Quattro Fontane**. Don't miss the masterful crypt and the exquisite cloister. Just outside are the eponymous four fountains, said to represent rivers. Two blocks along, take a right to the **Aula Ottagona** (see p137). The ancient bronzes of the Prince and the Boxer are amazing expressions of controlled power.

Take Via Bissolati to **Via Veneto**. Check out the shops before enjoying lunch at the elegant **Café Doney** (see p140).

AFTERNOON

Admire the *belle époque* **Westin Excelsior** hotel (see p172), especially its cupola and sexually ambiguous caryatids. Don't miss the public rooms of the sublime **Regina Baglioni** (see p171), which positively reek of luxury.

After soaking up all the opulence, walk down to visit the **Capuchin Crypt and Museum** to put things back in perspective. End your tour at **Piazza Barberini** and Bernini's marvellously life-affirming Triton Fountain.

See map on p136 ←

La Dolce Vita Venues

Opulent outdoor seating at the popular Harry's Bar

1 Café Doney
MAP E2 ■ Via Veneto 141

This historical café (see pp78–9) is a great place to sip a cappuccino under the magnolias and watch passers-by.

2 Crispy
MAP E2 ■ Via Francesco Crispi 80

An organic takeaway bistro and grocery store, Crispy is great both for buying fruit and vegetables and for a quick vegan meal. They also serve energy drinks and fruit shakes.

3 Gioielleria Capuano
MAP E2 ■ Via Veneto 195

This luxury store has been selling sophisticated jewellery from its own collection as well as pieces made by other Italian brands since the 1930s.

4 Zuma
MAP D2 ■ Via della Fontanella di Borghese 48

At the top of the celebrity Fendi Private Suites (see p170), this restaurant has grand views of Rome. It's perfect for a romantic tête-à-tête.

5 VIVA
MAP E2 ■ Via Sicilia 45

Enjoy mouthwatering seafood, including a fabulous tuna tartare, grilled octopus and caponata (aubergine side dish), at this Sicilian restaurant.

6 Harry's Bar
MAP E2 ■ Via Veneto 150

Noted for its American style and Bellini cocktails, this glamorous venue is still frequented by celebrities. It features a piano bar, a restaurant with gourmet Italian cuisine and a café with tables outside.

7 Brunello
MAP E2 ■ Via Veneto 72

Sumptuous interiors and a chic clientele make this hotel-restaurant a great place for watching the city's rich and beautiful crowd.

8 Jackie O'
MAP E2 ■ Via Boncompagni 11

A leading watering-hole since the 1960s, this restaurant and bar still attracts international stars. It has a piano bar and serves great cocktails and food.

9 Hard Rock Café
MAP E2 ■ Via Veneto 62/A/B

Great for people-watching, this chain café serving classic American fare, including great burgers and cocktails, has become somewhat of a landmark.

10 The Glove
MAP E2 ■ Via Veneto 106

This store sells gloves for every occasion, from warm mittens to elegant silk and leather gloves.

Places to Eat

1 **Sapori d'Ischia**
MAP E2 ▪ Via Marche 19
▪ 06 4201 2467 ▪ €€

The fish here is fresh and the menu filled with Neapolitan specialties such as mozzarella di bufala and sea food pastas. Visit on sundays for the occasional live music and karaoke.

2 **Pesceria Barberini**
MAP E2 ▪ Via San Nicola da Tolentino 23 ▪ 06 4290 3789 ▪ Closed Sun ▪ €€

Broad selection of fresh seafood, including oysters, sea urchin pasta, *carpaccios* and various types of fish.

3 **Colline Emiliane**
MAP E2 ▪ Via degli Avignonesi 22 ▪ 06 481 7538 ▪ Closed Sun D, Mon ▪ €€

Emilia-Romagna cuisine, consisting of a variety of *prosciutto* (ham) dishes and *tortellini in brodo* (meat-filled pasta in broth), is the speciality here.

4 **Trimani Wine Bar**
MAP F2 ▪ Via Cernaia 37/B ▪ 06 446 9630 ▪ Closed Sun ▪ €€

A full menu of soups, pastas and cured meats is served at this classy wine bar.

5 **Osteria Barberini**
MAP E2 ▪ Via della Purificazione 21 ▪ 06 474 3325 ▪ Closed Sun ▪ €€

This small restaurant, with a cosy interior and friendly staff, is renowned for its truffle dishes.

6 **Dagnino**
MAP E3 ▪ Via Vittorio Emanuele Orlando 75 ▪ 06 481 8660 ▪ Closed Sun ▪ €

This is Rome's best spot for Sicilian pastries such as *cassata* (iced cake).

7 **La Giara**
MAP E2 ▪ Via Toscana 46, at Via Sardegna ▪ 06 4274 5421 ▪ Closed Sun, Aug ▪ €€

This traditional *trattoria* with an unpretentious charm focuses on fish and seafood dishes.

Well-lit interiors of La Giara

8 **Matermatuta**
MAP E3 ▪ Via Palermo 51 ▪ 06 482 3962 ▪ Closed Sun ▪ €€

Specializing in seafood, this modern restaurant is a local favourite. Try the fish, which is served with great oysters and scallops, as well as the delicious mains such as octopus with green peas and cardamom. The service is exceptional.

9 **Sapori Sardi**
MAP E2 ▪ Via Piemonte 79 ▪ 06 474 5256 ▪ €€

Enjoy fine Sardinian dishes and mirto liqueur at this friendly restaurant.

10 **Africa**
MAP F2 ▪ Via Gaeta 26 ▪ 06 494 1077 ▪ Closed Mon ▪ €

Spicy vegetables and meats are served with spongy bread here.

Cassata at Dagnino

See map on p136

🔟 Trastevere and Prati

The Bohemian neighbourhood of Trastevere ("across the Tiber"), a former working-class area, has retained its medieval essence despite now being one of the most restaurant- and nightlife-packed zones of the city. The Borgo is Vatican turf, with kitsch religious souvenir shops and tourist-orientated cafés, while Prati to the north is one of Rome's most genuine, non-touristy, middle-class districts.

Statue, Ponte Sant'Angelo

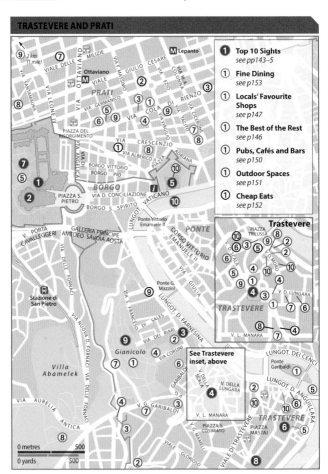

TRASTEVERE AND PRATI

1. **Top 10 Sights**
   see pp143–5
1. **Fine Dining**
   see p153
1. **Locals' Favourite Shops**
   see p147
1. **The Best of the Rest**
   see p146
1. **Pubs, Cafés and Bars**
   see p150
1. **Outdoor Spaces**
   see p151
1. **Cheap Eats**
   see p152

The magnificent St Peter's Basilica, Vatican City

1 Vatican City

One of the great museum complexes (see pp12–15) of the world includes Michelangelo's famous Sistine Chapel and the extensive Raphael Rooms.

2 St Peter's Basilica

The capital of Christendom (see pp16–17) is packed with works by Bernini and statues by Michelangelo. The panoramic views from the dome are breathtaking.

3 Villa Farnesina Chigi

MAP J5 ▪ Via della Lungara 230 ▪ Open 9am–5pm Mon–Sat & 2nd Sun of month ▪ Adm

Peruzzi's (1508–11) sumptuous villa (see p60) was built for papal banker Agostino Chigi, whose parties were legendary – he would toss silver platters into the Tiber after each course. In a downstairs room, Peruzzi painted Chigi's horoscope on the ceiling, Sebastiano del Piombo painted scenes from Ovid's *Metamorphoses*, and Raphael painted the sensual *Galatea*. Peruzzi's upstairs hall features a *trompe-l'oeil* balustrade overlooking hills. The 1527 graffiti by Charles V's troops is now protected as historic vandalism. The bedroom contains Sodoma's 1517 *Wedding Night of Alexander the Great*.

4 Santa Maria in Trastevere

MAP K6 ▪ Piazza S Maria in Trastevere ▪ Open 7:30am–9pm daily (8am–noon & 4–9pm daily in Aug)

Rome's oldest church (see p51) dedicated to the Virgin was founded on the site where a font of oil spouted the day Christ was born. The miracle is depicted in the stupendous *Life of the Virgin* mosaics (1291) by Pietro Cavallini in the apse. The current 12th-century church has ancient mismatched columns, 13th-century mosaics, a Cosmatesque pavement and a rare 7th-century panel painting of the *Madonna della Clemenza* in the chapel left of the altar.

Brilliant mosaics in Santa Maria

Façade of Museo di Castel Sant'Angelo

5 Museo di Castel Sant'Angelo

MAP J1 ■ Lungotevere Castello 50 ■ Open 9am–7:30pm daily ■ Adm (free first Sun of the month)

Rising above the river, Hadrian designed his massive circular tomb in 123–39. Aurelian fortified it in 271 as part of his city walls *(see p156)*. It was the papal castle for 1,000 years – a viaduct from the Vatican let the popes scurry here in times of crisis. Gregory the Great named it in 590 after a vision of

St Michael announced the end of a plague from its tower, marked by the bronze statue of a sword-bearing archangel. There are frescoed Renaissance papal apartments and a small arms and armour collection, plus stunning panoramas of the city from the ramparts.

6 Santa Cecilia in Trastevere

MAP D5 ■ Piazza di S Cecilia 22 ■ Open 9:30am–1pm & 4–7:15pm daily; frescoes open 10am–12:30pm ■ Adm for crypt and frescoes

This church is reputedly built over the house of the martyred Cecilia. Look for the Guido Reni painting of her decapitation. Under the apse's glittering 9th-century mosaics rests a 1293 *baldacchino* by Arnolfo di Cambio and Stefano Maderno's 1600 statue of the saint (he saw her incorrupt body when her tomb was opened in 1599). Ring the bell on the left aisle to see the top half of Pietro Cavallini's *Last Judgement* (1289–93), his only remaining fresco in Rome.

7 Vatican Gardens

MAP A2 ■ Viale Vaticano ■ 06 6988 4676 ■ Tours: daily except Wed & Sun (call ahead) ■ Adm (includes entry to Vatican museums) ■ www.vatican.va

Typical 16th-century Italianate gardens of lawns, woods, grottoes and fountains. Structures include the first Vatican radio tower, designed by Marconi in 1931, Pier Luigi Nervi's

The serene lawns of the Vatican Gardens

shell-shaped audience hall (1971) and the Mannerist Casina of Pius IV (1558–61), home to the Pontifical Academy of Sciences.

8 San Francesco a Ripa

MAP C5 ■ Piazza di S Francesco d'Assisi 88 ■ Open 7am–1pm & 4:30–7:30pm daily

Though altered during the Renaissance and Baroque eras, the church was built just 12 years after St Francis stayed at this hospice in 1219. Ask the sacristan's permission to visit the cell in which St Francis stayed, which contains a copy of his portrait by Margaritone d'Arezzo. The last chapel on the left houses Bernini's *Beata Ludovica Albertoni* (1671–4) shown in a state of religious ecstasy.

Bernini's *Beata Ludovica Albertoni*

9 Gianicolo

MAP B4

This long ridge separating Trastevere from the Vatican offers some of the best views of Rome (see p65). Its two equestrian monuments celebrate Garibaldi and his wife Anita, who is buried underneath hers.

10 Ponte Sant'Angelo

MAP J2

Hadrian built this bridge in 133–4 to access his mausoleum, but only the three central arches of that span remain. Clement VII had the statues of St Peter (by Lorenzetto) and St Paul (by Paolo Taccone) installed in 1534. Clement IX hired Bernini in 1688 to design the statues of 10 angels holding symbols of the Passion.

A TOUR OF TRASTEVERE

▶ MORNING

Begin at **San Crisogono** (see p146); ask the custodian to let you into the excavations downstairs. By 10am be at **San Francesco a Ripa** for the five minutes it takes to see Bernini's sculpture. Head down Via Anicia Antica, right on Via Madonna dell'Orto, and left on Via di S Michele to reach **Santa Cecilia**. Explore the crypt and pay the nuns a small donation to get up to see the Cavallini frescoes. Head out of the courtyard left onto Via di Genovesi, which leads to Viale Trastevere.

Crossing Piazza S Maria in Trastevere, bear right into Piazza S Egidio and fork left onto Via della Scala. Continue past Santa Maria della Scala and up Via della Lungara to **Villa Farnesina** (see p143). You'll be here before noon, time enough to spend 30 minutes admiring the frescoes. Take a breather amid the greenery at the **Orto Botanico** (see p146), then return to the heart of Trastevere to enjoy a pizza at **Pizzeria Dar Poeta** (see p152).

AFTERNOON

Peruse the collections of the **Museo di Roma in Trastevere** (see p146), visit the marvellous medieval church of **Santa Maria in Trastevere** (see p143) and walk up Via Garibaldi to peek through the grille at Bramante's Tempietto in the courtyard of **San Pietro in Montorio** (see p146). Or simply spend the afternoon wandering the medieval streets, awaiting the dinner hour when Trastevere comes to life.

See map on p142 ←

The Best of the Rest

The small Tiber Island, associated with medicine and healing

1 Tiber Island
MAP M6

It is said that the serpent of medical god Aesculapius jumped ship and swam ashore here in 293 BC. Rome's maternity hospital is still here.

2 Galleria Corsini
MAP J5 ■ Via della Lungara 10 ■ Open 10am–6pm Tue–Sun ■ Adm (free first Sun of the month)

This small painting collection features works by Fra Angelico, Van Dyck, Titian, Rubens and Caravaggio.

3 San Pietro in Montorio
MAP C4 ■ Piazza San Pietro in Montorio 2 ■ Church: open 9am–noon & 3–4pm daily ■ Temple: open 10am–6pm Tue–Sun

Bramante designed this mini-temple to mark the spot where St Peter was supposedly crucified.

4 Orto Botanico
MAP J5 ■ Largo Cristina di Svezia 24 ■ Open Apr–Sep: 9am–6:30pm; Oct–Mar: 9am–5:30pm Mon–Sat ■ Adm

Galleria Corsini's gardens are now Rome University's botanical museum.

5 Ponte Rotto
MAP N6

Rome's first stone bridge (181–142 BC) was ruined in 1598. Three arches were retained until 1886, when two were destroyed to make way for Ponte Palatino (rotto is Italian for broken).

6 Santa Maria della Scala
MAP K6 ■ Piazza S Maria della Scala 23 ■ Open 10am–1pm & 4–5:30pm daily

A charming Renaissance church, whose claim to fame is a *Virgin and Child* by Cavalier d'Arpino, who was Caravaggio's teacher.

7 Fontana Paola
MAP B5

This wide basin at the end of the Paola aqueduct is a favourite backdrop for wedding photos.

8 Villa Doria Pamphilj
MAP B5 ■ Via di S Pancrazio ■ Open 7am–sunset daily

Rome's largest public park (see p66) was established in 1644–52 by Camillo Pamphilj. It is a great place for picnics.

9 Museo di Roma in Trastevere
MAP K6 ■ Piazza di S Egidio 1b ■ Open 10am–8pm Tue–Sun ■ Adm

Housed in a beautifully restored former convent, this museum includes life-size dioramas of Ancient Roman rooms and shops.

10 San Crisogono
MAP L6 ■ Piazza S Sonnino 44 ■ Open 7am–noon & 3:30–7pm Mon–Sat, 8am–1pm & 3:30–7pm Sun ■ Adm

The 1626 façade copies the medieval one. Inside are 22 ancient columns and excavations of the original 5th-century basilica.

Locals' Favourite Shops

1 Coin Excelsior
MAP C2 ■ Via Cola di Rienzo 173
The flagship of the Coin department store specialises in famous international brands. Housed in an Art Nouveau building redesigned with contemporary touches, it offers high-end shopping, from beauty products and jewellery to shoes and fashion.

2 Carlo Cecchini Designer
MAP L6 ■ Via della Lungaretta, 65
This shop offers a selection of high-quality leather bags created by designer Carlo Cecchini. The designs are creative and imaginative, following the latest trends.

Speciality foods at Castroni

3 Castroni
MAP C2 ■ Via Cola di Rienzo 196
The gastronomic temple of Rome since 1932, this shop is piled high with packaged and prepared speciality foods from countries the world over, such as Japan, Greece, India, China and the Middle East.

4 Boutique Gallo
MAP C2 ■ Via Ovidio 18
Selling high-quality knitwear, this shop specialises in colourful socks and stockings, and also has clothes for women and children.

5 Peroni snc
Piazza dell'Unità 29
From baking pans to chocolate thermometers, Peroni sells an amazing range of baking equipment plus other kitchen goods.

6 Gente
MAP B2 ■ Via Cola di Rienzo 277
The place to go for the best Italian and international fashion brands, selected for women.

7 Ottimomassimo
MAP C5 ■ Via Manara 16/17
Superb illustrated books for children, including guidebooks, in Italian, English, French and Spanish, can be found at this bookshop. It also hosts activities and bookclubs.

8 Costantini
MAP C2 ■ Piazza Cavour 16
This fine wine cellar has an excellent selection at reasonable prices.

9 Sabon
MAP C2 ■ Via Cola di Rienzo 241
Luxurious soaps, toiletries and candles made with natural ingredients are sold here.

10 Polvere di Tempo
MAP L6 ■ Via del Moro 59
The non-mechanical timepieces at this shop, including hour glasses, sundials, candle clocks and astrolabes, are all made by the owner.

Timepieces at Polvere di Tempo

See map on p142

Pubs, Cafés and Bars

1 Ombre Rosse
MAP K6 ■ Piazza S
Egidio 12–13

This laid-back pub is a staple of Trastevere nightlife. The atmosphere is always lively, with tables on the piazza in summer.

2 Freni e Frizioni
MAP K5 ■ Via del Politeama 4

A former mechanic's garage has been transformed into a hip *aperitivo* spot serving a buffet during the summer. The bar overflows into a pretty outdoor courtyard.

Cool *aperitivo* bar Freni e Frizioni

3 Ma Che Siete Venuti a Fa
MAP K5 ■ Via Benedetta 25

This Italian pub, which has its name inspired by a football chant translating to "What did you come here for?", serves a range of artisanal beers .The waiters here provide impeccable service.

4 Caffè di Marzio
MAP K6 ■ Piazza di Santa
Maria in Trastevere 15

This café is a perfect place to sit and admire the façade of the basilica of Santa Maria in Trastevere – one of Rome's oldest – and watch life unfold in the lively piazza. They have good coffees, pastries and hot chocolate.

5 Caffè della Scala
MAP K6 ■ Via della Scala 4

Highly recommended for when a lazy evening *aperitivo* is called for, this pretty, Bohemian café has seats outside for people watching.

6 Ditta Trinchetti
MAP L6 ■ Via della
Lungaretta 76

This is a wonderful *tavola calda* (self-service buffet) and delicatessen – try the Puglian *burrata* (fresh cheese made from mozzarella and cream), superior sandwiches, and hot dishes that include great bean soup in winter.

7 Enoteca Trastevere
MAP L6 ■ Via della
Lungaretta 86

With a pleasingly dark wood interior and plenty of seating out front on the cobblestones, this thriving wine bar also serves light snacks and cocktails.

8 Enoteca Ferrara
MAP K5 ■ Piazza Trilussa 41

This bustling wine bar has a very loyal following of conoisseurs, which is not surprising as it is known for serving some of the best wines by the glass in the city. There's an in-house deli, and a lovely back garden for when the weather is good.

9 Meccanismo
MAP K5 ■ Piazza Trilussa 34

A trendy aperitivo bar with a great music selection. This is a perfect spot for light lunches during the day and abundant aperitivo buffets in the evening.

10 Forno la Renella
MAP K6 ■ Via del Moro 15–16

Romans flock here from all over the city for the high-quality bread, pizza, focaccia and biscuits. Try it and you'll understand why. Everything is baked in wood-fired ovens, and the toppings and fillings change according to season.

Previous pages The Vatican City from Ponte Umberto

Outdoor Spaces

1 Parco del Gianicolo
The beautiful park on top of the Janiculum Hill is known for offering the best view in Rome (see p145).

2 Villa Sciarra
A peaceful park (see p67) in the Gianicolo neighbourhood, filled with statues and fountains. It's perfect for a romantic stroll.

The busy Piazza Santa Maria

3 Piazza Santa Maria in Trastevere
Dotted with cafés and restaurants, this piazza (see p63) is perfect for watching the people of Trastevere go about their days.

4 Bar Gianicolo
MAP B5 ▪ Piazzale Aurelio 5
A small snack bar with lots of outdoor seating in the sun. A great reward for having made it to the top of the Janiculum Hill.

5 Vatican Gardens
The perfect place to catch your breath after exploring Vatican City (see p144).

6 Piazza in Piscinula
MAP C5
This, one of the prettiest piazzas in Trastevere, complete with arches, climbing plants and cobblestones, offers great photo opportunities.

7 Expedition of the Thousand
MAP B4 ▪ Piazza Giuseppe Garibaldi
Within the Janiculum park, a collection of large busts placed on the banisters overlooking the city depicts the patriots who unified Italy in the Expedition of the Thousand.

8 Mercato Trionfale
MAP B2 ▪ Via la Goletta 1
This huge and busy food market is considered to be one of the best by Rome's pickier gourmands. Check out the vegetable stalls and stock up on pastas, drieds herbs and preserved vegetables.

9 Via Cola di Rienzo
MAP C2 ▪ Via Cola di Rienzo
Busy Via Cola di Rienzo is a great place to spend an afternoon shopping for beauty products and fashion. Snap up a bargain from the sidewalk market stalls.

10 Caffetteria Le Terrazze
MAP J1 ▪ Lungotevere Castello 50
A quaint terrace café with a glorious view, located inside Castel Sant'Angelo (see p144).

The breathtaking Vatican Gardens

Cheap Eats

1 Sorpasso
MAP B2 ▪ Via Properzio 31–33
▪ 06 890 24554 ▪ Closed Sun ▪ €

Enjoy Mediterranean cuisine in a laid-back atmosphere here. There is also a deli counter selling delights to take away for a picnic.

2 La Pratolina
MAP C2 ▪ Via degli Scipioni 248 ▪ 06 3600 4409 ▪ €

The delicious pizzas here are baked in a unique lava-stone wood-burning oven. Try the *Pinsa*, which is an Etruscan-style pizza.

3 Gelateria La Romana
MAP C2 ▪ Via Cola di Rienzo 2 ▪ 06 3260 9251 ▪ €

Enjoy fabulous ice cream specialties served in cones that are filled with melted chocolate.

4 Pizzeria Ivo a Trastevere
MAP C5 ▪ Via S Francesco a Ripa 158 ▪ 06 581 7082 ▪ Closed L, Tue ▪ €

A lively football theme and ever-present crowds are the features of Rome's favourite pizzeria.

5 Trapizzino Trilussa
MAP C4 ▪ Piazza Trilussa 46 ▪ 06 581 7312 ▪ €

The eatery offers pizza-dough triangles filled with vegetables, meat, and cheese, that are immensely popular in Rome and make for the perfect lunch on the go.

The bar at Trapizzino Trilussa

6 Pizzeria Dar Poeta
MAP K6 ▪ Vicolo del Bologna 45–6 ▪ 06 588 0516 ▪ €

Innovative pizzas are made in a wood-fired oven here – Roman-style, but with a thick crust.

7 Osteria dell'Angelo
MAP B1 ▪ Via G Bettolo 24 ▪ 06 372 9470 ▪ Closed Sun ▪ €

Angelo prepares excellent traditional Roman cooking at equally admirable prices. The service charge is 15 per cent. Book ahead.

8 Pizzeria da Vittorio
MAP K6 ▪ Via S Cosimato 14A ▪ 06 580 0353 ▪ €

Good Neapolitan-style pizza and *antipasti* are offered at this local favourite. A pleasant fan-cooled interior plastered with photos of famous patrons makes this one of Rome's most enjoyable pizzerias.

9 Da Giovanni
MAP J4 ▪ Via della Lungara 41A ▪ 06 686 1514 ▪ Closed Sun ▪ €

This cosy, friendly trattoria *(see p77)* serves a variety of typical Roman dishes prepared with fresh ingredients, and fantastic desserts. It is small, so book ahead.

10 La Boccaccia
MAP K5 ▪ Via di Santa Dorotea 2 ▪ 32 0775 6277 ▪ Closed Mon ▪ €

Serving supremely delicious *pizza a taglio* (pizza by the slice), La Boccaccia is great for a snack on the go. It also has a few seats inside and a bench to squeeze onto outside.

Fine Dining

1 Sabatini
MAP K6 ■ Piazza di Santa Maria in Trastevere 13 ■ 06 581 8307 ■ €€€

Roman cuisine and seafood are served at Sabatini. Book ahead for a table out on the main square.

2 Ferrara
MAP K6 ■ Via del Moro 1a ■ 06 5833 3920 ■ Closed L (except Sat & Sun) ■ €€

The creative food is as good as the wine at this superb restaurant.

The laid-back Antico Arco

3 Antico Arco
MAP B5 ■ Piazzale Aurelio 7 ■ 06 581 5274 ■ €€

Try the signature risotto with Castelmagno cheese in Nebbiolo wine sauce at this easy-going, contemporary Italian restaurant. Book ahead for an outdoor table.

4 Glass Hostaria
MAP K2 ■ Vicolo del Cinque 58 ■ 06 5833 5903 ■ Closed Mon & Tue, L ■ €€€

This ultra-modern restaurant (see p75) offers inventive Italian fusion cuisine and a great wine list.

5 Roma Sparita
Piazza di Santa Cecilia 24 ■ 06 580 0757 ■ Closed Mon L & Sun ■ €€

Set on a picturesque, quiet piazza far from the crowds of central Trastevere, Roma Sparita serves simple Roman fare, brilliantly executed.

PRICE CATEGORIES

For a three-course meal for one with half a bottle of wine (or equivalent meal), taxes and extra charges.
....
€ under €40   €€ €40–60   €€€ over €60

6 Antica Pesa
MAP C4 ■ Via Garibaldi ■ 18 06 580 9236 ■ Closed Sun ■ €€€

Outstanding Roman food and an indulgent atmosphere define this Trastevere staple (see p75). There's a leafy outdoor patio for warmer nights.

7 L'Arcangelo
MAP C2 ■ Via Giuseppe Gioacchino Belli 59 ■ 06 321 0992 ■ Closed Sat L, Sun ■ €€

High-quality ingredients are used in the classic Roman trattoria food here. After a meal guests are given a complementary zabaglione liqueur with sweet biscuits. There are also some very good fixed-menu deals at lunchtime.

8 Margot
MAP C2 ■ Via Crescenzio 39 ■ 06 6819 3221 ■ €€

This small, romantic restaurant serves staple Italian cuisine, such as gnocchi (see p73) with clams and eggplant parmigiana, as well as several vegetarian and gluten-free dishes.

9 La Pergola
Rome Cavalieri Hotel, Via Alberto Cadlolo 101 ■ 06 3509 2152 ■ Closed L, Sun & Mon ■ €€€

Offering the finest dining experience in Rome, this is the only restaurant (see p74) in the city with three Michelin stars. Elegant dress code.

10 Osteria La Gensola
MAP M6 ■ Piazza della Gensola 15 ■ 06 5833 2758 ■ €€

With a pleasant atmosphere and an intimate setting, this restaurant (see p75) offers sumptuous seafood at reasonable prices.

See map on p142

🔟 Beyond the City Walls

The 3rd-century Aurelian Walls are still largely intact and served as the defence of the city for 1,600 years until Italian Unification in 1870. After that, the walls were pierced in several places so that traffic could bypass the old gates and the modern city quickly sprawled far and wide in every direction. It is undeniable that Rome's most dazzling sights lie within the walls, but venturing outside them can have spectacular rewards. Ancient roads, an entire ancient town, some of Rome's oldest churches, the mystical catacombs and even Mussolini's pretentious contributions to modern architecture are all must-sees away from the city centre.

Sarcophagus, Via Appia Antica

BEYOND THE CITY WALLS

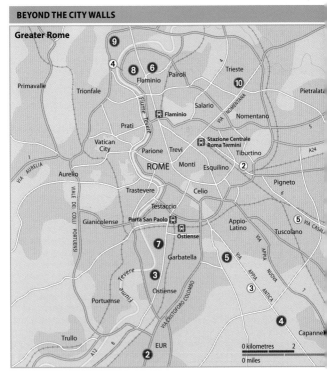

Greater Rome

1 Ostia Antica

Ancient Rome's trading heart has a wealth of fascinating ruins that evoke the city's earliest days, and a lovely rural site (see pp42–3).

2 EUR
Metro EUR Palasport and EUR Fermi

Built by Mussolini as a showcase to the world of the ideal Fascist metropolis, the EUR (l'Esposizione Universale di Roma) is disturbing to many visitors. The critic Robert Hughes described the Square Colosseum as "the most frightening building in the world", yet the aesthetic inspired many post-war architects. Today the area is largely a residential and business district. There's also a park with a lake, and Rome's aquarium, boasting sealed glass windows that face the lake.

Façade of San Paolo fuori le Mura

3 San Paolo fuori le Mura
Via Ostiense 190 ■ Metro Basilica S Paolo ■ Open 7am– 6:30pm daily

Rome's second largest church has had a history of violent ups and downs. It was built by Constantine in the 4th century, over the spot where St Paul was buried, and for about 400 years it was the largest church in Europe, until it was sacked by the Saracens in 846. It was rebuilt and fortified, but its position outside the walls left it mostly ignored until the mid-11th century, when it underwent a renewal. A fire in 1823 led to the reworking we see today. Fortunately, the cloisters, considered Rome's most beautiful, escaped the flames.

4 Via Appia Antica
Buses 118, 218

"The Queen of Roads" was completed in 312 BC by Appius Claudius, also the architect of Rome's first aqueduct. The most pastoral part begins at the circular Tomb of Cecilia Metella, which was made into a fortification in the Middle Ages. Starting here, you'll see more tombs and fragments of tombs, as well as grazing sheep and the private gates to fabulous modern villas. As you walk along, look to the east to see the arches of an ancient aqueduct marching towards the city.

Environs

0 km 20
0 miles 20

Orte
Viterbo ⑨
Vetralla ⑩
Tarquinia
③⑦
Civitavecchia
Sutri
Civita Castellana
Rieti
Lake Bracciano
Farfa
Morlupo
④ Cerveteri
Area of Greater Rome map, left
①⑥
② Tivoli
⑥⑧ ⑦
Frascati
⑤
① ⑧
Velletri
⑩ 180 km (110 miles)
Aprilia

Tyrrhenian Sea

Anzio
Latina
② 40 km (24 miles)

①	**Top 10 Sights** see pp155–7
①	**Places to Eat** see p159
①	**Day Trips from Rome** see p158

Concert halls of the Auditorium Parco della Musica

THE AURELIAN WALL

This ancient wall was begun by Emperor Aurelian (AD 270–75) and completed by his successor Probus (AD 276–82). It stretches 18 km (11 miles) around the city, with 18 gates and 381 towers, enclosing all seven of Rome's hills. In the 4th century, Emperor Maxentius raised it to almost twice its original height. To this day, most of the wall survives.

5 Appian Way Catacombs

San Sebastiano: Via Appia Antica 136; open 10am–5pm daily; adm ■ San Callisto: Via Appia Antica 110; open 9am–noon & 2–5pm Tue–Thu (online booking required); closed 1 Jan, Easter, 25 Dec & around 29 Jan–25 Feb; adm; www. catacombe.roma.it ■ Domitilla: Via delle Sette Chiese 282; open Feb–Dec: 9am–noon & 2–5pm daily; adm

The burial tunnels of Rome's early Christians are like a honeycomb under the consular roads out of Rome, especially along Via Appia Antica. Grave niches stacked like shelving are carved into the tufa. The soft volcanic rock is great for tunnelling, as it is softer when first exposed to air, hardening afterwards. There are precious remnants of fresco and engraved marble slabs.

6 Auditorium Parco della Musica

Viale Pietro de Coubertin 30 ■ 06 802 41281 ■ Open 11am–8pm daily (to 6pm in winter); closed Aug ■ Adm to concerts ■ www.auditorium.com

Italian architect Renzo Piano's "city of music" is the heart of Rome's cultural life, with three whale-shaped concert halls hosting daily classical, rock, pop and jazz performances. The "theatre hall" is for dance shows and electronic nights, while revolving art exhibitions adorn the complex's hallways. There is also a café, bookshop and playground.

7 Centrale Montemartini

Via Ostiense 106 ■ 06 0608 ■ Open 9am–7pm Tue–Sun ■ Adm ■ www.centralemontemartini.org

Rome's first power station (see p69) has been transformed into a stunning showcase for Greek and Roman art – parts of the Musei Capitolini collection (see pp28–9) that, until now, were kept in storage. The effect is extraordinary, playing off the might of modern technology against the human vulnerability of these ancient masterpieces.

8 MAXXI

Via Guido Reni, 4A ■ 06 320 1954 ■ Open 11am–8pm Tue–Sun (to 7pm Wed, Thu & Sun) ■ Adm ■ www.maxxi.art

Opened in 2010, MAXXI (Museo delle Arti del XXI secolo) (see p55), Rome's first contemporary art centre, was designed by the British-Iraqi architect

Futuristic buildings of MAXXI

Dame Zaha Hadid and is a jewel of modern architecture. The galleries are a series of long intertwining bands. The permanent collection contains more than 350 works, and the museum has two sections: visual arts and architecture.

⑨ Foro Italico and Stadio dei Marmi

Viale del Foro Italico

Originally called the Foro Mussolini, this sports complex was understandably renamed in the late 1940s, even though the 16-m (55-ft) obelisk still reads "Mussolini Dux" ("Mussolini the Leader"). In imitation of every Roman emperor, there was supposed to have been a 75-m (250-ft) statue of Il Duce as Hercules. The Classical-style statues of the Stadio dei Marmi, 60 colossal young Fascist athletes, are worth a look.

Apse mosaic at Sant'Agnese

⑩ Sant'Agnese fuori le Mura and Santa Costanza

Via Nomentana 349 ▪ Buses 36, 60, 62, 84, 90 ▪ Sant'Agnese: open 8am–7pm Mon–Sat; Santa Costanza: open 9am–noon & 3–6pm Mon–Sat, 3–6pm Sun

These 4th-century churches are located in the same Early Christian complex. Both are decorated with mosaics. Sant'Agnese depicts the martyred St Agnes as she appeared in a vision eight days after her death. The ambulatory around the circular Santa Costanza has detailed scenes of an ancient Roman grape harvest.

A MORNING WALK ON THE VIA APPIA ANTICA

▶ Start at the **Porta San Sebastiano**, the grandest city gate of them all, where you can visit the **Museo delle Mura** *(see p69)*, which illustrates the history of the Aurelian Wall. Climb the stairs for great views. From here, continue straight on along the **Via Appia Antica** *(see p155)*. One of the first sights you'll come to, on the left at a crossroads, is the small Domine Quo Vadis? church – this marks the spot where Peter, fleeing persecution, encountered Christ and decided to return to Rome and face his martyrdom like a saint. The church contains a replica of footprints in stone, said to be those of Christ, but it is actually an ancient pagan *ex voto*.

Quite a bit further ahead, you'll come to the **Catacombs of San Sebastiano** *(see p64)*. Take the guided tour, and don't miss the curious fresco of a bowl of fruit and a partridge, which, according to some ancient writers, was the most lascivious of all creatures. Continuing on, past a mobile bar where you can buy snacks and drinks, visit the **Circus of Maxentius**, an ancient racetrack. Note how *amphorae* were embedded in the bricks to lighten the construction of the upper grandstands. Your last stop will be the 1st-century BC **Tomb of Cecilia Metella**. The frieze of bulls' skulls and garlands is beautiful and the cone-shaped sanctum is peaceful.

For lunch, walk back to the **Ristorante l'Archeologia** *(see p159)* for a hearty meal. Then backtrack a few hundred metres to the bus ⬤ stop to catch the No 118 into town.

See map on pp154–5 ←

Day Trips from Rome

① Villa d'Este
Piazza Trento, Tivoli ■ COTRAL bus from Ponte Mammolo ■ 07 7433 2920 ■ Open 8:30am– 1hr before sunset Tue–Sun ■ Adm (free first Sun of the month)

Built in the 16th century, Villa d'Este is renowned for its gardens and features 100 fountains.

Canopus Pool, Hadrian's Villa

② Hadrian's Villa
Via Tiburtina, 6 km (4 miles) southwest of Tivoli ■ COTRAL bus from Ponte Mammolo ■ 07 7438 2733 ■ Open 9am–1hr before sunset daily ■ Adm (free first Sun of the month)

Built as Hadrian's summer retreat between AD 118 and 34, this vast area contained full-scale reproductions of the emperor's favourite buildings from Greece and Egypt. The ruins include temples and theatres.

③ Tarquinia Necropolis
Train from Termini or Ostiense or COTRAL bus from Lepanto ■ 07 6685 0080 ■ Open 8:30am–dusk Tue–Sun ■ Adm

The museum of Etruscan artifacts housed within this large necropolis is famous for its 4th-century BC terracotta horses.

④ Cerveteri Necropolis
Train from Termini to Cerveteri-Ladispoli ■ 06 994 0651 ■ Open 8:30am–1 hour before sunset Tue–Sun ■ Adm

Established in the 6th century BC, this town's necropolis has intact streets, houses and frescoes.

⑤ Castelli Romani
Metro Anagnina, then COTRAL buses ■ Palazzo Chigi Ariccia: Piazza di Corte 14, Ariccia; 06 933 0053; open 10am–1pm, 3:30–6:30pm Tue–Sun (to 6pm in winter, gardens Apr–Sep); adm

There is much to attract in this area of the Alban Hills. Swim in Lago di Albano, or visit Ariccia's Palazzo Chigi, a Baroque complex designed by Bernini in the 17th century.

⑥ Frascati
Metro Anagnina, then COTRAL bus ■ Villa Aldobrandini: Via Cardinale Massaia 18; 06 683 3785; open 9am–5:30pm Mon–Fri (gardens only), booking required

This small town is home to Villa Aldobrandini, whose gardens offer magnificent panoramas of Rome.

⑦ Palestrina
Metro Anagnina, then COTRAL bus ■ Museum: Palazzo Barberini ■ Open 9am–8pm daily ■ Adm

This town boasts Italy's greatest Hellenistic temple. Among its treasures is a 2nd-century BC mosaic.

⑧ Rome's Beaches
Trains depart from Porta San Paolo; ATAC bus or metro ticket required

The Ostia sea strip to the city's south is dotted with beach clubs and free beaches (spiaggia libera).

⑨ Viterbo
Most sights: open 8:30am–6:30pm Tue–Sat ■ Adm

Visit this medieval town's Papal Palace, Fontana Grande and Archaeological Museum.

⑩ Pompeii
Train from Termini to Naples, then Circumvesuviana train ■ 08 1857 5111 ■ Open 9am–5pm (to 7:30pm in summer) ■ Adm

Now a UNESCO World Heritage Site, this city was buried and preserved by the eruption of Vesuvius in AD 79.

Places to Eat

① Allo Sbarco di Enea, Ostia Antica

Via dei Romagnoli 675 ▪ Metro Piramide then local train ▪ 06 565 0034 ▪ Closed Mon L ▪ €€

The waiters dress up in Ancient Roman gear and the decor is like a low-budget epic movie at this kitsch but fun restaurant. The speciality is fish; try the *spaghetti alle vongole* (clams).

② Pizzeria Formula Uno

MAP G4 ▪ Via Degli Equi 13 ▪ 06 445 3866 ▪ Closed Sun ▪ €

A San Lorenzo institution, this lively, no-frills pizzeria has been serving thin-crusted, scrumptious pizzas with top-quality toppings for decades. The carciofi alla giudia and anchovies *(see p72)* are an absolute must, too.

Ristorante l'Archeologia

③ Ristorante l'Archeologia, Via Appia Antica

Via Appia Antica 139 ▪ Bus 118 ▪ 06 788 0494 ▪ €€

Dine around the fireplace in winter and in the garden in summer at this restaurant in an elegant converted farmhouse. It serves rustic regional fare, such as roast lamb and home-made pasta dishes.

④ Aroma Osteria Flaminio

Lungotevere Flaminio 62D ▪ 06 3265 1751 ▪ €

At this beautiful restaurant near MAXXI *(see p156)* enjoy dishes pre-pared with high-quality ingredients. The cod cooked with cheese and pepper sauce is delicious.

PRICE CATEGORIES
For a three-course meal for one with half a bottle of wine (or equivalent meal), taxes and extra charges.

€ under €40 €€ €40–60 €€€ over €60

⑤ Osteria Bonelli

Viale dell'Acquedotto Alessandrino, 172/174 ▪ 329 863 3077 ▪ Closed Sun ▪ €

Classic dishes at this friendly, lively *osteria* include pasta, lamb and fabulous roasted beef cheeks.

⑥ La Sibilla, Tivoli

Via della Sibilla 50 ▪ COTRAL bus from Ponte Mammolo ▪ 07 7433 5281 ▪ Closed Mon ▪ €€

Overlooking Villa Gregoriana, this restaurant is in a spectacular location.

⑦ Ambaradam, Tarquinia

Piazza Matteotti 14 ▪ 07 6685 7073 ▪ Closed Wed L ▪ €

Conveniently located on the main piazza, this homely and typical trattoria is known for its delicious ravioli and attentive service.

⑧ Pinocchio, Frascati

Piazza del Mercato 21 ▪ Metro Anagnina, then COTRAL bus ▪ 06 941 7883 ▪ Closed Mon–Sat L ▪ €

Pinocchio (also a hotel) specializes, as does this entire area, in the celebrated *porchetta* (pork roast).

⑨ Il Porticciolo

Via del Porto 13 ▪ 331 729 4816 ▪ €

Wonderful seafood is served here with a gorgeous sea view, right on the Sperlonga harbour.

⑩ Piccola Trattoria da Patrizio, Viterbo

Via della Cava 50 ▪ Train from Roma Ostiense or COTRAL bus from Saxa Rubra ▪ 07 6126 7741 ▪ €

This family-run, cosy trattoria offers reasonably priced delicious food in generous portions.

See map on pp154–5 ←

Streetsmart

Roman street scene

Getting Around

Arriving by Air

Rome has two airports, Fiumicino and Ciampino, both served by international flights and with excellent transport links to the city centre.

Fiumicino (FCO), 30 km (19 miles) southwest of Rome, is the main hub. From here, the **Leonardo Express**, run by Trenitalia, takes 35 minutes non-stop to Termini station in the city. There is also a slower train to Tiburtina station (50 minutes), stopping at Trastevere and Ostiense. Buy tickets at the station or online.

Several bus companies, including **Terravision** and **Sit Bus Shuttle**, run services to Termini station, taking about an hour. Touts will usually approach you with their latest ticket offer.

Taxis charge a flat fare from Fiumicino to the city centre and can be booked online. Minibus taxis, such as **AirportShuttle**, charge per person.

Ciampino (CIA) is 15 km (9 miles) southeast of the city. The fastest way to Rome is by bus to Termini station (40 minutes). Bus companies include **Atral**. Taxis charge a flat fare to the city centre.

International Train Travel

Regular high-speed international trains connect Italy to the main towns and cities in Austria, Germany, France and Eastern Europe. Reservations for these services are essential and tickets are booked up quickly.

You can buy tickets and passes for multiple international journeys via **Eurail** or **Interrail**; however, you may still need to pay an additional reservation fee depending on which rail service you travel with. Always check that your pass is valid before boarding.

Regional and Local Train Travel

Trenitalia is the main train operator in Italy. Tickets can be bought online but there are only a fixed number available so book ahead.

Trenitalia (FS) and **Italo Treno** (NTV) both run a high-speed rail service. Reservations are essential. Rome's main stations are Termini and Tiburtina.

There is a useful train line to Ostia Antica and Ostia Lido from Stazione Porta San Paolo, next to Piramide Metro station.

Tickets must be validated by stamping them before boarding. Machines are positioned at the entrance to platforms in railway stations for this purpose. Heavy fines are levied if you are caught with an unvalidated ticket.

Public Transport

ATAC is Rome's main public transport authority. Safety and hygiene measures, timetables, ticket information, transport maps and more can be obtained from ATAC kiosks, the customer service office or the ATAC website.

Tickets

Tickets (*biglietti*) are available from kiosks, stations, bars, newsstands or any shop with the ATAC sticker in the window. Be aware that ticket machines only accept cash. Tickets cannot be bought on board – they must be bought in advance (there are automatic ticket machines at main bus stops and Metro stations) and must be validated on the day of travel.

Tickets are valid on all modes of public transport, including buses, trams, Metro and local train lines. Regular one-way tickets (BIT) valid for 75 minutes cost €1.50, day tickets (BIG) cost €7, three-day tickets (BTI) cost €18 and weekly passes (CIS) are €24. Children under 10 travel for free with an adult.

Metro

Rome's Metro (*Metropolitana*) has three lines – A, B and C. Line A runs from west to southeast and Line B runs from northeast to south. A and B meet at Termini station, and A and C at San Giovanni. Regional rail services connect with the Metro to serve the surrounding areas and the airports. Line C runs from Pantano station to San Giovanni, where it links with Line A.

Trains run every 4–10 minutes 5:30am–11:30pm daily, and 5:30am–1:30am on Friday and Saturday nights.

On street level, Metro stations are clearly marked by red and white "M" signs. At the station, use the maps to identify which line you need and then insert your ticket through the barrier to access the platform. The machine will return your ticket to you and you should keep it on you in case of inspection. Screens on the platform show the waiting time for the next train. Once you are onboard, Look out for your stop, as it may not be announced.

Trams

Trams cover the outskirts of the city centre and are a good way to get to the main sights while avoiding travelling through the crowded, and congested, centre. The most useful tram routes are No 2 (to MAXXI) and No 19 (connecting Vatican City with Villa Borghese).

Tram stops display the tram numbers that serve them and a list of stops on each route. Approaching trams display the route number and their destination.

Useful routes include Route 2 (along Via Flaminio) and Route 8 (between Largo Argentina and Trastevere).

Trams operate 5:30am–10:30pm or midnight daily, depending on the route (Route 8 runs until 3am on Friday and Saturday nights). Tickets must be stamped on board in the yellow machines.

Buses

Buses cover most of the city. When not stuck in traffic they are a quick way to reach the main sights and attractions of Rome.

The city's main bus terminus is on Piazza dei Cinquecento outside Termini station, but there are other major route hubs throughout the city, most usefully those at Piazza del Risorgimento and Piazza Venezia.

Bus stops display the bus numbers that serve them and a list of stops on each route. Regular services generally run every 10 to 20 minutes.

After 11:30pm a night bus service operates until 5.15am. Night buses are

marked with the letter "N" (for *notturno*) before the route number.

Buses must be flagged down. Enter at the front or back doors and exit via the middle door. Tickets must be stamped in the yellow machines located at the front or back of the bus. Press the button to request a stop.

For day trips, **COTRAL** blue buses run from several Rome terminals out into the suburbs and surrounding countryside.

Long-Distance Bus Travel

Long-distance coaches terminate at Tiburtina, which is the city's main coach station. Tickets and information for coaches to European cities are available from the **Eurolines**, **Flixbus** or **Italybus** websites.

Local buses, serving villages and towns within the Lazio region, are run by COTRAL. All bus stations used by COTRAL in Rome are linked to Metro stations. Tickets are purchased on the spot and cannot be booked in advance.

DIRECTORY

ARRIVING BY AIR

AirportShuttle
🔲 airportshuttle.it

Atral
🔲 atral-lazio.com

Ciampino and Fiumicino
🔲 adr.it

Leonardo Express
🔲 trenitalia.com

Sit Bus Shuttle
🔲 sitbusshuttle.com

Terravision
🔲 terravision.eu

INTERNATIONAL TRAIN TRAVEL

Eurail
🔲 eurail.com

Interrail
🔲 interrail.eu

REGIONAL AND LOCAL TRAIN TRAVEL

Italo Treno
🔲 italotreno.it

Trenitalia
🔲 trenitalia.com

PUBLIC TRANSPORT

ATAC
🔲 atac.roma.it

BUSES

COTRAL
🔲 cotralspa.it

LONG-DISTANCE BUS TRAVEL

Eurolines
🔲 eurolines.com

Flixbus
🔲 flixbus.it

Italybus
🔲 italybus.it

Guided Bus Tours

Big Bus Tours offers hop-on-hop-off tours of the city aboard double-decker buses. While travelling between stops, ticket holders can listen to audio guides, which are available in eight languages and detail the history of sites outside the windows as you pass by. Tours run every 15 to 20 minutes each day, with a first departure at 9am and a last departure at 7pm (6pm in winter). Buses can be boarded at any of the eight stops, which include the Colosseum, Trevi Fountain, Piazza Barberini and the Vatican. You can also buy "combo" tickets that include entry to the Colosseum and the Vatican, or night tours.

The **Roma Cristiana** bus is a similar tour, but with a Christian emphasis. It runs from Termini to Piazza San Pietro with stops close to religious sights, and also includes audio guides.

Taxis

Taxis in Rome are some of the most expensive in Europe and note that not all accept credit cards. They cannot be hailed; to take one, make for an official taxi stand, which are located at stations, main piazzas or close to key tourist sights – the most useful are at Termini, Piazza Venezia, Piazza di Spagna, Piazza del Popolo and Piazza Barberini. You can also reserve **Radiotaxi 3570** online, **Chiama Taxi** by phone or use the Uber app. When you order a

taxi by phone, the meter will run from the time of your call. Official taxis are white, have a "taxi" sign on the roof and their official taxi licence number is displayed on the doors.

When travelling to and from the airport, bear in mind that extra charges are added for each piece of luggage placed in the boot, for rides between 10pm and 7am, on Sundays and public holidays, and for journeys to and from airports. Report any problems with taxi drivers by calling 06 0608.

Driving to Rome

Rome is easily reachable from other European countries via E-roads, the International European Road Network connecting major roads across national borders within Europe, or by national (N) and secondary (SS) roads from neighbouring France, Switzerland, Austria and Slovenia. The city is also easily accessible from the rest of Italy.

Tolls are payable on most motorways (*autostrade*), and payment is made at the end of the journey in cash, by credit card or pre-paid magnetic VIA cards, available from tobacconists and the **ACI** (*Automobile Club d'Italia*). If you wish to avoid toll roads, there is almost always an alternative route signposted.

Note that if you bring your own foreign-registered car to Italy, you must carry a Green Card, the vehicle's registration documents and a valid driver's licence.

Car Rental

To rent a car in Italy you must be over 21 and have held a valid driver's licence with no points for at least one year.

Driving licences issued by any of the European Union member states are valid throughout the EU, including Italy.

If visiting from outside the EU, you may need to apply for an International Driving Permit (IDP). Check with your local automobile association before you travel.

Driving in Rome

Driving in Rome is not recommended – roads are congested and parking is extremely difficult, even for locals.

City centre streets are designated ZTL (*Zona a Traffico Limitato*) which means that only residents can drive and park there. Those arriving in the city by car are advised to leave it in a car park outside the city centre, and to travel into Rome by public transport from there. The **European Car Parking Guide** and **Saba** list free car parks on Rome's periphery. There are also car parks located near Villa Borghese and Piazza Partigiani. Look for a white "P" sign on a blue background. Metered parking is permitted in parking spaces identified by a blue line from 8am until 8pm.

If your vehicle is towed, call the municipal police. You can reach them by dialling 06 0606. Tell them where you parked and they will direct you to the nearest tow lot.

Once you have located your vehicle, you will have to pay a fee to retrieve it, in addition to the penalty for the parking violation.

Rules of the Road

It is important to abide by the following rules. Drive on the right, use the left lane only for passing and yield to traffic from the right. Seat belts must be worn by all passengers seated in both the front and back of the vehicle. Heavy fines are levied for using a mobile phone while driving.

The legal drink-drive limit is strictly enforced (p169). If you are drinking alcohol, use public transport or take a taxi.

During the day dipped headlights are compulsory when driving on motorways, dual carriageways and on all out-of-town roads. A red warning triangle and fluorescent vests must be carried at all times, for use in the event of an emergency.

If you have an accident or breakdown, switch on your hazard warning lights and place a warning triangle at least 50 m (55 yd) behind your vehicle. In the event of a breakdown, call the ACI emergency number (803 116) or the emergency services (112 or 113). The ACI will tow any foreign-registered car to the nearest ACI-affiliated garage for free.

Hitchhiking

Hitchhiking (autostop) is illegal on motorways, and is not commonplace in large cities such as Rome. In more rural areas it is a common transport method for travellers on a budget. Always consider your own safety before entering an unknown vehicle or letting someone into yours.

Cycle and Scooter Hire

Cycling in Rome can be a challenging task due to the city's hilly nature, the heavy traffic and the lack of bike paths, but it is still a green and convenient way to get around the city. If you are not up for urban cycling, a ride in Villa Borghese park can be a gentler and more enjoyable alternative. Bikes, tandems and rickshaws can all be hired by the entrance of the Pincio Gardens.

You can rent bicycles, motorcycles and scooters hourly or by the day. You may have to leave your passport with the rental shop as a deposit, and you must have a valid licence to hire a scooter or motorcycle. **Bici & Baci** and **Barberini Scooters for Rent** offer bike and scooter rental by the hour and by the day.

Motorcyclists, scooter drivers and any of their passengers must wear helmets by law; these can be rented from most hire shops. Unless you are an experienced moped or scooter rider, it is wise not to ride in Rome.

Walking

Everything from St Peter's and the Janiculum to Villa Borghese and beyond can be seen without having to use public transport. In fact, much of the city is made up of narrow lanes and alleys, which are impenetrable to buses, and many streets are pedestrianized.

Wandering through Rome's historic centre is one of the most enjoyable aspects of any visit to the city. You can take in the architectural details, absorb the streetlife and peek into any church, shop or bar that catches your interest.

To travel safely on foot, wear sensible shoes, cross streets only when the green avanti sign is lit and wait at the crossing when the red alt sign is lit. In summer, keep to the shady, narrow streets rather than main piazzas, as they can be very hot.

DIRECTORY

GUIDED BUS TOURS

Big Bus Tours
W bigbustours.com

Roma Cristiana
W operaromana
pellegrinaggi.org

TAXIS

Chiama Taxi
C 060609

Radiotaxi 3570
W 3570.it

DRIVING TO ROME

ACI
W aci.it

DRIVING IN ROME

**European Car
Parking Guide**
W car-parking.eu/italy/
rome/pr

Saba
W sabait.it

CYCLE AND
SCOOTER HIRE

**Barberini Scooters
for Rent**
W rentscooter.it

Bici & Baci
W bicibaci.com

Practical Information

Passports and Visas

For entry requirements, including visas, consult your nearest Italian embassy or check the **Polizia di Stato** website. Citizens of the UK, US, Canada, Australia and New Zealand do not need a visa for stays of up to three months, but, from 2024, must apply in advance for the European Travel Information and Authorization System (**ETIAS**). Visitors from other countries may also require an ETIAS, so check before travelling. EU nationals do not need a visa or an ETIAS.

Government Advice

Now more than ever, it is important to consult both your and the Italian government's advice before travelling. The **UK Foreign and Commonwealth Office**, the **US State Department**, the **Australian Department of Foreign Affairs and Trade** and the Italian **Ministero della Salute** offer the latest information on security, health and local regulations.

Customs Information

You can find information on the laws relating to goods and currency taken in or out of Italy on the **ENIT** (Italy's national tourist board) website.

For EU citizens there are no limits on most goods taken in or out of Italy provided they are for personal use only. Exceptions include firearms and weapons, endangered species and some types of food and plants. Non-EU residents can claim back sales tax on purchases over €155.

Insurance

We recommend taking out a comprehensive insurance policy covering theft, loss of belongings, medical care, cancellations and delays, and read the small print carefully.

UK citizens are eligible for free emergency medical care in Germany provided they have a valid European Health Insurance Card (EHIC) or UK Global Health Insurance Card (**GHIC**).

Health

Italy has a world-class healthcare system. Emergency medical care in Italy is free for all EU and Australian citizens. If you have an EHIC card, present this as soon as possible. You may have to pay after treatment and reclaim the money later.

For other visitors, payment of medical costs is the responsibility of the patient. It is important to arrange comprehensive medical insurance before travelling.

No vaccinations are necessary for visiting Italy, and there are few health hazards in Rome. Wear hats and sunscreen, stay out of the sun, and drink plenty of water in summer. Tap water is drinkable.

Pharmacies are indicated by a green cross. Many will sell common drugs including antibiotics without a prescription. If you run out of medicine you take regularly, most pharmacists will sell replacements, especially if you have the packaging.

There are two 24-hour clinics aimed at tourists, which are run by the **Guardia Medica Turistica**. English is spoken in both.

Smoking, Alcohol and Drugs

Smoking is banned in enclosed public places in Rome. Possession of narcotics is prohibited and could result in a prison sentence.

Italians tend to drink only with meals and are unlikely to be seen drunk – obvious drunkenness is frowned upon.

Italy has a strict limit of 0.05 per cent BAC (blood alcohol content) for drivers. This means that you cannot drink more than a small beer or a small glass of wine if you plan to drive. For drivers with less than three years' driving experience the limit is 0.

ID

By law you must carry identification with you at all times in Italy. A photocopy of your passport photo page (and visa if applicable) should suffice. If you are stopped by the police you may be asked to present the original document within 12 hours.

Personal Security

Italy is relatively safe, and even in a big city like Rome street violence is rare. The historic centre is well policed, but pickpocketing is common, particularly on public transport and at popular tourist sites. Take particular care on crowded bus routes such as 23, 40 and 64. When you're travelling in the city, keep your belongings in a safe place and with you at all times.

Bag-snatching scooter drivers are a problem, so hold bags on the inside of the pavement where possible, especially in crowded tourist areas.

There are two police forces, the **Carabinieri**, the military branch, and the **Polizia di Stato**, the civil branch. Crimes can be reported to either, and both can issue the crime or loss reports *(denuncia di furto o smarrimento)* that you will need when making an insurance claim for theft or loss. Contact your embassy if you have your passport stolen, or in the event of a serious crime or accident.

For **emergency police**, **ambulance** or **fire brigade services** dial 112 – the operator will ask which service you require. For **ambulance** emergencies you can also dial 118 and for the **fire brigade** the direct number is 115.

As a rule, Romans are very accepting of all people, regardless of their race, gender or sexuality. Homosexuality was legalized in 1887 and in 1982, Italy became the third country to recognize the right to legally change your gender. If you do feel unsafe, the **Safe Space Alliance** pinpoints your nearest place of refuge.

Women may receive unwanted and unwelcome attention, especially around tourist areas. If you feel threatened, head straight for the nearest police station.

Travellers with Specific Requirements

Rome's historic towns and cobbled streets are ill-equipped for disabled access. Many buildings do not have wheelchair access or lifts. Always call ahead to ensure that your needs will be met.

Assistance at airports can be arranged by notifying your airline company or travel agent of your particular needs in advance of your trip. **ADR Assistance** can coordinate assistance at Rome's Ciampino or Fiumicino or airports. Train travellers with Trenitalia *(see p163)* can arrange special reservations and assistance at stations.

Some museums, including the Vatican, offer tours in Italian Sign Language (LIS) and American Sign Language (ASL), as well as multi-sensory tactile tours.

DIRECTORY

PASSPORTS AND VISAS

Polizia di Stato
w poliziadistato.it

ETIAS
w etiasvisa.com

GOVERNMENT ADVICE

Australian Department of Foreign Affairs and Trade
w dfat.gov.au
w smartraveller.gov.au

Ministero della Salute
w salute.gov.it

UK Foreign and Commonwealth Office
w gov.uk/foreign-travel-advice

US State Department
w travel.state.gov

CUSTOMS INFORMATION

ENIT
w italia.it

INSURANCE

GHIC
w ghic.org.uk

HEALTH

Guardia Medica Turistica
MAP D2 & C5
■ Via Canova 19 and Via Morosini 30
C 06 7730 6112

PERSONAL SECURITY

Ambulance
C 118

Carabinieri
C 112
w carabinieri.it

Fire Brigade
C 115

Police, Ambulance and Fire Brigade
C 112

Polizia di Stato
C 113

Safe Space Alliance
w safespacealliance.com

TRAVELLERS WITH SPECIFIC REQUIREMENTS

ADR Assistance
w adr.it

Time Zone

Italy operates on Central European Time (CET), which is 1 hour ahead of Greenwich Mean Time (GMT) and 6 hours ahead of US Eastern Standard Time (EST). The clock moves forward 1 hour during daylight saving time from the last Sunday in March until the last Sunday in October.

Money

Italy is one of the 19 European countries using the euro (€). Most establishments accept major credit, debit and prepaid currency cards.

Contactless payments are becoming increasingly common in Rome, but it's always a good idea to carry some cash for smaller items such as coffee, gelato, pizza-by-the-slice, and when visiting markets or more remote areas. Ticket machines at stations also tend to accept cash over debit and credit cards.

Wait staff should be tipped €1–2 and hotel porters and housekeeping will expect €1 per bag or day.

Electrical Appliances

The electricity supply in Italy is 220–230 volts. Power sockets are type F and L, fitting plugs with two and three round-pronged pins. As there are two types of socket, some Italian appliances require an adaptor – ask as you make a purchase. All electrical appliances with non-Italian plugs will also need adaptors.

Mobile Phones and Wi-Fi

Fast speed internet and Wi-Fi is available in cafés and hotels all over the city. The city council also provides free Wi-Fi in many piazzas throughout the city – all Wi-Fi zones are clearly marked – but you need to have an Italian mobile number, as registration is done online and accounts are validated users dialling a free number that is only accessible domestically. The WiFi°Italia° app allows you to connect quickly and easily to free Wi-Fi hotspots throughout Rome and Italy.

Italy's dialling code is 39. In Italy the regional phone code is an integral part of every number, and always has to be dialled. Rome's area code is 06.

Visitors with EU tariffs will be able to use their devices abroad without being affected by roaming charges. This means that you pay the same rates as you would at home. Americans will need a triband phone. Your home provider will have roaming options, but check rates carefully. A cheaper alternative may be to purchase an Italian SIM card (you will need ID).

Postal Services

The Italian postal system, **Poste Italiane**, can be appallingly slow. If using Poste Italiane, avoid sending registered mail as it tends to accumulate at the collection point before being sent on. If speed is of the essence for destinations within Italy, use the postal system's courier service, Posta Celere; for international destinations use a private courier such as **DHL**. Stamps (*francobolli*) are on sale at post offices and tobacconists, and often (unofficially) at any shop selling postcards.

The Vatican City and San Marino have their own post systems and stamps. Only letters bearing San Marino or Vatican stamps can be posted in San Marino and Vatican postboxes.

Weather

Rome has a temperate climate. High season is Easter to July and September to October. Most of the city's shops and restaurants close through much of August as residents head to the beaches or mountains to escape the heat, but there are still a few tourists around.

Opening Hours

The days when Rome's museums and sights closed for *riposo*, the long lunch break are fast becoming history. Most major museums and sights stay open all day, as do an increasing number of supermarkets and international chain stores. But some shops, churches and other small businesses still follow tradition and shut for a few hours in the afternoon. Many museums, art galleries and archaeological sites are closed on Monday and last admission is usually an hour before closing time. On Sunday, restaurants usually close for lunch.

The COVID-19 pandemic proved that situations can change suddenly. Always check before visiting attractions and hospitality venues for up-to-date hours and booking requirements.

Visitor Information

The first port of call for general tourist information are **06 0608**, the city's information service and the **ENIT** (Italian State Tourism Board). The Roma Turismo website also has a lot of well-organized tourist information.

The 2- and 3-day **Roma Pass** cards are excellent value for visitors as they include travel on all public transport plus free entry to two museums and discounted entry to many others.

The **Omnia Rome and Vatican Pass** (€129 for three days) offers a similar package, but also includes the Vatican Museums.

Many national and city museums offer free entry to under 18s, and discounts for students. During the Beni Culturali (Culture and Heritage week) in the Spring, admission to all state-run sites is free.

Local Customs

Italians are relatively relaxed when it comes to etiquette. Strangers usually shake hands, while friends and family greet each other with a kiss on each cheek. But there are some strict rules. You can be fined for dropping litter, sitting on monument steps or eating or drinking outside historic sites, churches and public buildings.

When visiting churches and cathedrals, strict dress codes apply: cover your torso and upper arms, and ensure shorts and skirts cover your knees. Shoes must be worn.

It is an offence to swim or bathe in – or, in some cases, even sit on – public fountains. You can also be fined for buying something from illegal street traders.

Language

Italian is the official language spoken in Rome. The level of English spoken in the city varies. Many of those working in the major tourist areas speak very good English. However, a little knowledge of the local language goes a long way, and locals appreciate visitors' efforts to speak Italian, even if you can only manage a few words.

Taxes and Refunds

VAT (IVA) in Italy is usually 22 per cent. Under certain conditions, non-EU citizens can claim a rebate.

Either claim the rebate before you buy an item (show your passport to the shop assistant and complete a form), or you can claim it retrospectively by presenting a receipt to a customs officer as you leave. Stamped receipts will be sent back to the vendor to issue a refund.

Accommodation

Rome has a great range of memorable places to stay, from opulent grand hotels and chic boutique places to lodgings run by religious organizations and hostels. The ENIT website provides an extensive list of options. To avoid disappointment, and inflated prices, book well in advance.

All accommodation in Rome – five-star hotels, rented rooms, flats and even campsites – is by law obliged to add the city tourist tax to its rates. This varies between €3 and €7 per night – always check if it is included in the rate quoted to you. The tax is charged for a maximum of 10 nights.

Under Italian law, hotels are required to register guests at the local police headquarters and to issue a receipt of payment (ricevuta fiscale), which you must keep until you leave Italy.

DIRECTORY

POSTAL SERVICES

DHL
w dhl.it/en.html

Poste Italiane
w poste.it

VISITOR INFORMATION

06 0608
t 06 0608
w 060608.it

ENIT
w italia.it
w enit.it

Roma Pass
w romapass.it

Omnia Rome and Vatican Pass
w romeandvatican pass.com

Places to Stay

PRICE CATEGORIES
For a standard, double room per night (with breakfast if included), taxes and extra charges.

€ under €150   €€ €150–350   €€€ over €350

Luxury Hotels

Atlante Star
MAP B2 ■ Via Vitelleschi 34 ■ 06 686 386 ■ www.atlantehotels.com ■ €€€
In a grand 19th-century building with old-world charm, this hotel offers its guests attentive service and extras such as a free airport pick-up and Jacuzzis. The rooftop garden and restaurant is famous for its spectacular panorama of the nearby St Peter's Basilica.

Giulio Cesare
MAP B2 ■ Via degli Scipioni 287 ■ 06 321 0751 ■ www.hotelgiulio cesare.com ■ €
Formerly the patrician villa of a countess, this hotel's atmosphere is still aristocratic. Chandeliers, antiques, art, Oriental carpets and a grand piano typify the quiet elegance of the public rooms. Mirror-lined hallways lead to elegant bedrooms with marble baths. You can eat at outdoor tables in a lovely terrace garden. It is located on a quiet street close to the Vatican.

De Russie
MAP D2 ■ Via del Babuino 9 ■ 06 328 881 ■ www.roccofortehotels.com ■ €€€
This historic hotel, a favourite of Picasso, has been refurbished in a sumptuous, understated style. Delights include terraced garden cafés; an excellent restaurant; the Stravinskij (see p122), one of Rome's most renowned cocktail bars; a spa and gym and a secret garden on the Pincio. All of its bedrooms are decorated in elegant muted colours and provide sheer comfort.

Fendi Private Suites
MAP D2 ■ Via della Fontanella di Borghese 48 ■ 06 9779 8080 ■ www.fendiprivate suites.com/en ■ €€€
Owned by the renowned fashion designer, this grand Palazzo has seven suites that focus on luxury and privacy, each with a view of the city. The decor combines old-school elegance and modern comfort. There is a "pillow menu" for picky sleepers, and even iPads featuring exclusive ideas for walking tour. A superb Japanese restaurant, Zuma (see p140), offers views overlooking the city, perfect for a special occasion or a romantic meal.

Grand Hotel Flora
MAP E2 ■ Via Veneto 191 ■ 06 489 929 ■ www.marriott.com ■ €€€
Set in a Neo-Classical building, this gracious and elegant hotel has the air of refinement you expect on Via Veneto, combined with efficient service. The decor features marble, antiques and soft colours. The Ailanto Roof Garden restaurant boasts views of the great dome of St Peter's Basilica, the Villa Borghese park and the beautiful skyline of the city. There is also a piano bar. The hotel is part of the Marriott chain.

Hassler
MAP D2 ■ Piazza Trinità dei Monti 6 ■ 06 699 340 ■ www.hotelhassler roma.com ■ €€€
In one of the few genteel hotels that's not yet part of a luxury chain, the honey-coloured tones of the public rooms set the mood of timeless luxury. The sumptuous suites and the terrace restaurant offer some of the most magnificent views in the city. Its elegant restaurant, Imàgo (see p74), has been awarded a Michelin star for its imaginative Italian fusion cuisine.

J.K. Place
MAP L1 ■ Via Monte D'Oro 30 ■ 06 982 634 ■ www.jkroma.com ■ €€€
Providing a truly deluxe experience, J.K. Place has impeccably furnished rooms and suites. The decor combines antiques and modern design pieces to create a "Dolce Vita" retro feel. Service is informal but attentive, and the café, which is open all day, has a great menu of Italian and international classics.

Dharma Luxury
MAP E3 ■ Torino 123 ■ 06 481 4085 ■ www.dharmagroup.it ■ €€
Each of the 29 rooms at Dharma Luxury has its own unique decor

inspired by the history of the building, always with a charming, contemporary touch. The suites have private spas, including a jacuzzi and steam bath. Piazza della Repubblica and Termini Station are only a short walk away and there is a 10 per cent discount on offer for the nearby restaurants, Cotto and Cucina Nazionale.

Regina Baglioni
MAP E2 ▪ Via Veneto 72 ▪ 06 421 111 ▪ www. baglionihotels.com ▪ €€€
A setting fit for a king, which it has been more than once. With extravagant Italian Art Nouveau styling, wall silks, opulent carpets, paintings, marble floors and antiques, this hotel is a palace inside and out. A beautiful wrought-iron staircase, watched over by a statue of Neptune, leads up to the rooms from the reception area. Suites on the seventh floor have panoramic views.

St Regis Grand
MAP E3 ▪ Via V E Orlando 3 ▪ 06 470 91 ▪ www.marriott.com ▪ €€€
The extravagant St Regis Grand was set up by César Ritz in 1894, and continues to live up to the illustrious hotelier's name. Completely restored, it attracts guests drawn from the ranks of royalty, heads of state, captains of industry and famous celebrities. A world-class restaurant, Vivendo, a business centre and a fitness club complete its offerings.

Romantic Hotels

Grand Hotel del Gianicolo
MAP B4 ▪ Viale delle Mura Gianicolensi 107 ▪ 06 5833 3405 ▪ www.grand hotelgianicolo.it ▪ €€
Located on the hill above Trastevere, this former convent offers every amenity, including roof gardens, beautiful lawns and a swimming pool. The location is serene, despite nearby traffic. Public rooms feature Venetian glass fixtures.

San Anselmo and Villa San Pio
MAP D5 ▪ Piazza Sant' Anselmo 2 and Via di Santa Melania ▪ 06 570 057 ▪ www.aventino hotels.com ▪ €€
Nestled on a tranquil hill, both these adjacent establishments are spacious and pleasant. Rococo decor predominates, and includes elegant tapestries and chandeliers. Shiatsu massages are also available on request.

Farnese
MAP C1 ▪ Via Alessandro Farnese 30 ▪ 06 321 2553 ▪ www.hotelfarnese.com ▪ €€
This *belle époque* mansion is furnished with period authenticity. Captivating *trompe l'oeil* fresco decorations, modern bathrooms and a roof garden are just a few of its attractions. Rich fabrics and high ceilings are typical of the rooms.

Lifestyle Suites Rome
MAP L3 ▪ Piazza Navona 93 ▪ 06 686 4568 ▪ www. lifestylesuitesrome.com ▪ €€€
Housed in a 15th-century building, this lovely hotel blends historical charm with contemporary comfort. The gorgeous rooftop terrace makes for fabulous aperitivos and offers stunning views of Piazza Navona.

Lord Byron
MAP B2 ▪ Via G de Notaris 5 ▪ 06 322 0404 ▪ www.lordbyronhotel. com ▪ €€€
This refined boutique hotel was originally a monastery, but there is nothing ascetic about it nowadays. The decor is an eclectic mix of styles and periods, but all of it evokes opulence. Its location provides serene solitude that makes a perfect antidote to the hectic life of the centre.

Piranesi Palazzo Naier
MAP D2 ▪ Via del Babuino 196 ▪ 06 328 041 ▪ www.palazzo naier.com ▪ €€€
Located just off the Piazza del Popolo, this is a romantic boutique hotel run by a charming family. The bedrooms have wooden floors and are beautifully decorated with brocade. There are fine views of the city from the pretty roof terrace.

Crossing Condotti
MAP N1 ▪ Via Mario de' Fiori 28 ▪ 06 6992 0633 ▪ www.crossingcondotti. com ▪ €€€
This private residence offers the comfort of a wonderful downtown house, complete with a shared kitchenette with tea and coffee-making facilities. The nine rooms are decorated with the owner's art and antiques.

Portrait Roma
MAP D2 ▪ Via Bocca di Leone 23 ▪ 06 6938 0742 ▪ www.lungarno collection.com ▪ €€€

The classic Italian home inspired this luxury boutique hotel, created with couples in mind. The suites are elegant and romantic, with designer furnishings and customized service.

Raphael
MAP L3 ▪ Largo Febo 2 ▪ 06 682 831 ▪ www. raphaelhotel.com ▪ €€€

Set behind Piazza Navona in a burnt-siena palazzo, the location could not be more perfect. The foyer is full of unusual art treasures and most of the rooms are originally decorated.

Westin Excelsior
MAP E2 ▪ Via Veneto 125 ▪ 06 470 81 ▪ www. marriott.com ▪ €€€

The grande dame of Rome's hotels, noted for its commanding location and *belle époque* architecture, boasting sculpted balconies with caryatids. Notes of grandeur abound everywhere you look, with sumptuous rooms and classic decor. There is a spa with a pool and several fine restaurants.

Rooms with a View

Albergo del Senato
MAP M3 ▪ Piazza della Rotonda 73 ▪ 06 678 4343 ▪ www.alber godelsenato.it ▪ €€

Situated in a 19th-century palazzo, this charming hotel features sumptuous rooms with gorgeous wooden floors. Some rooms also have valuted ceilings and original decorations. The large terrace offers breathtaking views of the Pantheon.

Homs
MAP D2 ▪ Via della Vite 71–2 ▪ 06 679 2976 ▪ www.hotelhoms.it ▪ €€

On a quiet shopping street, this mid-sized hotel with antique furnishings has a gracious feel. Out of the two roof terraces, one is indoors for year-round breakfasts, from which you can admire Rome's skyline.

The Vista Rooms and Terrace
MAP M3 ▪ Via di Torre Argentina, 76 ▪ 06 3972 3919 ▪ www.thevista roomsandterrace.com ▪ €€

A centrally located, beautifully decorated no-frills hotel with a view over the rooftops of Rome. There is a great breakfast available, as well as cooking classes and a co-working area.

Abruzzi
MAP M3 ▪ Piazza della Rotonda 69 ▪ 06 9784 1351 ▪ www.hotel abruzzi.it ▪ €€

Located in the heart of the city centre, this hotel offers large rooms decorated with charming images of ancient Rome. Ask for a room that opens onto the dazzling view of the piazza and Pantheon.

Inn at the Spanish Steps
MAP D2 ▪ Via dei Condotti 85 ▪ 06 6992 5657 ▪ www.theinn atspanishsteps.com ▪ €€

This upmarket hotel is in a 17th-century building once lived in by Danish author Hans Christian Andersen. It offers great views of the Spanish Steps from its attractive rooftop garden. The well-equipped rooms feature an iPod docking station and a coffee machine.

Scalinata di Spagna
MAP D2 ▪ Piazza Trinità dei Monti 17 ▪ 06 458 6150 ▪ www.hotel scalinata.com ▪ €€

With its coveted location housed in an 18th-century villa at the top of the Spanish Steps, this intimate jewel boasts marvellous views from many of its rooms and from the trellis-covered terrace. The rooms are not large but are beautifully appointed. Book well in advance.

Sole al Pantheon
MAP M3 ▪ Piazza della Rotonda 63 ▪ 06 678 0441 ▪ www.hotelsoleal pantheon.com ▪ €€€

Noted as an inn since 1467, this distinguished hotel was the choice of Renaissance writer Ariosto. Facing the Pantheon, it has painted period decoration in many of the rooms and modern touches such as Jacuzzis and double-glazing.

Torre Colonna
MAP P4 ▪ Via delle Tre Cannelle 18 ▪ 06 8360 0192 ▪ www.torre colonna.it ▪ €€

Housed inside a medieval defensive tower, this boutique hotel sits right on top of the Imperial Fora. Each of the five individually decorated rooms has a Jacuzzi and there is also one on the terrace, with wonderful views overlooking the Fora.

Albergo Mozart
MAP D2 ▪ Via dei Greci 23B ▪ 06 3600 1915 ▪ www.hotelmozart.com ▪ €€

Great value and refined furnishings define this hotel, which is an eight-minute walk away from Piazza di Spagna. There is a fireplace for the winter months and a marvelous roof terrace with picturesque views.

Sofitel Villa Borghese
MAP E2 ▪ Via Lombardia 47 ▪ 06 478 021 ▪ www. sofitel.accor.com ▪ €€€

Housed in a renovated palazzo, this luxurious hotel has a classically elegant, modern interior and offers superb views of the Villa Borghese park from its top floor terrace.

Comfort, Style and Value Hotels

Des Artistes
MAP F3 ▪ Via Villafranca 20 ▪ 06 445 4365 ▪ www. hoteldesartistes.com ▪ €

A cheerful hotel with accommodation options to suit all budgets. Warm fabrics, modern art and marble bathrooms create an air of luxury, and all of the rooms have data ports. There's a floor with rooms set aside for travellers on a budget and a pleasant roof terrace. One of the best choices near Termini.

Oxford
MAP E2 ▪ Via Boncompagni 89 ▪ 06 420 3601 ▪ www. hoteloxford.com ▪ €€

Just a few steps away from the famous Via Veneto, this hotel offers well-equipped, classic

rooms and a reliably good American-style buffet breakfast.

La Rovere
MAP B3 ▪ Vicolo Sant' Onofrio 4 ▪ 06 6880 6739 ▪ www.hotel larovere. com ▪ €€

This quiet, family-run hotel is a short walk from the centro storico. The rooms here are a charming mix of modern and classic styles.

Mecenate Palace
MAP F3 ▪ Via Carlo Alberto 3 ▪ 06 4470 2024 ▪ www.mecenatepalace. com ▪ €€

With views of Santa Maria Maggiore (see p131), this comfortable hotel's name recalls a great patron of the arts from the time of Augustus Caesar. The terrace café is ideal for small conferences and the meeting hall holds up to 40 people.

Teatropace 33
MAP L2 ▪ Via del Teatro Pace 33 ▪ 06 687 9075 ▪ www.hotelteatropace. com ▪ €€

In a quiet street just a few minutes' walk from Piazza Navona, Teatropace 33 occupies a beautiful ochre former cardinal's palazzo, wonderfully restored. Every room in the stylish interior is different. No lift.

Tritone
MAP P1 ▪ Via del Tritone 210 ▪ 06 6992 2575 ▪ www. tritonehotel.com ▪ €€

Near the Trevi Fountain and Piazza Barberini, Tritone has comfortable rooms and good-quality decor. The emphasis is on tranquillity, ensured by double-glazing and wall-to-wall carpeting.

The superior rooms feature wood-veneered walls. Breakfast in the roof garden is a joy.

9Hotel Cesàri
MAP N2 ▪ Via di Pietra 89A ▪ 06 674 9701 ▪ www. 9-hotel-cesari-rome.it ▪ €€

Close to the Pantheon next to the Temple of Hadrian, this little gem was famous in the 1800s, when French writer Stendhal stayed here. The exterior is little changed. The interior, however, has been kept up to date, set off with antiques and old prints. All rooms have blue marble bathrooms.

Condotti
MAP N1 ▪ Via Mario de' Fiori 37 ▪ 06 679 4661 ▪ www.hotelcondotti. com ▪ €

Amid the designer boutiques along this street, the Condotti Hotel offers comfort and period furnishings. All rooms are soundproofed, and many feature views over the rooftops; one has a terrace. The staff are unfailingly attentive.

Dei Borgognoni
MAP P1 ▪ Via del Bufalo 126 ▪ 06 6994 1505 ▪ www.hotelborgognoni. it ▪ €€

Although just around the corner from the bustling historic centre, this up-to-date period building feels removed from it all. Subdued lighting and colours enhance the antique accents, and the hushed garden is very inviting. Some rooms have private patios. Fitness clubs and sports facilities are also available at this hotel.

For a key to hotel price categories see p170

Pantheon
MAP M3 ▪ Via dei Pastini 131 ▪ 06 678 7746 ▪ www.hotelpantheon.com ▪ €€€
Close to the eponymous temple (see pp18–19), this establishment has public areas with stained glass, mosaics and beamed ceilings. The door to each room has an antique print of a Rome obelisk.

Santa Maria
MAP K6 ▪ Vicolo del Piede 2 ▪ 06 589 4626 ▪ www.hotelsantamaria trastevere.it ▪ €
Occupying a 16th-century cloister, this is an oasis of calm within the bustling Trastevere area. Ground-floor rooms (one is adapted for disabled guests) surround a courtyard garden, filled with citrus trees. A wine bar serves snacks and drinks. Single-rate as well as multiple-occupancy rooms are available.

Business Hotels

Dei Consoli
MAP B2 ▪ Via Varrone 2D ▪ 06 6889 2972 ▪ www.hoteldeiconsoli.com ▪ €€
Elegant hotel with all the facilities, including Wi-Fi, hydromassage and meeting rooms. Enjoy breakfast on the roof terrace with views of St Peter's.

Forum
MAP P4 ▪ Via Tor de' Conti 25–30 ▪ 06 679 2446 ▪ www.hotelforum.com ▪ €€
Set in an 18th-century converted convent, this hotel has a sunny roof garden restaurant and bar which overlooks the Imperial Fora (see pp26–7). The meeting room can seat up to 100 people and is equipped with full facilities.

Nazionale a Montecitorio
MAP M1 ▪ Piazza Montecitorio 131 ▪ 06 695 001 ▪ www.hotel nazionale.it ▪ €€€
Located next to the Italian Parliament, in the heart of the historic city center, this hotel in a 16th-century palace has welcomed many politicos. It has a regal atmosphere, especially in the marble-floored restaurant.

Parco dei Principi
MAP E2 ▪ Via G Frescobaldi 5 ▪ 06 854 421 ▪ www.parcodei principi.com ▪ €€€
Just at the edge of Villa Borghese park stands this modern high-rise, yet inside all is over-the-top Italian court decor. Panoramas from every room take in greenery and the city's domes. There's a gym, a pool, patios, lounges and a business centre as well.

Radisson Blu GHR Hotel
MAP F3 ▪ Via Filippo Turati 171 ▪ 06 444 841 ▪ www.radissonhotels.com/en-us/destination/italy/rome ▪ €€
A contemporary hotel with high-tech conference facilities, and a rooftop bar and restaurant.

Sina Bernini Bristol
MAP Q1 ▪ Piazza Barberini 23 ▪ 06 488 931 ▪ www.sinahotels.com ▪ €€€
This brick building faces Bernini's Triton fountain (see p138). The decor is simple and the hotel has excellent facilities. There's a roof garden, and top rooms have fine views.

Grand Hotel Plaza
MAP D2 ▪ Via del Corso 126 ▪ 06 6992 1111 ▪ www.grandhotelplaza.com ▪ €€€
Dating from 1860, the Grand Hotel Plaza is one of Rome's oldest hotels, and is replete with Edwardian lavishness. Grand salons with frescoes, stained-glass skylights, chandeliers and antiques combined with modern amenities produce a comfortable ambience. Some of the rooms have a private terrace, and the two large rooftop terraces offer views of the city.

Anantara Palazzo Naiadi
MAP E3 ▪ Piazza della Repubblica 47 ▪ 06 489 381 ▪ www.nh-hotels.com ▪ €€€
Set in a majestic palazzo overlooking the Baths of Diocletian (see p137), this five-star luxury hotel provides top service and quality. The decor recalls Neo-Classical elegance and the roof terrace is a perfect place for a business lunch.

Rome Cavalieri Waldorf Astoria
MAP B1 ▪ Via Cadlolo 101 ▪ 06 350 91 ▪ www.romecavalieri.com ▪ €€€
This hotel is possibly the best place in Rome for doing business on a grand scale, thanks to its two restaurants – La Pergola (see p74) has three Michelin stars and is Rome's finest dining experience – four bars, indoor and outdoor pools, beauty salon, spa, fitness centre, tennis courts and parks.

Budget Hotels

Columbia

MAP E3 ▪ Via del Viminale 15 ▪ 06 488 3509 ▪ www.hotel columbia.com ▪ €€

Located in Termini, this quiet gem of a hotel is close to the Baths of Diocletian and has good transport options for sightseeing. Dark wood and light-coloured fabrics create an airy feel. The breakfast buffet can be enjoyed on the beautiful roof terrace.

Locanda Carmel

MAP K6 ▪ Via Goffredo Mameli 11 ▪ 06 580 9921 ▪ www.hotelcarmel.it ▪ €

A *pensione*-style place with spartan decor and modest rooms. There's a vine-covered terrace and most rooms have double-glazing. A unique touch is the kosher kitchen for Jewish guests. A wide selection of Italian and kosher wines are also available here.

Adriatic Hotel

MAP B3 ▪ Via Giovanni Vitelleschi, 25 ▪ 06 6880 8080 ▪ www. adriatichotel.com ▪ €

A good-value hotel in a well-positioned location, between Castel Sant' Angelo and the Vatican. Rooms have private bathrooms, with air conditioning available for an extra fee.

TMark Hotel Vaticano

MAP B2 ▪ Viale Vaticano 99 ▪ 06 3974 5562 ▪ www.tmarkhotel vaticano.it ▪ €€€

Close to the Vatican, with an attractive foyer and large rooms. Terraces and a roof garden with great views are outstanding features for this price range. Staff provide quality service. On a fairly quiet shopping street, handy for public transport. Free cable TV and airport shuttle.

Artorius

MAP R4 ▪ Via del Boschetto 13 ▪ 06 482 1196 ▪ www.hotelartorius rome.com ▪ €€

On one of Monti's prettiest roads, this two-star family-run hotel offers a relaxing experience at reasonable prices. The rooms are spacious, comfortable and elegant, and there's a pleasant bar.

Buonanotte Garibaldi

MAP C4 ▪ Via Garibaldi 83 ▪ 06 5833 0733 ▪ www. buonanottegaribaldi.com ▪ €€

This small, luxury B&B in the heart of Trastevere was carved out of an art studio and is a perfect romantic getaway. Breakfast is served in the elegant dining room or in the lush courtyard. Take a pick from the Rome, Chocolate or Tinto rooms, which have all been decorated by the owner herself.

Campo de' Fiori

MAP L4 ▪ Via del Biscione 6 ▪ 06 6880 6865 ▪ www. hotelcampodefiori.com ▪ €€€

This cosy boutique hotel is housed in a medieval building, which has been restored and decorated with mirrors, frescoes and antique coffered ceilings to highlight its orginal features. The roof terrace offers a panoramic view of the spires and domes of Rome's ancient quarter. Friendly staff provide an excellent service.

Hotel King

MAP Q1 ▪ Via Sistina 231 ▪ www.hotelkingroma. com ▪ €

With the Spanish Steps just a short walk away, this hotel is wonderfully located. Rooms are modern – each one is equipped with a satellite TV and air conditioning. A play area, pleasant veranda and gym are also available.

Sant'Anna

MAP B3 ▪ Borgo Pio 134 ▪ 06 6880 1602 ▪ www.santannahotel. net ▪ €€

This fashionable, small hotel in the medieval Borgo next to St Peter's Basilica has frescoes in the breakfast room and a fountain in the courtyard. The rooms are spacious and those situated at the top have their own tiny balconies. The area, so close to the Vatican, is quiet and still retains the feel of old Rome.

Smeraldo

MAP M4 ▪ Vicolo dei Chiodaroli 9 ▪ 06 687 5929 ▪ www.smeraldo roma.com ▪ €€

An excellent choice both in terms of location and quality. The name honours the emerald-green marble entrance, and there are marble accents throughout the building. Rooms are clean and simple and some have private balconies. There are two terraces.

For a key to hotel price categories see p170

Hostels and Religious Institutions

B&B Il Covo
MAP R4 ▪ Via del Boschetto 91 ▪ 06 484 894 ▪ www.bbilcovo.com ▪ €
A simple but charming B&B in the heart of Monti, with wooden beams and brick-vaulted ceilings. Breakfast is served downstairs at the café.

The Beehive
MAP K4 ▪ Via Marghera 8 ▪ 06 4470 4553 ▪ www.the-beehive.com ▪ €
Run by an American couple, this contemporary hotel-cum-hostel is near Roma Termini but is quiet with a secluded walled garden. It offers free Internet access and national phone calls.

Centro Diffusione Spiritualità
MAP J5 ▪ Via dei Riari 44 ▪ 06 6880 6122 ▪ No credit cards ▪ No air conditioning ▪ www.villariari.it ▪ €
This religious house, next to the botanical gardens in Trastevere, is a bit characterless but clean and well organized, and has a lovely garden. There is an 11pm curfew.

Fraterna Domus
MAP C3 ▪ Via di Monte Brianzo 62 ▪ 06 6880 2727 ▪ www.fraterna-domus.it/english.html ▪ €
A small hostel built around a 6th-century church and run by a group of friendly nuns, Fraterna Domus has small, clean and comfortable rooms and offers excellent homemade meals at a fraction of the price of those at other *centro storico* places. It has well-equipped conference facilites.

Generator Hostel
MAP K4 ▪ Via Principe Amedeo, 251 ▪ 06 492 330 ▪ www.staygenerator.com ▪ €
Set over seven floors, this hostel is just a short walk from the Colosseum and Termini station, and offers good value for money. It also features women-only dorms, a bar and a travel shop.

Hostel Alessandro and Alessandro Downtown
MAP E2 ▪ Via Vicenza 42 and Via Carlo Cattaneo 23 ▪ 06 446 1958/44 340 147 ▪ www.hostelsalessandro.com ▪ €
Friendly staff, a 24-hour reception, no curfew, a shared kitchen, internet access and free coffee, tea and pastries make these two hostels a popular choice. They also offer locker services, free maps and provide tourist information. Hostel Alessandro is situated to the north of Termini, while Alessandro Downtown is on the other side, near Via Cavour.

Hostel Sandy
MAP E3 ▪ Via Cavour 136 ▪ 335 225945 ▪ www.hostelworld.com ▪ No credit cards ▪ No air conditioning ▪ €
Located close to the Colosseum, this friendly hostel, with young and spirited staff, can accommodate up to three to eight people in their dormitories. Hostel Sandy provides shared and private rooms with individual lockers.Free internet access is also provided. There is no curfew and they can arrange walking/bus tours for you.

Hotel Panda
MAP D2 ▪ Via della Croce 35 ▪ 06 678 0179 ▪ www.hotelpanda.it ▪ €
An affordable option in the Piazza di Spagna area. Rooms are simple and clean and the staff are very friendly. The hotel has a breakfast deal with the bar downstairs.

Orsa Maggiore for Women Only
MAP C4 ▪ Via S Francesco di Sales 1/a ▪ 06 689 3753 ▪ www.orsamaggioreroma.com ▪ No air conditioning ▪ €
Run by the International Women's House in a 17th-century convent, this Trastevere hostel offers 13 rooms for women only (boys under 10 years of age allowed). The rooms are single, double and multiple-occupancy, and all are spacious, bright and quiet, overlooking either the garden, cloister or city rooftops. There's also an organic café.

Blue Hostel
MAP F3 ▪ Via Carlo Alberto 13 ▪ 340 925 8503 ▪ www.bluehostel.it ▪ No credit cards ▪ €€
A high-level hostel with fantastic double or triple rooms in the Esquiline. Each room of the Blue Hostel has wooden floors and ceilings, and offers en suite bathroom and Wi-Fi. Perfect place to stay for families or small groups.

Residences and Apartments

Adagio Aparthotel
Via Damiano Chiesa 8 ■ 06 301 98 ■ www.adagio-city.com ■ €
Situated in a lush area of the city, close to Monte Mario, Adagio Aparthotel has spacious apartments. All units feature a private balcony, a flat-screen TV, and a fully-equipped kitchen with a microwave, stove and fridge. They also offer breakfast. Private parking is available.

Aldrovandi Residence
Via Aldovrandi 11 ■ Tram No. 19 ■ 06 322 1430 ■ www.aldrovandiresidence.it ■ €
This elegant residence is outside the city centre, just beyond Villa Borghese in the peaceful Parioli district, full of greenery. The furnishings are handsome and the service is deferential. Guests are welcome to use the pool of the Hotel Aldrovandi next door. There is a minimum one-week stay requirement.

Apartment Rentals
Rome Sweet Home; 06 6992 4091; www.romesweethome.com ■ Cross-Pollinate; 06 9028 8130; www.cross-pollinate.com ■ €
Numerous services offer more unconventional apartment rentals. Prices vary depending on type of apartment, length of stay and number of people.

Aurelia Residence
Via Aurelia 145 ■ 06 393 8648 ■ www.aurelia residence.it ■ €
This residence-style accommodation near the Vatican is perfect for families. The rooms are stylish and clean and the shopping area is just a few minutes' walk away. The roof garden offers views of St Peter's dome. Minimum two-night stay.

Marco Aurelio 49
MAP F5 ■ Via Marco Aurelio 49 ■ 06 7720 9761 ■ www.appartamenti marcoaurelio49.com ■ €
Located on a quiet street right by the Colosseum, this set of six studio apartments are furnished in a colorful and a characterful fashion. Some of the apartments have balconies or terraces, and are fully equipped with kitchens, air-conditioning and Wi-Fi.

Residenza Bollo Apartments
MAP K4 ■ Vicolo del Bollo 4 ■ 06 320 7625 ■ www.bolloapartments.com ■ €
In a quiet pedestrian street an easy walk from Piazza Navona, this 17th-century palazzo has a range of apartment options, characterized by large windows, wood floors and beamed ceilings. At reception you can rent a bike and arrange guided tours.

Residenza Farnese
MAP K4 ■ Via del Mascherone 59 ■ 06 6821 0980 ■ www.residenza farneseroma.it ■ €
Housed in a restructured 15th-century palazzo in an area loaded with history, Residenza Farnese offers space and comfort just a stone's throw from the lovely Piazza Farnese and the river.

Trastevere
MAP K6 ■ Via L Manara 24A–25 ■ 06 581 4713 ■ www.hoteltrastevere.it ■ €
Located just a block away from the main piazza, this unassuming, and modest establishment captures the charm of Trastevere. The rooms have views of the local market. There are also small, clean apartments with kitchens.

Vatican Suites
MAP A3 ■ Via Nicolò V 5 ■ 06 633 306 ■ www.vatican-suites.com ■ €
Three historic mansions in Prati have been transformed into residence hotels offering studio apartments and one- and two-bedroom suites of varying sizes, all simply decorated and clean, with well-equipped kitchenettes.

Santa Chiara
MAP M3 ■ Via S Chiara 21 ■ 06 687 2979 ■ www.albergosantachiara.com ■ €€
Santa Chiara is situated just behind the Pantheon in three historic buildings and has been run by the same family for 200 years. Rooms as well as three apartments for two to five people are available. The topmost has beamed ceilings, a fireplace and a terrace with an unforgettable view of the huge ancient dome. All rooms are spacious and full of character. Design features include oak headboards, marble-topped desks and travertine bathrooms.

For a key to hotel price categories see p170

General Index

Acknowledgments

This edition updated by

Contributor Daniel Mosseri
Senior Editor Alison McGill
Senior Designer Vinita Venugopal
Project Editor Tijana Todorinovic
Picture Researcher Vagisha Pushp
Publishing Assistant Halima Mohammed
Jacket Designer Jordan Lambley
Senior Cartographer Subhashree Bharti
Cartography Manager Suresh Kumar
Senior DTP Designer Tanveer Zaidi
Senior Production Editor Jason Little
Senior Production Controller Samantha Cross
Managing Editors Shikha Kulkarni,
Hollie Teague
Deputy Editorial Manager Beverly Smart
Managing Art Editors Sarah Snelling,
Priyanka Thakur
Art Director Maxine Pedliham
Publishing Director Georgina Dee

DK would like to thank the following for
their contribution to the previous editions:
Reid Bramblett, Jeffrey Kennedy, Ros Belford,
Kathryn O'Donoghue, Helena Smith, Solveig
Steinhardt and Arianna Vatteroni.

The publisher would like to thank the
following for their kind permission to
reproduce their photographs:

Key: a-above; b-below/bottom; c-centre;
f-far; l-left; r-right; t-top

4Corners: SIME/Luigi Vaccarella 3tr, 160–61;
SIME/Giovanni Simeone 4t.

Alamy Stock Photo: Vito Arcomano 43cr; 131bl,
132bl, 139cla; Marko Beric 81tr; Carlo Bollo 26-7c;
CFimages 94t, 120tr; Tristan Deschamps 71cra;
Adam Eastland 28cl; eye35.pix 44-45; PE
Forsberg 67b; Granger, NYC. 69cl; Francesco
Gustincich 84tl; Hemis 147cl; Hemis 80b; hemis.fr
/ SERRANO Anna 4b; imageBROKER / Stefan
Auth 40cl; imageBROKER 78t; John Kellerman
98tl, 116bl; Gunter Kirsch 63cl; LaPresse /
MARCELLA GASTINI 81cl; Elio Lombardo 138ca;
Valerio Mei 68tl, 128cla; nagelestock.com 11tl; B.
O'Kane 52br; Stefano Paterna 58t; Danilo Poccia
110bl; Realy Easy Star/Tullio Valente 79clb; Boaz
Rottem 134cra; Kumar Sriskandan 109clb;
Fabrizio Troiani 67cra; Martyn Vickery 120bl; Alvaro
German Vilela 113cl; Ed Warner 121tr, Tim E
White 83tr.

Alimentari Ruggeri: 111tr.

AWL Images: Stefano Politi Markovina 1

Babingtons Tea Rooms: 122b.

Caffe Sant'Eustachio: 78bl.

Casina Valadier: 123cra.

Cinecitta si Mostra: 69bc.

Corbis: 35crb; Elena Aquila 127tl; C.E. Bolles
58cb; Demotix/eidon photographers, 85tr; Design
Pics/Peter M. Wilson 4cr; dpa/Lars Halbauer
102cla; Chris Hellier 23tl; Duncan James 72bc;
Andrea Jemolo 100br; Bob Krist 60br; Leemage

4clb, 34clb, 37clb, 37b, 46tr; Massimo Listri 29tr;
R. Ian Lloyd 89br; Araldo de Luca 29cla, 31t; Mauro
Magliani 24cla, 24clb, 25cra; Masterfile/Siephoto
156t; Mario Matassa 72cl; National Geographic
Society/Tino Soriano 2tl, 8–9; 136t, Vittoriano
Rastelli 47br; Paul Seheult 31bc; Sylvain Sonnet
51tr; Vatican Museu /Alessandra Benedetti 57t;
Roger Wood 59br; Marco Zeppetella 85cl.

Danon: 119tl

Depositphotos Inc: ChiccoDodiFC 84br.

Dorling Kindersley: Courtesy of the Capitoline
Museum, Rome (Musei Capitolini)/Mike Dunning
30tl, 30cr; Galleria Borghese, Roma, Courtesy of
the Ministero della Pubblica Instruzione/John
Heseltine 6crb, 10crb; Courtesy of MAXXI/Mockford
and Bonetti 5b, 55b, 83bl; Courtesy of Basilica San
Clemente/Mockford and Bonetti 64tl; Courtesy of
Villa Medici/Mockford and Bonetti 116cra.

Dreamstime.com: 36189341 20–21, 32–3;
22tomtom 135cl; Adisa 131tr; Ajafoto 79tc;
Alexirina27000 24br; Anton Aleksenko 118br;
Alessandro0770 158cla; Anitasstudio 4cla, 101tr,
15crb; Antonyesse 141bl; Azurita 73cl; Yehuda
Bernstein 146t; Maurizio Biso 137b; Goran
Bogicevic/Boggy 26tl; Ciolca 130cla; Danflcreativo
156br; Dennis Dolkens 155tr; Donyanedomam
144b; Pierre Jean Durieu 18br; Ekaterinabelova
151cla; Emicristea 26clb, 144cla; F11photo 143t;
Gekaskr 151b; Nataliya Hora 7tr, 10bl; Anna
Hristova 107cr; Ilfede 14t; Inkwelldodo 117clb;
Mariusz Jurgielewicz 157tr; Kedofoto 5tr;
Marcovarro 66clb; Maurodp75 104–105; Salvatore
Micillo 88cla; Monkey Business Images 73ca;
Luciano Mortula 7cr; Juan Moyano 89tl; Roland
Nagy 115tr; Nicknickko 48t; Anna Pakutina
42-43c; Dzmitry Paliakou 72tr; Thomas Perkins
79tl; William Perry 11bl, 16bl; Perseomedusa
91bl; Phant 38–9; Photogolfer 55tl; Janusz
Pieńkowski 133bl; Olimpiu Alexa-pop 92bl; Marek
Poplawski 27cr, 125bl; Preisler 10cla; Valerio
Rosati 140t; Sborisov 18cl, 63cla; Scaliger 17bl,
49clb, 124cra, 148–9; Jozef Sedmak 52cla, 53tl,
97bl, 132t; Olga Shtytlkova 2tr; Sjankauskas 82bc;
Krzysztof Slusarczyk 48bc; Dariusz Szwangruber
6cla, 19tc; Tasstock 100tl; Tinamou 34br, 35cl;
Tomas1111 97t; Stefano Valeri 108t; Yorgy67
16cra; Zerbor 73br.

Explora Rome: 70t.

Fiaschetteria Beltramme da Cesaretto: 123bl.

Freni e Frizioni: 150cla.

Getty Images: Gonzalo Azumendi 36bl; Paolo
Cordelli 93cl; Giorgio Cosulich 138br; AFP /
Tiziana Fabi 119br; DEA /G. Nimatallah 56cl;
Heritage Images 15bc; Don Klein 82tc; Digitaler
Lumpensammler 12–13c; Mondadori 47clb;
Alberto Pizzoli 75crb; Stock Montage 59clb; Slow
Images 4crb; Universal
Images Group/Hulton Fine Art 49tr; Guy
Vanderelst 4cl; Visions Of Our Land 3tl, 86–7.

Glasshostaria: 75t.

IDEARIA srl / Trapizzino Trilussa: 152b.

Il Pagliaccio: 74bl.

iStockphoto.com: 8vFanl 126b; powerofforever
51clb, 99cla.

La Giara: 141cr.

La Gatta Mangiona: 76tr

Leam Rome: 134bl.

Polvere di Tempo: 147br.

Ristorante Antico Arco: 153cla.

Ristorante l'Archeologia: 159cl.

Roscioli: 76clb.

Photo Scala, Florence: 11ca, 17tc, 42bl; DeAgostini Picture Library 23cb, 36tr; Fondo Edifici di Culto – Min. dell'Interno 38br; Ministero Beni e Att. Culturali 11cb, 34cra, 40crb, 40bl, 41tr, 41cl, 42cla.

ColosseumSuperStock: 38cla; DeAgostini 12cl; Universal Images Group 29bl.

Too Much: 93br.

Volpetti: 129bl.

Cover
Front and spine: **AWL Images:** Stefano Politi Markovina; Back: **Alamy Stock Photo:** Classic Image tr, Iain Masterton cla; **AWL Images:** Stefano Politi Markovina b; **Depositphotos Inc:** VividaPhoto crb **Dreamstime.com:** Ekaterinabelova tl

Pull out map cover
AWL Images: Stefano Politi Markovina

All other images are: © Dorling Kindersley. For further information see: www.dkimages.com.

Illustrator Chris Orr & Associates

Commissioned Photography Demetrio Carrasco, Mike Dunning, John Heseltine, Mockford and Bonetti, Kim Sayer, Stuart West, Rough Guides/Chris Hutty, Rough Guides/James McConnachie, Rough Guides/Roger d'Olivere Mapp, Rough Guides/Natascha Sturny, Kim Sayer.

Penguin Random House

First edition 2002

Published in Great Britain by
Dorling Kindersley Limited,
DK, One Embassy Gardens, 8 Viaduct Gardens, London SW11 7BW, UK

The authorised representative in the EEA is Dorling Kindersley Verlag GmbH. Arnulfstr. 124, 80636 Munich, Germany

Published in the United States by
DK Publishing, 1745 Broadway, 20th Floor, New York, NY 10019, USA

Copyright © 2002, 2023 Dorling Kindersley Limited

A Penguin Random House Company

23 24 25 26 10 9 8 7 6 5 4 3 2 1

A CIP catalogue record is available from the British Library.

A catalogue record for this book is available from the Library of Congress.

ISSN 1479-344X
ISBN 978 0 2416 2125 7
Printed and bound in Malaysia

www.dk.com

As a guide to abbreviations in visitor information blocks: **Adm** = *admission charge;* **D** = *dinner;* **L** = *lunch.*

MIX
Paper | Supporting responsible forestry
FSC™ C018179
www.fsc.org

This book was made with Forest Stewardship Council™ certified paper – one small step in DK's commitment to a sustainable future.
For more information go to www.dk.com/our-green-pledge

Phrase Book

In an Emergency

Help!	**Aiuto!**	*eye-yoo-toh*
Stop!	**Ferma!**	*fair-mah*
Call a doctor.	**Chiama un medico.**	*kee-ah-mah oon meh-deekoh*
Call an ambulance.	**Chiama un' ambulanza.**	*kee-ah-mah oon am-boo-lan-tsa*
Call the police.	**Chiama la polizia.**	*kee-ah-mah lah pol-ee-tsee-ah*
Call the fire brigade.	**Chiama i pompieri.**	*kee-ah-mah ee pom-pee-air-ee*

Communication Essentials

Yes/No	**Sì/No**	*see/noh*
Please	**Per favore**	*pair fah-vor-eh*
Thank you	**Grazie**	*grah-tsee-eh*
Excuse me	**Mi scusi**	*mee skoo-zee*
Hello	**Buongiorno**	*bwon jor-noh*
Goodbye	**Arrivederci**	*ah-ree-veh-dair-chee*
Good evening	**Buona sera**	*bwon-ah sair-ah*
What?	**Che?**	*keh*
When?	**Quando?**	*kwan-doh*
Why?	**Perchè?**	*pair-keh*
Where?	**Dove?**	*doh-veh*

Useful Phrases

How are you?	**Come sta?**	*koh-meh stah*
Very well, thank you.	**Molto bene, grazie.**	*moll-toh beh-neh grah-tsee-eh*
Pleased to meet you.	**Piacere di conoscerla.**	*pee-ah-chair-eh dee coh-noh-shair-lah*
That's fine.	**Va bene.**	*va beh-neh*
Where is/ are…?	**Dov'è/ Dove sono…?**	*dov-eh/ doveh soh-noh*
How do I get to…?	**Come faccio per arrivare a…?**	*koh-meh fah-cho pair arri-var-eh a*
Do you speak English?	**Parla inglese?**	*par-lah een-gleh-zeh*
I don't understand.	**Non capisco.**	*non ka-pee-skoh*
I'm sorry.	**Mi dispiace.**	*mee dee-spee-ah-cheh*

Shopping

How much does this cost?	**Quant'è, per favore?**	*kwan-teh pair fah-vor-eh*
I would like…	**Vorrei…**	*vor-ray*
Do you have…?	**Avete…?**	*ah-veh-teh*
Do you take credit cards?	**Accettate carte di credito?**	*ah-chet-tah-teh kar-teh dee creh-dee-toh*
What time do you open/close?	**A che ora apre/ chiude?**	*a keh ora ah-preh/ kee-oo-deh*
this one	**questo**	*kweh-stoh*
that one	**quello**	*kwell-oh*
expensive	**caro**	*kar-oh*
cheap	**a buon prezzo**	*ah bwon pret-soh*
size (clothes)	**la taglia**	*lah tah-lee-ah*
size (shoes)	**il numero**	*eel noo-mair-oh*
white	**bianco**	*bee-ang-koh*
black	**nero**	*neh-roh*
red	**rosso**	*ross-oh*
yellow	**giallo**	*jal-loh*
green	**verde**	*vair-deh*
blue	**blu**	*bloo*

Types of Shop

bakery	**il forno/ panificio**	*eel forn-oh/ panee-fee-cho*
bank	**la banca**	*lah bang-kah*
bookshop	**la libreria**	*lah lee-breh-ree-ah*
cake shop	**la pasticceria**	*lah pas-tee-chair-ee-ah*
chemist	**la farmacia**	*lah far-mah-chee-ah*
delicatessen	**la salumeria**	*lah sah-loo-meh-ree-ah*
department store	**il grande magazzino**	*eel gran-deh ma-gad-zeenoh*
grocery	**alimentari**	*ah-lee-men-tah-ree*
hairdresser	**il parrucchiere**	*eel par-oo-kee-air-eh*
ice-cream parlour	**la gelateria**	*lah jel-lah-tair-ree-ah*
market	**il mercato**	*eel mair-kah-toh*
newsstand	**l'edicola**	*leh-dee-koh-lah*
post office	**l'ufficio postale**	*loo-fee-choh pos-tah-leh*
supermarket	**il supermercato**	*eel su-pair-mair-kah-toh*
tobacconist	**il tabaccaio**	*eel tah-bak-eye-oh*
travel agency	**l'agenzia di viaggi**	*lah-jen-tsee-ah dee vee-ad-jee*

Sightseeing

art gallery	**la pinacoteca**	*lah peena-koh-teh-kah*
bus stop	**la fermata dell'autobus**	*lah fair-mah-tah dell-ow-toh-booss*
church	**la chiesa basilica**	*lah kee-eh-zah bah-seel-ee-kah*
closed for holidays	**chiuso per ferie**	*kee-oo-zoh pair fair-ee-eh*
garden	**il giardino**	*eel jar-dee-no*
museum	**il museo**	*eel moo-zeh-oh*
railway station	**la stazione**	*lah stah-tsee-oh-neh*
tourist information	**l'ufficio del turismo**	*loo-fee-choh del too-ree-smoh*

Staying in a Hotel

Do you have any vacant rooms?	**Avete camere libere?**	*ah-veh-teh kah-mair-eh lee-bair-eh*
double room	**una camera doppia**	*oona kah-mairah doh-pee-ah*
with double bed	**con letto matrimoniale**	*kon let-toh mah-tree-moh-nee-ah-leh*
a room with bath/ shower	**una camera con bagno/ doccia**	*oona ka-mair-ah kon ban-yoh/ dot-chah*
twin room	**una camera con due letti**	*oona kah-mairah kon doo-eh let-tee*

single room	una camera	oona kah-mairah
	singola	sing-goh-lah
I have a	Ho fatto una	oh fat-toh oona
reservation.	prenotazione.	preh-noh-tah-
		tsee-oh-neh

Eating Out

Have you got	Avete un	ah-veh-teh
a table for...?	tavolo per...?	oon tah-voh-loh pair
I'd like to	Vorrei prenotare	vor-ray preh-noh-
reserve a table.	un tavolo.	ta-reh oon tah-voh-loh
breakfast	colazione	koh-lah-tsee-oh-neh
lunch	pranzo	pran-tsoh
dinner	cena	cheh-nah
the bill	il conto	eel kon-toh
waitress	cameriera	kah-mair-ee-air-ah
waiter	cameriere	kah-mair-ee-air-eh
fixed-price	il menù a	eel meh-noo ah
menu	prezzo fisso	pret-soh fee-soh
dish of	piatto del	pee-ah-toh dell
the day	giorno	jor-no
starter	l'antipasto	lan-tee-pass-toh
first course	il primo	eel pree-moh
main course	il secondo	eel seh-kon-doh
vegetables	i contorni	ee kon-tor-noh
dessert	il dolce	eel doll-cheh
wine list	la lista dei	lah lee-stah day
	vini	vee-nee
glass	il bicchiere	eel bee-kee-air-eh
bottle	la bottiglia	lah bot-teel-yah
knife	il coltello	eel kol-tell-oh
fork	la forchetta	lah for-ket-tah
spoon	il cucchiaio	eel koo-kee-eye-oh

Menu Decoder

l'acqua	lah-kwah	mineral water
minerale	meenair-ah-leh	
gassata/	gah-zah-tah/	fizzy
naturale	nah-too-rah-leh	still
agnello	ah-niell-oh	lamb
aglio	al-ee-oh	garlic
al forno	al for-noh	baked
alla griglia	ah-lah greel-yah	grilled
la birra	lah beer-rah	beer
la bistecca	lah bee-stek-ah	steak
il burro	eel boor-oh	butter
il caffè	eel kah-feh	coffee
la carne	la kar-neh	meat
carne di	kar-neh dee	pork
maiale	mah-yah-leh	
la cipolla	la chip-oh-lah	onion
il formaggio	eel for-mad-joh	cheese
le fragole	leh frah-goh-leh	strawberries
il fritto	eel free-toh	mixed fried
misto	mees-toh	seafood
la frutta	la froot-tah	fruit
frutti di	froo-tee dee	seafood
mare	mah-reh	
i funghi	ee foon-ghee	mushrooms
i gamberi	ee gam-bair-ee	prawns
il gelato	eel jel-lah-toh	ice cream

l'insalata	leen-sah-lah-tah	salad
il latte	eel laht-teh	milk
il manzo	eel man-tsoh	beef
l'olio	loh-lee-oh	oil
il pane	eel pah-neh	bread
le patate	leh pah-tah-teh	potatoes
le patatine	leh pah-tah-teen-eh	chips
fritte	free-teh	
il pepe	eel peh-peh	pepper
il pesce	eel pesh-eh	fish
il pollo	eel poll-oh	chicken
il pomodoro	eel poh-moh-dor-oh	tomato
il prosciutto	eel pro-shoo-toh	ham
cotto/	kot-toh/	cooked/
crudo	kroo-doh	cured
il riso	eel ree-zoh	rice
il sale	eel sah-leh	salt
la salsiccia	lah sal-see-chah	sausage
il succo	eel soo-koh	orange
d'arancia	dah-ran-chah	juice
il tè	eel teh	tea
la torta	lah tor-tah	cake/tart
l'uovo	loo-oh-voh	egg
vino	vee-noh	white wine
bianco	bee-ang-koh	
vino rosso	vee-noh ross-oh	red wine
lo zucchero	loh zoo-kair-oh	sugar
la zuppa	lah tsoo-pah	soup

Numbers

1	uno	oo-noh
2	due	doo-eh
3	tre	treh
4	quattro	kwat-roh
5	cinque	ching-kweh
6	sei	say-ee
7	sette	set-teh
8	otto	ot-toh
9	nove	noh-veh
10	dieci	dee-eh-chee
11	undici	oon-dee-chee
17	diciassette	dee-chah-set-teh
18	diciotto	dee-chot-toh
19	diciannove	dee-cha-noh-veh
20	venti	ven-tee
30	trenta	tren-tah
40	quaranta	kwah-ran-tah
50	cinquanta	ching-kwan-tah
60	sessanta	sess-an-tah
70	settanta	set-tan-tah
80	ottanta	ot-tan-tah
90	novanta	noh-van-tah
100	cento	chen-toh
1,000	mille	mee-leh

Time

one minute	un minuto	oon mee-noo-toh
one hour	un'ora	oon or-ah
a day	un giorno	oon jor-noh
Monday	lunedì	loo-neh-dee
Tuesday	martedì	mar-teh-dee
Wednesday	mercoledì	mair-koh-leh-dee
Thursday	giovedì	joh-veh-dee
Friday	venerdì	ven-air-dee
Saturday	sabato	sah-bah-toh
Sunday	domenica	doh-meh-nee-ka

Street Index